STEPHEN MINISTRY
TRAINING MANUAL

VOLUME 2 • MODULES 15–25

Stephen Ministry Training Manual
ISBN: 0-9633831-8-3

C: 1/1/2000 R: 12/15/2006

13	11	09	07
8	7	6	5

Table of Contents

Volume 2

(continued on the next page)

Bringing the Caring Relationship to a Close

Preclass Reading

Contents

▶ Caring Relationships End

Caring relationships always eventually end. They can end in many different ways.

Sally and Claire

Sally had been talking a couple of times a week with her Stephen Minister, Claire, for almost three years. First Sally's mother had died in an accident, then there was the divorce. Sally and Claire had been through a lot together.

Recently, though, their visits had been more like getting together with a friend than care receiver and Stephen Minister. Sally remembered how for more than a year she had cried every time they got together. She would dump her feelings of anger and helplessness, and Claire would patiently listen. Slowly Sally moved beyond her anger and sadness and built a new life. For the last few months they had talked about Claire's family almost as much as Sally's issues.

Claire thought it was time to talk with Sally about bringing closure to the caring relationship. She consulted with her Supervision Group, and they agreed.

When Claire and Sally next met, Claire said, "It sounds as if it's time for us to talk about closure." Sally's first reaction was panic, followed by sadness. Then Claire explained that closure didn't mean the end of their relationship. Rather, they would acknowledge how their relationship had changed and end their formal caring relationship so their friendship could continue to grow. After that Sally felt better about the closure, although she still felt sad.

Sally and Claire began meeting less frequently. They talked a lot about the three years they had been together. Their friendship grew even deeper as they tapered off their official caring visits. As they concluded their final caring visit, they hugged and thanked each other. Then they made plans to have lunch together the next week. Sally said, "I'm buying."

Lawrence and Bruce

The first time Bruce met Lawrence was in the hospital. Lawrence had just had surgery to remove a tumor, and Bruce had been assigned as his Stephen Minister.

They quickly developed a very close relationship. Lawrence confided in Bruce, talking about his fear of dying and his sadness at eventually having to leave his family behind. One of the biggest challenges Bruce had ever faced was to stick with Lawrence and not flinch as Lawrence shared his raw suffering. Lawrence recognized how much Bruce was giving, and they came to love each other like two soldiers fighting together on the front lines.

Lawrence's cancer went into remission, and they started talking about what Lawrence might do if he had five or ten more years to live. Lawrence wanted to spend the time he had left with his family, and he and Bruce talked about how Lawrence could get more involved in his children's lives.

Then one day Bruce showed up for a caring visit and found a note on the front door that said only "At the Hospital." He rushed to the hospital and learned that Lawrence had died that afternoon. Bruce sat with Lawrence's family until late into the night.

Bruce grieved Lawrence's death as deeply as he had grieved his own father's death. His Supervision Group cared for him and listened to him. Finally they recommended that Bruce have his own Stephen Minister. "I never expected being a Stephen Minister to be like this," Bruce said. "But once I got to know Lawrence, I knew that when he died, it would be as if a part of me died too."

Jerome and Martin

Jerome had talked with the pastor about his faith struggles; he was finding it harder to believe in Jesus, especially because of his job as a research assistant at a genetics laboratory where his coworkers attacked anyone who took faith in God seriously. The pastor wanted to meet with Jerome every month or so, but he also wanted Jerome to meet with a Stephen Minister every week.

Jerome was Martin's first care receiver. Martin didn't know very much about Jerome's situation when they started their caring relationship. He asked incisive questions to learn about Jerome's problems. The third time they got together, Jerome poured out his doubts about God and his fears about his spiritual well-being. He also told Martin about a Sunday school teacher who had made lewd suggestions to him when he was a child and how he had struggled with trusting God since that time.

About an hour before their next visit, Jerome called and said he couldn't meet. When Martin tried to reschedule the visit, Jerome said, "I'll have to get back to you." But Jerome didn't call, and he never returned Martin's repeated calls.

Finally, on the advice of his Supervision Group, Martin sent Jerome a letter. He expressed his concern and his hopes for Jerome's future. He said he would be available if Jerome ever wanted to call and talk.

Anita and Wanda

For the past two years, Anita had lived with her invalid mother, Elizabeth, and cared for her every morning and evening. When the nurse's aide who cared for Elizabeth during the day didn't show up, Anita would have to call in to work to say she couldn't be there and stay home with her mother. Anita had been caring for her mother like this for two years, and she felt lonely, overwhelmed, and frustrated. Once when Pastor Mary visited Elizabeth, she noticed how unhappy Anita looked and suggested a Stephen Minister.

Anita's Stephen Minister was Wanda. Wanda had joined the church when her husband's job moved them to the city. She was close to Anita's age, and they became close friends quickly.

After a couple of months, Wanda showed up for the caring visit looking very sad. "Roger just got a new job, and we have to move to Connecticut. It came completely out of the blue. The company is going to move us and take care of selling our house, and we have to be in

Connecticut in two weeks. I'm so sorry." Anita was also sorry and sad.

They met two more times, but the visits felt awkward and rushed. The Stephen Leaders assigned a new Stephen Minister to care for Anita. Wanda and Anita talked on the phone once in a while for about half a year, but over time their relationship slowly faded.

▶ Key Facts about Closure

Closure is the process of bringing your caring relationships to a good end. While this may sound simple, closure can be quite challenging. In this Preclass Reading you will learn some of the basics about closure and see how a normal closure process will take place. Then, in the In-Class Session, you will learn about some of the more challenging aspects of closure and practice handling some closure challenges.

Closure Is Essential for a Successful Caring Relationship

You may begin your caring relationships well and conduct them with compassion and insight, but if you don't also bring good closure, the caring relationship will not be as effective. In fact, poorly done closure can undo much of the good that the caring relationship brought about. Through an effective closure process, both the care receiver and the Stephen Minister can say good-bye to the caring relationship and move on. Without effective closure, the care receiver and the Stephen Minister may get stuck in the caring relationship, never grieving the loss of it and never able to move on from it.

Closure Is a Loss

At the end of a caring relationship, care receivers may feel as though they have lost an important part of their lives. Here are some possible real or perceived losses for care receivers.

▶ The security of the caring relationship

▶ The Stephen Minister's friendship

▶ Regular, reliable weekly visits with their Stephen Minister

▶ Someone to listen to them talk about their life challenges

▶ A trusted confidant

▶ The help of a friend who shared their burdens—now they have to go it alone

▶ The sense of being a special person who has a Stephen Minister

▶ The congregation's special concern that has been evidenced by the care of the Stephen Minister

Individual care receivers may experience other losses. If the care receiver perceives the ending of the relationship as a loss, then he or she will need the Stephen Minister's understanding and care to help grieve that loss.

Stephen Ministers also experience real and perceived losses at the end of a caring relationship.

▶ The care receiver's friendship

▶ A sense of being useful in another's life

▶ The sense of being needed by the care receiver. There may be something sad about ending the caring relationship; it may feel like sending a child off to live on his or her own.

▶ Enjoyable conversations with the care receiver

▶ The challenge of providing care

► Weekly caring visits with the care receiver

Stephen Ministers may experience other losses as well.

The amount of grief over closure depends on how close the relationship was and how it ends. Some people will not feel closure as much of a loss at all. For others it will be a definite cause for sadness. If the relationship ends with the death of one of the parties, the grief may be strong and long-lasting.

Stages of Grief in Closure

Since closure is a loss that brings about some grief, care receivers and Stephen Ministers may go through the stages of grief as part of closure.

Shock

Once a care receiver or a Stephen Minister realizes that closure is a possibility, he or she may try to pretend that it is not taking place or that there are no grief feelings. One or both may also avoid the subject of closure as a way of denying the feelings associated with it.

As part of their denial, one or both may try to bargain their way out of the necessity of closure. Care receivers may promise their Stephen Ministers that they will work harder at recovery or offer to meet more frequently or less often. Stephen Ministers may promise their Supervision Groups that they will be more insightful about their care receivers or that they will get around to closure, but just not now. A Stephen Minister may say, "Just give us three more months."

Recoil

Stephen Ministers and care receivers may be angry that the relationship is going to end. They will probably feel sadness as they come to terms with the loss. One or both may feel guilty. They may feel lonely as the caring visits get farther and farther apart.

Rebuilding

Bringing the caring relationship to a good end means accepting change and feeling excited about new possibilities. Ending the caring relationship is a step into the future. The care receiver will find new sources of support and friendship, which has been one of the goals of the caring relationship all along. The Stephen Minister will receive a new caring ministry assignment after a while.

Depending on the nature of the relationship, the care receiver and the Stephen Minister will continue to relate in some way. That may mean several follow-up phone calls over time or a rich friendship for the rest of their lives.

Stephen Ministers Help Care Receivers Grieve

Part of the Stephen Minister's job in the closure process is to help the care receiver recognize and grieve his or her loss. Stephen Ministers will use their listening skills and their sensitivity to feelings to draw out their care receivers and encourage them to talk about their feelings associated with the loss.

Closure Involves the Supervision Group

Stephen Ministers always consult with their Supervision Groups before closure. They describe reasons for considering closure and then look to the Supervision Group for confirmation or for reasons why closure might not be the best choice at that time. The group provides support and encouragement as Stephen Ministers deal with closure issues. They will also care for the Stephen Minister as he or she goes through closure and help him or her grieve the end of the caring relationship.

▶ How to Know It's Time for Closure

You may be able to tell from the care receiver's words or actions that it is time to initiate closure. Reference Box A contains some clues.

REFERENCE BOX A

Clues That It May Be Time for Closure

1. Your care receiver's behavior shows that he or she has pretty much recovered from the crisis that brought you together. For example, he or she is demonstrating consistent work habits, or establishing a new life after the death of a spouse, or dealing with visitation issues following a divorce, or employed again and no longer feeling depressed.

2. Your care receiver no longer has crucial problems to discuss and does not appear to be hiding any.

3. Your care receiver is consistently, genuinely happy.

4. Your care receiver cries less and has few reasons to cry.

5. Your care receiver has accepted the reality of a loss that he or she experienced and has moved on to establish a new life.

Pray

When you notice such clues, ask the Holy Spirit to give you the wisdom to know when it is time for closure. Ask to be emptied of your agenda for the care receiver and filled with God's agenda for that person.

Consult with Your Supervision Group

Talk to your Supervision Group about closure. Tell them what has happened to make you believe it may be time for closure and see what they say.

If in Doubt, Continue

If you aren't sure that it's time for closure, and if your Supervision Group can't help you come to a confident conclusion, you should probably continue with the caring relationship. Look for other issues that you and your care receiver need to talk about or for additional signs that it is time to close the relationship.

▶ The Normal Closure Process

When a caring relationship comes to normal closure (as opposed to the closure challenges you will learn about in the In-Class Session), there is a period of tapering off during which the

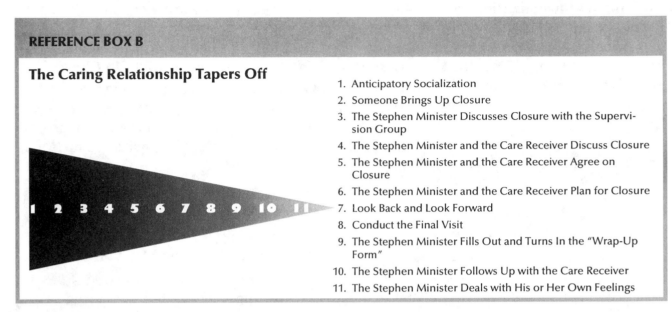

The Caring Relationship Tapers Off

1. Anticipatory Socialization
2. Someone Brings Up Closure
3. The Stephen Minister Discusses Closure with the Supervision Group
4. The Stephen Minister and the Care Receiver Discuss Closure
5. The Stephen Minister and the Care Receiver Agree on Closure
6. The Stephen Minister and the Care Receiver Plan for Closure
7. Look Back and Look Forward
8. Conduct the Final Visit
9. The Stephen Minister Fills Out and Turns In the "Wrap-Up Form"
10. The Stephen Minister Follows Up with the Care Receiver
11. The Stephen Minister Deals with His or Her Own Feelings

Stephen Minister and the care receiver work through closure. The diagram in Reference Box B illustrates this normal closure process.

1. Anticipatory Socialization

Anticipatory socialization means mentioning now something that may happen later in order to prepare people. Then, when the event does happen, they are not caught off guard and it is not so much of a shock.

For example, a person who knows that retirement can be a sad time as well as a happy one, and who understands why, can deal with uncomfortable feelings that surface. If the person only expects retirement to be positive, however, he or she might be blindsided by some of the negatives.

Anticipatory socialization is especially important in the process of bringing closure. Care receivers will be able to deal with closure better if they have thought about it ahead of time.

Anticipatory socialization regarding the closure process might begin as early as the very first caring visit, particularly if the care receiver asks something like, "How long will we be meeting together?" The anticipatory socialization in the caregiver's response may go something like the one in Reference Box C.

An Example of Anticipatory Socialization

Caregiver: That's difficult to say now, but sooner or later we will probably stop meeting. When that time comes, I think both of us will know and we can talk about it. Right now, let's just focus on what's happening currently, and we'll meet together as long as is necessary.

In this example the caregiver did not tell the person when the relationship would end, but did make him or her aware that there would be an eventual point of closure.

Anticipatory socialization might also offer the care receiver some idea of what it will be like once closure has actually happened. When you are in the closure process, you might want to say something like the statement in Reference Box D.

REFERENCE BOX D

What It Will Be Like after Closure

Caregiver: We've been talking lately about no longer meeting together. What do you think it might be like for you when we aren't getting together anymore?

After giving your care receiver an opportunity to respond to this question, listen for some of the possible feelings and reactions that he or she might have, such as:

▶ feeling happy because of the growth and progress he or she has made;

▶ feeling proud and confident in his or her ability to cope with the situation;

▶ feeling sad about not seeing the caregiver regularly; or

▶ feeling depressed, alone, and perhaps frightened.

Look for opportunities to mention that the two of you will not be meeting as care receiver and caregiver forever. That way he or she can feel comfortable bringing up the topic and will not be shocked if you mention closure.

2. Someone Brings Up Closure

The next step in the normal closure process is for the care receiver, the Stephen Minister, or the Supervision Group to mention ending the caring relationship.

The Care Receiver Brings Up Closure

Given the anticipatory socialization you will do, it is possible your care receiver will introduce the topic of closure by saying something like what is in Reference Box E.

REFERENCE BOX E

A Care Receiver Brings Up Closure

Care receiver: When we first started meeting, we said that this caring relationship would not last forever. You said we would meet as long as I needed to. I think I may have reached the point where we could stop meeting. I've adjusted to living here, I've made new friends, and I don't feel so sad about missing where we used to live. Do you think it might be time for you to care for someone else?

You would want to ask your care receiver to say more and to listen carefully to make sure you understand everything he or she is thinking and feeling about ending the caring relationship.

The Stephen Minister Brings Up Closure

After noticing clues that it is time to end the caring relationship, you might have a conversation like the one in Reference Box F.

A Stephen Minister Brings Up Closure

Care receiver: As I was driving yesterday, the thought suddenly popped into my head that life isn't so bad after all. Why, two years ago I would have never had such an optimistic thought.

Caregiver: You've come a long way since your husband died.

Care receiver: I guess I have. In those months right after his death, I thought I'd never make it.

Caregiver: I remember that it was very rough for you.

Care receiver: It was. But so much has happened since then. The new apartment, so many activities, and my friends. It's almost as if I've started a new life.

Caregiver: As I said before, I think that you have come a long way. I feel very good about the progress you've made. In fact, I'm wondering how much longer we need to meet. I think we might talk about bringing our relationship to a close. What do you think about that?

Bringing Up Closure Doesn't Necessarily Mean You'll Close the Relationship

After either of the conversations above, you might encounter one of several different reactions.

One reaction might be shock or denial. One or both of the people might quickly back off from the idea of closure and not bring it up again for a long time.

Another possible reaction is for the care receiver or the Stephen Minister or both to start thinking of many different issues that they still need to talk about and work through. This may be a helpful fresh start for a caring relationship that has gone flat. It could also be a form of denial. As you explore the issues that surface, you will learn whether they are substantial enough to warrant continuing the caring relationship.

Even when you don't end up closing the caring relationship, discussions about closure can bring new focus, energy, and commitment to the relationship.

3. The Stephen Minister Discusses Closure with the Supervision Group

As soon as possible after closure comes up, the Stephen Minister talks with his or her Supervision Group about it during the brief check-in at the beginning of the supervision meeting. If you have concerns about closure, you may want to ask the group to let you discuss your caring relationship at the next supervision meeting even if it isn't your turn. If you are concerned about the care receiver's ending the caring relationship before you have a chance to talk with the Supervision Group, you could call your Stephen Leader.

4. The Stephen Minister and the Care Receiver Discuss Closure

Once the topic of closure comes up, you and your care receiver need to discuss it until the two of you decide what you want to do. This may be a quick discussion, or you may talk about closure for weeks or months before you come to a decision. That decision may be to continue with your caring relationship and postpone closure or to proceed with bringing the caring relationship to a close.

5. The Stephen Minister and the Care Receiver Agree on Closure

When closure proceeds normally, the Stephen Minister and the care receiver will agree to end the caring relationship. This needs to be a mutual decision. If your care receiver doesn't want to end the caring relationship, you need to respect his or her need for it to continue. (In the In-Class Session you will learn how to deal with situations where the care receiver hangs on to the caring relationship beyond the point where it is doing any good.) If your care receiver wants to end the caring relationship but you believe he or she needs to continue in it, do your best to convince him or her of the need to continue. (You also will learn about how to deal with premature closure in the In-Class Session.)

6. The Stephen Minister and the Care Receiver Plan for Closure

Work out a mutually acceptable plan for bringing the caring relationship to a close.

Tapering Off

One way to plan for closure is to taper off. Tapering off means decreasing the frequency of your caring visits. If you have had weekly visits, you might taper your visits to once every two weeks, and then, once a month.

Tapering off allows the care receiver to see how well he or she gets along without weekly support and allows time for the care receiver to work at strengthening other support systems. This also provides the care receiver the opportunity to share feelings about these experiences when you do meet.

Be sure to explain your reasons to your care receiver as you suggest tapering off. Also, don't push for closing the relationship too quickly. Allow the care receiver to move at his or her own pace.

Set a Specific Date for the Final Session

Include in your plan a date for the final caring visit. Designate one caring visit that both the caregiver and the care receiver recognize as their final session.

The final caring visit needs to be set by mutual agreement at least one session, and preferably several sessions, ahead of time. You might say something like what is in Reference Box G.

REFERENCE BOX G

Setting Definite Dates

Caregiver: Since we won't be meeting too much longer, let's set some definite dates. How about meeting two weeks from now, and then two weeks after that we will have our last meeting?

It might be helpful to remind your care receiver in the next-to-last session that you have only one more scheduled session. This prevents his or her being caught off guard.

7. Look Back and Look Forward

As you taper the frequency of your caring visits, focus your conversations on your care receiver's thoughts and feelings about the closure process. How does it feel for the care receiver to be ending the caring relationship? How was it to go two weeks between visits? How confident is your care receiver about making his or her own way without the caring relationship? Look back over your caring relationship and remember it together. Comment about how your care receiver has grown, and invite him or her to reflect on how he or she has changed. Share your own feelings about ending the caring relationship, and let your care receiver care for you if that seems appropriate. Do what you can to help the care receiver recognize, accept, and express his or her feelings about the end of the caring relationship and the future without the caring relationship.

8. Conduct the Final Visit

Your final caring visit provides a formal end to the caring relationship. Following are some elements you should be sure to include.

Reminder during the Final Session

As your final visit begins, remind your care receiver that this is the last time that the two of you will meet in a formal caring relationship. This will prevent any misunderstanding.

Review the Caring Relationship

During the final session, talk about what has happened during the caring relationship, as you have been doing. As you proceed through this review, focus on some specific, concrete changes that have taken place. You might say something like what is written in Reference Box H.

REFERENCE BOX H

Noting Changes

Caregiver: Since your husband's death, you've found a new place to live, made many new friends, and have gotten involved at church and in the community. How do you feel about all these things you've done?

Talk about Feelings

Another topic for discussion is the care receiver's feelings about this being the last session for the two of you. Reference Box I contains examples of how to help your care receiver talk about his or her feelings.

REFERENCE BOX I

Facilitating Talk about Feelings

Caregiver: How do you feel about today's being our last meeting?

[or]

Caregiver: What's going on inside as you think about ending our caring relationship?

You will probably want to share your feelings with your care receiver as well. Reference Box J contains an example of what you might say.

Sharing Your Own Feelings

Caregiver: We've always been honest with each other, and especially about our feelings. I feel both happy and sad. I'm happy because you've come such a long way and your life is so much more enjoyable for you now. I'm sad because we'll no longer be seeing each other on any kind of formal, regular basis. It's been a very rewarding and meaningful relationship for me. I will miss getting together with you.

Impart Hope

During the final session, try to impart a sense of hope to the care receiver. Discuss the progress or growth the care receiver has made and point out the strengths or skills he or she has attained during the time you have been together. Remind your care receiver that he or she has not only survived this crisis but also has grown from it. By surviving, the care receiver has gained new coping skills that will help in the future. There is an example of what you might say in Reference Box K.

Imparting Hope

Caregiver: You're really a different person than the one I knew right after your wife died. You've learned to take care of yourself. For example, you now know more about the tasks around the house that she always took care of. *[Give details.]*

You have become more outgoing with so many new friends. As much sorrow, grief, and loss as your wife's death caused you, you certainly are now much better equipped to take care of yourself and to face problems that may arise in the future. I feel really good about where you are with all of this.

Leave the Door Open

Let your care receiver know that he or she may call you if problems arise or if he or she just needs to talk. State this explicitly. You might say something like the message in Reference Box L.

Offering Additional Future Care

Caregiver: I want to let you know that if something important comes up in the future and you need someone to help you see it through or talk with you about it, I'm just a phone call away.

Mark the Occasion

The last visit can be a solemn occasion, which deserves to be marked formally. You may want to have a special worship service with prayers, Bible reading, and thanksgiving. You might be able to share Holy Communion together to mark your last visit. Another idea would be to commission each other for your life and ministry after the caring relationship by laying hands on each other and praying for each other. If you think such a formal activity would be appropriate for your caring relationship, discuss it with your care receiver.

Say Good-bye

The last component of the final session is to say good-bye. Just as there is a formal final session, there should also be a formal good-bye.

During this ritual of saying good-bye, don't deny your care receiver the privilege of complimenting you or expressing affection. Assertiveness training has equipped you to accept compliments and expressions of affection. Reference Box M contains examples of what to say and what not to say in this situation.

REFERENCE BOX M

How to Receive an Expression of Appreciation

Care receiver: This is difficult for me to say, but I want to tell you that I really appreciate all that you have done for me. As far as people go in my life, you are one of the greatest.

Don't say: It was nothing. You did all the work. There's nothing special about me.

Do say: That's very nice of you to say that. We did work through this together, and I'm grateful that you let me be a part of your life during some tough times.

---

9. The Stephen Minister Fills Out and Turns In the "Wrap-Up Form"

After your final caring visit, fill out the "Wrap-Up Form." There's a sample in appendix A on page 357. The instructions on the back tell how to fill it out. Give it to your Supervision Group Facilitator or one of your Stephen Leaders.

The appropriate Stephen Leader will review the form and then dispose of it.

10. The Stephen Minister Follows Up with the Care Receiver

Once you have ended your formal caring relationship, you need to follow up with your former care receiver. This follow-up may be anything from a couple of telephone calls in the month or so after the caring relationship ends to a lifelong friendship.

Why Have a Follow-Up Relationship?

By keeping in touch you can continue to serve as a stabilizing influence even if you just make occasional contacts. This might be especially helpful if your care receiver has no family living in the area, or if his or her family is not supportive.

You might also want to have a follow-up relationship simply because it would be meaningful and growth-producing for your care receiver. Your continued care is not necessary for the care receiver, but a follow-up relationship may be beneficial to him or her.

This is also a good situation to discuss with your Supervision Group. They will help you ask the question, "Whose needs are being met?" and develop the best plan for continuing contact.

You may want to have a follow-up relationship because you and your care receiver have become friends. Although you definitely should not push to be friends with your care receiver, if it happens naturally in the course of working together, that's okay.

Be careful that neither you nor your care receiver simply just hangs on to the relationship. That would indicate inappropriate boundaries and would not be helpful for you or your care receiver. If you suspect that is the case, bring it up with your Supervision Group.

Ways of Maintaining a Follow-Up Relationship

You may want to give a care receiver an occasional phone call. At appropriate times of the year, such as Christmas and his or her birthday, you may want to send the person a card. You may correspond by mail or by e-mail. Keep track of significant dates such as the anniversary of a loved one's death, and check in on those days to see how your former care receiver is doing.

You and your care receiver will decide whether to have a follow-up relationship beyond a couple of check-in phone calls. Don't feel obligated to have a long-term relationship if you don't think it is necessary or if you don't want to. Do what is natural and comfortable for you.

11. The Stephen Minister Deals with His or Her Own Feelings

You may have strong feelings of grief after the caring relationship is officially over. Be aware of those feelings, accept them, and express them. Your Supervision Group is the proper place to talk about those feelings.

Your conversations with your Supervision Group, possibly along with a few weeks off, may be all you need to work through your feelings and get ready for another care receiver.

If your care receiver dies, however, you may experience much more intense grief. Stephen Ministers whose care receivers have died have sometimes needed months to work through their grief. Supervision Groups need to provide extra care for Stephen Ministers whose care receivers die.

If your feelings are very strong and troubling, you may want to request a Stephen Minister to care for you. If you start feeling moderately to severely depressed or have other needs that are beyond a Stephen Minister's care, your Stephen Leaders will help you seek care from a mental health professional.

▶ Getting Ready for the In-Class Session

In preparation for the In-Class Session, think of a time when you have ended a relationship. This ending may have come about for many different reasons—from someone's moving away to someone's dying. Make sure you have in mind a situation about which you won't mind sharing in class.

Appendix A

Wrap-Up Form

CONFIDENTIAL   **Stephen Ministry® Form**

Date _____

1. Name of caregiver _____

2. Caring relationship originally initiated by _____

3. Date of initial contact _____

4. Date of final contact _____

5. Total number of caring contacts _____ Number of hours spent with care receiver _____

6. Type of caring_____
    _____

7. Reason for bringing closure:
    ❏ completed formal caring relationship   ❏ withdrawal by care receiver
    ❏ referral to another Stephen Minister   ❏ referral to community resource
    ❏ other
    Explain:

8. Type of follow-up (check all applicable):
    ❏ visits by Stephen Minister   ❏ phone calls by Stephen Minister
    ❏ social meeting   ❏ other
    ❏ no follow-up
    Explain:

9. If you do plan follow-up, how often do you plan to follow up? _____

10. Name (or code number) of care receiver _____

(continued on the next page)

How to Use the Wrap-Up Form

1. Write in the name of the caregiver.

2. Record who originally initiated the caring relationship, e.g., the care receiver, the minister, a relative, or a friend.

3. Fill in the date of the first caring visit.

4. Fill in the date of the last formal caring visit.

5. Fill in the total number of caring visits and number of hours spent with the care receiver.

6. Record the type(s) of caring that went on, e.g., caregiver visiting care receiver, phone calls, a combination of both visits and phone calls.

7. Check the reason for bringing closure and explain.

8. Indicate the type of follow-up you plan to have with the care receiver, if any.

9. If you plan to have a follow-up, record how often you plan to have contact with the care receiver.

10. Fill in the name of the care receiver. Your Referrals Coordinator may have assigned an identifying code number for your care receiver to maintain confidentiality during supervision. If so, use that number here.

11. This form should be filled out and turned in as soon as possible after the date of the last formal caring visit.

Bringing the Caring Relationship to a Close

Outline and Focus Notes

Let him who walks in the dark, who has no light, trust in the name of the LORD and rely on his God.

Isaiah 50:10b

I. Caregiving Is an Act of Faith

II. LIFE: Experiences of Closure or No Closure

FOCUS NOTE 1

Personal Experiences of Closure

1. How far in advance did you know that the relationship was ending?

2. What did you or the other person do to bring the relationship to a close?

3. How did the two of you say good-bye?

4. What continuing contact did you have, or have you had, with the person?

5. On a scale of one to ten, how good was your experience of closure of this relationship? (One = the worst, ten = couldn't have been better.)

6. What makes for a good experience of closure?

▶ both perspectives heard

▶ feelings

▶ bringing a sense of hope

▶ choice of relationship status → ongoing

▶

▶

TM-15 OFN Bringing the Caring Relationship to a Close.doc C: 1/1/2000 R:

>
>
>
>
>
>
>
>

III. Closure Challenges

A. Premature Closure by the Care Receiver

1. Reasons for Premature Closure

a. Moving

b. Inaccurate Assumptions

c. Threateningly Intense Feelings

d. Embarrassment over Sharing Too Much

e. Threat of Change

f. Impatience

FOCUS NOTE 2

Statements Care Receivers May Say to Express Impatience

▶ "I don't think this is doing any good. I feel worse now than I did when we started meeting."

▶ "My life is miserable, just as it's always been. We just seem to be wasting time."

▶ "All this doesn't seem to be getting me anywhere."

▶ "I haven't seen any changes in myself or my situation. What's the use of continuing these visits?"

---

g. Conflict

h. Interference

FOCUS NOTE 3

Ways in Which Outside Interference Might Be Expressed

▶ "You don't need help. You're strong; you can stand on your own two feet."

▶ "It's such a bother. Why do you spend the time?"

▶ "Are you still talking to that Stephen Minister?"

---

i. Lack of Interest

2. *Responding to Premature Closure by the Care Receiver*

a. Consult with Your Supervision Group

b. Listen and Understand

c. Address the Care Receiver's Concerns

d. Express Your Opinion

e. Try to Schedule at Least One More Meeting

FOCUS NOTE 4

Advantages of at Least One More Meeting

▶ You will have a chance to understand and respond fully to your care receiver's reasons for wanting to end the caring relationship.

▶ Your care receiver may want to end the caring relationship because of strong feelings that will dissipate over a week's time. By scheduling more caring visits, you can help your care receiver not end the caring relationship by a rash decision.

▶ You can have a more normal closure experience and work through the feelings that come with ending a caring relationship.

▶ With time to talk, you and your care receiver may discover other issues that your care receiver would benefit from working on.

▶ You will have a chance to talk to your Supervision Group or at least one of the Stephen Leaders.

FOCUS NOTE 5

What to Say to Get at Least One More Caring Visit

▶ "This is very sudden and I would like some time to think about it. Could we get together at least one more time?"

▶ "Could we agree to get together a couple of more times in order to talk about your desire to end our caring relationship?"

▶ "There is a whole process of ending a caring relationship. Both you and I are likely to have some fairly strong feelings about not meeting anymore. Typically closure takes place over several visits, and there's a process of gradually reducing the frequency of caring visits. Could we work through that closure process instead of just ending abruptly?"

▶ "We have been meeting for many weeks *[months/years]* now and I would like to have at least one more visit so we can work together to end our caring relationship well."

---

f. Do Your Best to Reestablish Contact

g. There May Be Nothing You Can Do

B. Premature Closure by the Stephen Minister

1. Reasons for Stephen Ministers to Bring Premature Closure

2. Dealing with Premature Closure by the Stephen Minister

a. Explain to Your Care Receiver

b. Make the Closure As Normal As Possible

c. Meet the Care Receiver's Continuing Needs

C. Closure Because of Referral to a Community Resource

D. Reluctance to Close

1. When the Care Receiver Is Reluctant to Bring Closure

2. When the Stephen Minister Is Reluctant to Bring Closure

FOCUS NOTE 6

Signs of Stephen Minister Boundary Problems

A Stephen Minister may be experiencing boundary problems if he or she exhibits any one of or combination of the following:

▶ Seems to need the care receiver or the caring relationship in order to be happy

▶ Takes on an unreasonable degree of responsibility for the care receiver's growth and well-being

▶ Is very self-critical about the care receiver's lack of progress

▶ Is unreasonably optimistic about the possibilities for his or her care receiver

▶ Seems unable to accept reality about the care receiver or the caring relationship

---

FOCUS NOTE 7

A Very Useful Question

"Whose needs are being met?"

E. If the Care Receiver Dies

IV. Practicing Closure

FOCUS NOTE 8

Stephen Minister's Instructions for Skill Practice 1

Read all the instructions in this Focus Note. Then review steps 2–6 of "The Normal Closure Process" on pages 350–352 in your Preclass Reading. Do not read the care receiver's instructions in Focus Note 9.

Description of your care receiver:

Your care receiver is an adult whose mother and father died in an automobile accident two and a half years ago. About six months after the accident, you began your caring relationship with him or her. During the two years you have been meeting, your care receiver has moved from deep sadness, through anger with God, into guilt for not paying enough attention to his or her parents, and finally to a point of being able to talk about good memories of his or her parents and about how to deal with life as an orphan. You were very worried about your care receiver earlier in the caring relationship, but now you feel confident that he or she will be fine.

Steps in your skill practice:

▶ Your care receiver will begin the skill practice. He or she will bring up the possibility of closure.

▶ Listen to your care receiver and explore his or her thoughts about ending the caring relationship. Discuss the pros and cons of closure with your care receiver.

▶ Work out a plan for tapering off the caring relationship and set a date for the last meeting.

▶ End the skill practice within five minutes.

Care Receiver's Instructions for Skill Practice 1

Spend five minutes studying the information in this Focus Note and preparing to play your role.

Your situation:

Two and a half years ago, both of your parents died in an automobile accident. You took responsibility for the funeral and dealing with their affairs, but you felt terribly sad and couldn't seem to get over it. You talked with your pastor, who suggested a Stephen Minister, and you have been meeting with your Stephen Minister for about two years now.

During those two years you have gone through several stages. For a long time you were deeply sad and could hardly talk about it. Then you felt very angry with God, and your Stephen Minister helped you get back to where you could pray and worship. You had several months of feeling guilty for not paying enough attention to your parents while they were alive. Now you are at a point where you can share your memories of your parents with your Stephen Minister and laugh or cry about those memories without going to pieces. Recently you have been coming to terms with the fact that you are now an orphan and you realize that you have to learn to live your life without your parents to lean on. ∗

In recent caring visits you have enjoyed your Stephen Minister's company, but you didn't have any weighty issues you needed to talk about. You know you will remain friends with your Stephen Minister, but you wonder whether it is time to stop meeting regularly as Stephen Minister and care receiver.

Think about your role and about how you could add your own details in order to make the role your own.

Steps in your skill practice:

▶ Begin the skill practice by saying, "I've been thinking about our meetings and wondering whether it's time for us to think about closure."

▶ Tell your Stephen Minister your thoughts about ending the caring relationship and discuss them with him or her.

▶ End the skill practice within five minutes.

FOCUS NOTE 10

Observer's Instructions for Skill Practice 1

Read both the Stephen Minister's instructions in Focus Note 8 and the care receiver's instructions in Focus Note 9. Also review the discussion questions in Focus Note 11 below to prepare to lead the discussion after the skill practice.

FOCUS NOTE 11

Discussion Questions

1. What feelings came up as you talked about closure?

2. How did the Stephen Minister do with the task of moving the caring relationship toward an appropriate closure?

3. What barriers did you run into that made closure more challenging?

4. What would you do differently if a situation like this ever came up again?

FOCUS NOTE 12

Observer's Instructions for Skill Practice 2

Read both the Stephen Minister's instructions in Focus Note 13 and the care receiver's instructions in Focus Note 14. Also review the discussion questions in Focus Note 11 above to prepare to lead the discussion after the skill practice.

FOCUS NOTE 13

Stephen Minister's Instructions for Skill Practice 2

Read the instructions in this Focus Note. Then review Focus Notes 4 and 5 on pages 361–362 about the advantages of having one more caring visit. Do not read the care receiver's instructions in Focus Note 14.

Description of your care receiver:

Your care receiver moved to your area five months ago because his or her spouse had received a promotion and a job transfer. He or she has been married more than six years and has no children.

Your care receiver has had a lot of trouble adjusting to his or her new home. He or she has felt sad about all the old friends he or she never sees anymore. Your care receiver has not made much of an effort to find new friends. He or she describes his or her new job as "boring and menial." In your last caring visit your care receiver shared some of his or her feelings of anger and resentment toward his or her spouse, who is working long hours and is never home. Your care receiver wondered aloud if his or her marriage was going to make it through this difficult time.

Steps in your skill practice:

▶ Your care receiver will begin the skill practice.

▶ Explore his or her plans and try to get him or her to say more about his or her feelings.

▶ Do your best to get your care receiver to agree to at least one more caring visit. Even if he or she refuses, don't give up trying to convince him or her to meet with you one more time.

▶ End the skill practice within five minutes.

FOCUS NOTE 14

Care Receiver's Instructions for Skill Practice 2

Spend five minutes studying the information in this Focus Note and preparing to play your role.

Your situation:

You and your spouse have been married more than six years. You have no children.

You moved into this area five months ago from the community where you had grown up. You didn't want to move, but your spouse received a promotion together with a transfer, and the two of you agreed you could not turn it down because of the large amount of additional money. You reluctantly agreed to the move, but you are still not happy about it.

As soon as you decided to move, your spouse immersed him- or herself in his or her new job and left you to handle all the details of the move on your own. He or she chose the new house and agreed to buy it without your ever having seen it. Now that you are in your new home, your spouse is rarely there. He or she rarely gets home before 8:30 in the evening and brings work home. You have been feeling angry and resentful toward your spouse.

You have tried to talk with your spouse, but he or she doesn't have time. Besides that, he or she is so wrapped up in work that he or she isn't very interested in your problems. The one time you expressed your anger, your spouse said, "I'm doing this for you, you know. Could you please deal with your responsibilities and let me concentrate on mine?"

You have decided that you have had enough of this new life and you are going back home. Your friend has offered to let you live with him or her. You have packed your bags and are planning to leave tomorrow. You secretly hope that your spouse will see your packed bags and ask you to stay.

Think about your role and about how you could add your own details in order to make the role your own.

Steps in your skill practice:
- Begin the skill practice by saying, "I really appreciate what you have done for me, but I need to tell you that this is the last time I'll be able to meet with you."
- Explain your situation and your decision.
- When your Stephen Minister asks you to meet with him or her at least one more time, say you can't because of the plans you have made. Finally, however, agree to one more caring visit the next week.
- End the skill practice within five minutes.

FOCUS NOTE 15

Care Receiver's Instructions for Skill Practice 3

Spend five minutes studying the information in this Focus Note and preparing to play your role.

Your situation:

You started meeting with your Stephen Minister when you were hospitalized for cancer surgery. Your Stephen Minister has been with you through the surgery, the radiation and chemotherapy treatments, and the joyous news that you were cancer-free. Your Stephen Minister has also helped you deal with the stresses your family has gone through and your guilt feelings about putting them through all this.

You have been meeting with your Stephen Minister for about 18 months, and about two months ago he or she recommended that you move toward bringing closure to your caring relationship. Your Stephen Minister said you are ready to resume your normal life and that, while he or she will always be available if you need him or her, you don't need the regular caring relationship anymore.

You haven't been as sure as your Stephen Minister that you don't need the caring relationship anymore, but you trust the person and have taken his or her word for it. During the past few months you and your Stephen Minister have been talking a lot about the past and how things have changed, and your Stephen Minister has helped you see the progress you've made. The two of you have also talked about your feelings, which, for the most part, have been sadness about no longer meeting with your Stephen Minister every week.

Now it is time for your final caring visit. You have been thinking a lot about what you want to say. You still aren't sure about being on your own, and you have a secret fear that the cancer will come back and you won't have anyone to rely on when it does. You have never mentioned this fear to your Stephen Minister.

Think about your role and about how you could add your own details in order to make the role your own.

Steps in your skill practice:

▶ Begin the skill practice by saying, "Well, here it is. I've been dreading this day."

▶ Tell your Stephen Minister what you have been thinking and feeling about ending the caring relationship. Tell him or her about your secret fear.

▶ End the skill practice within five minutes.

FOCUS NOTE 16

Observer's Instructions for Skill Practice 3

Read both the care receiver's instructions in Focus Note 15 and the Stephen Minister's instructions in Focus Note 17. Also read the discussion questions in Focus Note 11 on page 366 to prepare to lead the discussion after the skill practice.

Stephen Minister's Instructions for Skill Practice 3

Read these instructions and then review "Conduct the Final Visit" on pages 353–355 in your Preclass Reading. Do not read the care receiver's instructions in Focus Note 15.

Description of your care receiver:

Your care receiver is a cancer survivor. You began your caring relationship when he or she was in the hospital for surgery, and you stayed with him or her through radiation treatments and chemotherapy. The physician said they had gotten all the cancer and that your care receiver is cancer-free.

You have also listened as your care receiver has described his or her feelings about how the illness was affecting his or her family. You helped your care receiver figure out how to talk with the family about his or her feelings.

Your care receiver is back on his or her feet and ready to resume a normal life, and so you suggested closure. Your care receiver wasn't too sure about the idea but agreed once you explained that your relationship wouldn't end, it would just change. You have been tapering down your caring relationship and meeting once every other week. During this tapering-off period, you and your care receiver have talked about his or her recovery and feelings about the end of the caring relationship. You feel sad that the caring relationship is ending, but you also feel proud of your care receiver and of all the progress he or she has made.

Now it is time for your last caring visit. You have been thinking about how you are going to fit in all the necessary parts of a last caring visit, which are listed in the steps below.

Steps in your skill practice:

▶ Your care receiver will begin the skill practice.
▶ Work through as many of the elements of the final visit as you can in the time available. Those elements are:
  ▶ Remind the care receiver that this is the final visit.
  ▷ Review the caring relationship.
  ▷ Talk about feelings.
  ▷ Impart hope.
  ▷ Leave the door open.
  ▷ Mark the occasion.
  ▷ Say good-bye.
▶ End the skill practice within five minutes.

V. Caregiver's Compass Review

_____

_____

_____

_____

_____   _____

_____   _____

_____   _____

_____   _____

_____

_____

_____

_____

VI. Looking Ahead

Prayer Partner Requests and Thanksgivings

My prayer partner is _____

Prayer requests and thanksgivings to share with my prayer partner

_____

_____

Prayer requests and thanksgivings shared by my prayer partner

_____

_____

Supervision: A Key to Quality Christian Care—Part 1

Contents

▶ Caregiving Challenges

When Wanda went to visit Gertrude, she prayed all the way there. Gertrude had just found out that she had inoperable cancer and that she was likely to die within six months. Wanda prayed, "God, how can I help Gertrude? How can I stand all of Gertrude's pain?" After the visit Wanda was utterly exhausted. "I don't know where I'm going to find the courage to keep doing this," she said to herself.

Seth had been caring for Alan for a year and a half. Alan's father had died suddenly, and the intensity of Alan's grief had surprised and overcome him. Seth patiently listened as Alan worked through many different feelings about his father. Now, however, Alan seemed ready to move on, and Seth thought it might be time for closure.

Erin's relationship with her care receiver, Mary, had always been close. Mary was now 94 years old and had suffered a number of losses of aging. After their latest visit, however, Erin realized that she and Mary had never prayed together. "I wonder why that is," Erin thought. "I know that Stephen Ministry is Christian caregiving, but we don't seem to have any Christian element in our caring relationship."

Sam felt bamboozled by the problems his care receiver, Jack, was facing. Jack had lost his job at age 59 and had been looking for another job for almost a year. Jack had taken a temporary position, but that position was ending and Jack didn't know what to do. He needed a job, but no one seemed interested in hiring him. Jack was starting to feel down, and Sam didn't know what to do.

The last time Brenda met with her care receiver, she had trouble paying attention to what Renee was saying. She wanted to be there and she cared about Renee, but her mind wandered. Whenever she tried to think about Renee, Brenda would feel guilty and very uncomfortable. She wondered how she was going to be able to continue caring for Renee, feeling the way she did.

The next Tuesday night Wanda, Seth, Erin, Sam, and Brenda met together in their Supervision Group. As they prayed together to open the meeting, all five of them let out deep sighs. They were all relieved to be back with friends who cared about one another and their Stephen Ministry. Just being with their Supervision Group reminded them, once again, that they were not alone in their caregiving.

▶ Supervision Is a Key

Small Group Peer Supervision is absolutely essential for successful Stephen Ministry. You will get and give even more in supervision than you have in your 50 hours of training, and the success of your caring relationships depends on supervision more than any other element, except for God's help and guidance. In fact, your supervision session is one of the main times when God will give you help and guidance.

So that you'll be fully prepared to participate in small group supervision, you will have two In-Class Sessions and two reading assignments.

The Preclass Reading will tell you how supervision works and introduce you to some of the tools that you will use in supervision. That will prepare you to participate fully in the In-Class Session.

▶ The Structure of Small Group Peer Supervision

To participate fully in Stephen Series Small Group Peer Supervision, you need to understand not only how supervision works, but also why it works that way.

Frequency of Meetings

Once Stephen Ministers have finished their initial 50 hours of training and have been commissioned, they participate in twice-monthly supervision meetings. These twice-monthly meetings continue year-round.

What Happens in Supervision Meetings?

Supervision and continuing education meetings last two and a half hours. The schedule in Reference Box A shows how much time is given to various activities.

REFERENCE BOX A

Meeting Schedule

Group Size	Time	Activities
Whole Class	5 minutes	Opening, devotion, song, prayer
Whole Class	40 minutes	Continuing education (or more supervision)
Whole Class	15 minutes	Break
Small Group	90 minutes	Small Group Peer Supervision

Total 150 minutes (two and one half hours)

Note that some congregations have supervision before the break and continuing education after it. You will learn detailed information about what happens during the 90 minutes of Small Group Peer Supervision during part one of the In-Class Session, "Supervision: A Key to Quality Christian Care."

Attendance

Part of a Stephen Minister's covenant is faithfully attending supervision meetings. One hundred percent attendance is the expected norm. Sometimes Stephen Ministers will miss supervision meetings because they are ill, because they have to deal with an emergency, or because they are unavoidably out of town. When Stephen Ministers have to miss supervision meetings, they are expected to notify their Supervision Group Facilitator ahead of time.

Stephen Ministers attend supervision faithfully for three very good reasons.

For the Sake of the Care Receivers

Supervision enables the best care possible for those whom Stephen Ministers serve. Stephen Ministers cannot minister most effectively unless they participate faithfully in supervision.

For the Sake of the Other Stephen Ministers

At supervision meetings Stephen Ministers not only receive supervision, they also give it. Stephen Ministry supervision is peer supervision. Stephen Ministers care about one another so much that they attend supervision faithfully in order to help supervise one another and help one another grow to become even better caregivers.

For Their Own Sakes

Stephen Ministers know the benefits they receive personally from supervision. They see how they grow as Christians, as persons, and as caregivers through the supervision process. They attend supervision faithfully as a way of caring for themselves.

Size and Makeup of Supervision Groups

The Supervision Coordinator assigns all commissioned Stephen Ministers to small groups of five to seven members.

Supervision Groups Are Periodically Reorganized

Supervision Groups are reorganized at certain times, and the Supervision Coordinator assigns the members to new groups. This happens:

▶ when a new class of Stephen Ministers is commissioned;

▶ once a year; or

▶ when the Supervision Coordinator and the rest of the Stephen Leader Team believe it would be beneficial to form new groups.

Beginning new Supervision Groups periodically helps keep the supervision process fresh and alive. Stephen Ministers benefit from new insights that a new small group brings. Groups don't have time to get stuck in a rut. Reorganizing Supervision Groups also gives Stephen Ministers the opportunity to get to know more people in close, trusting small groups.

Another reason for assigning Stephen Ministers to new Supervision Groups periodically occurs when new Stephen Ministers are trained and commissioned. The new Stephen Ministers need to be integrated into supervision, and this works best when they are placed in groups that also contain some veteran

Stephen Ministers. Periodically reorganizing Supervision Groups gives Stephen Ministers practice in the process of group building so they can more quickly include the newly commissioned Stephen Ministers. Periodic reshuffling also helps veteran Stephen Ministers become accustomed to grieving when groups are broken up and reorganized. This prepares them emotionally to welcome the newly commissioned Stephen Ministers into their new Supervision Groups.

Benefits of Conducting Supervision in Small Groups

Supervision Groups with five to seven members are just the right size for peer supervision. They are small enough for everyone to participate fully, but are also big enough to offer the exchange of a variety of ideas and insights.

Stephen Ministers benefit from peer supervision for several reasons.

Stephen Ministers Grow by Contributing and Giving

By thinking through the needs in the caring relationships of other Stephen Ministers, their own knowledge and skills improve and their wisdom deepens.

Stephen Ministers Grow by Listening

By listening to the struggles and responses of fellow Stephen Ministers, they learn the best ways to care in a variety of situations.

Stephen Ministers Grow by Caring

By practicing caring skills (listening, reflecting feelings, and assertiveness, for example) with fellow Stephen Ministers in supervision, the skills are refined and reinforced.

Small Groups Foster Trust

Stephen Ministers learn to know and trust one another as they work together in small groups. Trust makes it possible for them to share openly and honestly so they can receive adequate supervision.

Small Groups Enable Growth as Persons and as Caregivers

The most important caring tool caregivers bring to the caring relationship is their own authentic, congruent selves. Supervision provides the opportunity for Stephen Ministers not only to grow in skills, but also to integrate caring skills into who they are. Instead of merely being people who listen, they become listeners; instead of being people who sometimes care, they become caregivers. Stephen Ministers who care with such congruency offer the best care possible to their care receivers.

▶ Leading Small Group Peer Supervision

There are three levels of leadership for supervision.

The Supervision Coordinator

The Supervision Coordinator is the Stephen Leader who has primary responsibility for making supervision happen in the congregation. He or she oversees the entire supervision process.

- ▶ Assigning Stephen Ministers to Supervision Groups
- ▶ Choosing, training, and supervising Supervision Group Facilitators

- ▶ Scheduling, planning, and coordinating supervision meetings
- ▶ Helping make sure the continuing education sessions meet the ministry needs of Stephen Ministers
- ▶ Planning for and administering all aspects of supervision

Supervision Group Facilitators

Supervision Group Facilitators can be Stephen Leaders or Stephen Ministers whom the Supervision Coordinator chooses for this task. They receive five hours of additional training to prepare them to facilitate Supervision Groups. Supervision Group Facilitators:

- ▶ convene the Supervision Group and keep it focused;
- ▶ communicate the needs of the Stephen Ministers in their small groups to the Supervision Coordinator, and communicate instructions and information from the Supervision Coordinator to the Supervision Group members;
- ▶ help Supervision Group members function more effectively together; and
- ▶ make sure Stephen Ministers see and meet care receivers' needs for referrals to other caring resources or for closure of the caring relationship.

Stephen Ministers

Stephen Ministers need to be integrally involved in leading Supervision Groups. Unless Stephen Ministers are deeply committed to Small Group Peer Supervision, and unless they work hard at providing excellent supervision for one another, supervision—and consequently Stephen Ministry—can be severely harmed at their congregation.

Quality Supervision Means Quality Ministry

Stephen Series supervision—structured and implemented in this way—has proven over the years to result in high-quality lay caring ministry. Stephen Ministers and Stephen Leaders who commit themselves to achieving this level of Stephen Series Small Group Peer Supervision will be rewarded with a personally enriching experience and a Stephen Ministry that will serve the congregation effectively for a long time.

▶ True-False Quiz about Supervision

This is an easy quiz because the answers and explanations are written right after each question. See whether there are any surprises in it for you.

1. Supervision is primarily a means to control the behavior of Stephen Ministers.

False.

Supervision ensures the best possible care for care receivers. It is not intended to police Stephen Ministers. Supervision serves Stephen Ministers and helps them provide the care their care receivers need.

Supervision helps Stephen Ministers remain accountable for their ministry. During supervision sessions Stephen Ministers turn in the records of their visits with their care receivers and discuss their caring relationships. But supervision cannot control people. Rather, it helps them control themselves and fulfill their caring ministry commitments.

2. It doesn't really matter what happens in supervision, just so you do something.

False.

Stephen Series supervision is structured. It is Small Group Peer Supervision. The specific activities that Stephen Ministers do in supervision have been proven to help them provide quality care. Supervision Group Facilitators lead the Supervision Groups and help participants receive and give effective peer supervision.

3. If you don't have a current care receiver, or if you aren't having problems in your caring relationship, you don't really need to be at supervision meetings.

False.

Supervision is not an optional activity for Stephen Ministers. Every Stephen Minister needs to be at every supervision meeting to:

▶ provide peer supervision to the other Stephen Ministers;

▶ receive supervision for his or her own caring relationship;

▶ grow in caregiving skills by learning from others' caring relationships, as well as his or her own;

▶ build the trust, group cohesiveness, and Christian community necessary for effective supervision; and

▶ receive continuing education to grow as an effective caregiver.

4. Supervision meets the needs of Stephen Ministers.

True.

Stephen Ministers need support to carry out their ministry. They need others who will:

▸ listen to them;

▸ help them care most effectively for their care receivers;

▸ help them grow in faith and in their ability to provide distinctively Christian care;

▸ help them grow in other caregiving skills and insights; and

▸ help them understand features of their caring relationships that they might not otherwise see.

While supervision certainly addresses Stephen Ministers' own needs, the needs of care receivers are always more important. Supervision meets the needs of Stephen Ministers to help them care for their care receivers as well as possible.

5. **In supervision sessions, one person does the supervising and the others wait their turns to receive supervision.**

   False.

   Stephen Series supervision is peer supervision. If one person is always monopolizing the conversation and others do not actively participate in supervising, then it is not *peer* supervision, and it is not working right.

   Stephen Ministers not only receive supervision, they also assist in supervising other Stephen Ministers in their Supervision Group. Everyone in the Supervision Group is involved in a cooperative process of:

   ▸ caring for one another;

   ▸ listening to one another;

▸ helping one another understand the needs of their care receivers; and

▸ meeting one another's needs for ideas, support, and encouragement.

6. **Many Stephen Series congregations have had very successful Stephen Ministries without conducting regular supervision.**

   False.

   When Stephen Series congregations do not conduct regular supervision, their Stephen Ministry is very likely to be unsuccessful and die.

   ▸ There is no support, so Stephen Ministers feel deserted. They carry a large responsibility all on their own. As a result, Stephen Ministers burn out and quit.

   ▸ There is no oversight of the care that Stephen Ministers provide. There is no guarantee of consistent, dedicated, high-quality care. The care receivers sometimes fall between the cracks and are lost.

   ▸ Word gets out in the congregation that the Stephen Ministry doesn't really do what it claimed it would. Congregation members form negative impressions of Stephen Ministry, and they refuse to volunteer to serve as Stephen Ministers or to receive care from Stephen Ministers.

   Often, without quality supervision, the congregation eventually just gives up on Stephen Ministry.

7. **Caring relationships are not only the concern of Stephen Ministers and care receivers; they are also of concern to Stephen Leaders and to the entire congregation.**

   True.

   Stephen Ministers give Christ's care. They are commissioned to deliver care on behalf of the entire congregation. Stephen Ministers are therefore accountable to the congregation for their care. The congregation has the right to make sure Stephen Ministers' care is high-quality and Christ-centered. The congregation has selected Stephen Leaders to oversee through supervision the care that Stephen Ministers provide.

8. **Stephen Leaders also benefit from supervision.**

   True.

   Stephen Leaders receive many benefits from supervision.

   ▸ Supervision provides the structure Stephen Leaders need to equip Stephen Ministers to deliver Christ's care.

   ▸ Supervision allows Stephen Leaders to work closely with Stephen Ministers, care for them, and enjoy fellowship with them.

   ▸ Supervision helps Stephen Leaders learn about Stephen Ministers' needs for continuing education.

   ▸ The Small Group Peer Supervision process enables Stephen Leaders to make sure that Stephen Ministers are equipped and supported to meet special needs of care receivers, such as the following:

   ▹ the need to recommend another care provider;

   ▹ the need for other types of wholistic care (food, clothing, medical care, a pastoral visit, or opportunities to get out, for example); or

   ▹ the need to bring closure to the caring relationship.

   ▸ Supervision helps Stephen Leaders assure that Stephen Ministry will work and last in their congregation.

▶ Six Tools for Effective Supervision

Look over these brief descriptions of each of the tools you will use when you participate in Small Group Peer Supervision, then turn to the indicated pages to study each tool carefully.

"Contact Record Sheet"

The "Contact Record Sheet" (see pages 382–383) is a simple tool for keeping track of your visits, telephone calls, and other contacts with your care receiver. You'll learn more about this tool in module 17, "How to Make a First Caring Visit."

"Check-In Statement Form"

At the beginning of a supervision session, each person in the group briefly tells how things are going in his or her caring relationship. This is called a check-in statement. This document (see page 384) is the tool you'll use to prepare your check-in statement before each supervision session.

"Stephen Minister's Progress Report"

At each supervision session, two Stephen Ministers report in more detail about their caring relationships and receive in-depth supervision from the group. The "Stephen Minister's Progress Report" (see pages 385–386) is one of the two tools Stephen Ministers can choose to prepare their in-depth reports.

"Distinctively Christian Care Report"

This form, "Distinctively Christian Care Report" (see pages 387–388), is the second option Stephen Ministers may use in preparing their in-depth reports.

"Questions for Regular Supervision Group Evaluation"

At the end of supervision sessions, group members take a few minutes to evaluate their work together. "Questions for Regular Supervision Group Evaluation" (see page 389) is the tool you will use most of the time.

"Questions for Periodic Supervision Group Evaluation"

Occasionally your group will engage in a more thorough evaluation using "Questions for Periodic Supervision Group Evaluation" (see pages 390–394).

▶ Getting Ready for the In-Class Session

Bring questions about this Preclass Reading to class. In class you will see a video that demonstrates a supervision session and learn about the parts of a session. Your Preclass Reading and In-Class Sessions will prepare you to get the most from (and give your best to) Small Group Peer Supervision.

Contact Record Sheet

CONFIDENTIAL

Stephen Minister _____

Contact Number	Date	Initiated by	Type of Contact	Length of Contact	Notes

(continued on the next page)

Explanation of Categories

Contact Number
Beginning with your first contact, all encounters with your care receiver should appear on this sheet regardless of their nature (phone, in person, or correspondence, for example).

Date
Date of contact

Initiated by
Note whether the Stephen Minister, the care receiver, or a third party initiated the contact. Be sure not to use the care receiver's name or initials.

Type of Contact
Phone call, visit, correspondence, happenstance encounter, or other

Length of Contact
Amount of time taken for the encounter in minutes

Notes
Record here, very briefly, notes for future reference. They can serve also as a "memory jogger" for your preparation of check-in statements and in-depth reports on the caring relationship. You might include such matters as these:

▶ The primary impression you received from the contact
▶ The location of the visit
▶ Anything special that took place during the contact
▶ A special need, concern, question, or issue that was raised
▶ An intense feeling you or the care receiver experienced
▶ The reason for the contact
▶ Any follow-up activities that are necessary
▶ Any change in the care receiver's situation, attitude, feeling, or behavior

▶ Check-In Statement Form

Write one- or two-sentence answers to the following questions, then share those answers briefly with your Supervision Group at the check-in time.

1. Describe your care receiver's primary need or problem.

2. What does your care receiver need from the caring relationship?

3. What are your current process-oriented goals for the caring relationship?

4. What is going well in the caring relationship, and what is not going well?

5. How can your Supervision Group help you be a better caregiver in this caring relationship, now, or the next time you report in-depth?

Stephen Minister's Progress Report

Stephen Ministry® Form

1. How many weeks have you been meeting with your care receiver? _____

2. How often have you been meeting with your care receiver? (Weekly, more than weekly, less than weekly) _____

   ▶ Has your pattern of visitation changed since your last in-depth report? ❑ Yes   ❑ No
   If yes, what brought about the change?

3. What other caregivers are involved in caring for your care receiver? (Professional therapist or counselor, social worker, medical doctor, visiting nurse, or others)

   ▶ Has this changed since your last in-depth report? ❑ Yes   ❑ No
   If yes, what brought about the change?

4. In one paragraph, tell how you understand your care receiver's current need, concern, or challenge.

5. Say more about your process-oriented ministry goals for working with your care receiver.

6. In one paragraph, summarize what you are doing to carry out those goals.

7. Evaluate the progress of your caring relationship.

   a. How do you feel about your relationship with your care receiver?

(continued on the next page)

b. How has your care receiver responded to your ministry?

c. What has been going well in your caring relationship?

d. What has been challenging, frustrating, or problematic for you in your caring relationship?

e. What do you believe should be the future focus of your caring relationship? (Continuing with your current focus? Closure? Referral to a mental health professional or other community resource? Focusing on spiritual concerns? Something else?)

8. With what questions, concerns, issues, or areas of need do you want the Supervision Group to help you at this time?

9. What Focus Question Set and Focus Questions might your Supervision Group use to discuss your caring relationship?

►Distinctively Christian Care Report

1. How many weeks have you been meeting with your care receiver? _____

2. How often have you been meeting with your care receiver? (Weekly, more than weekly, less than weekly) _____

   ► Has your pattern of visitation changed since your last in-depth report? ❏ Yes ❏ No
   If yes, what brought about the change?

3. What other caregivers are involved in caring for your care receiver? (Professional therapist or counselor, social worker, medical doctor, visiting nurse, or others)

   ► Has this changed since your last in-depth report? ❏ Yes ❏ No
   If yes, what brought about the change?

4. In one paragraph, tell how you understand your care receiver's current need, concern, or challenge.

5. Say more about your process-oriented ministry goals for working with your care receiver.

6. In one paragraph, summarize what you are doing to carry out those goals.

7. What happens in your caring relationship that you would describe as distinctively Christian?

8. How well do you think you understand your care receiver's spiritual needs right now?

(continued on the next page)

9. What does your care receiver need from God right now?

▶ How do you know?

10. Briefly describe how you are using a distinctively Christian caring tool—the Bible, prayer, forgiveness, blessings, "a cup of cold water"—in your caring relationship.

▶ How has your care receiver let you know that he or she needs you to use that tool?

▶ How has your care receiver responded to your use of that tool?

▶ How might your Supervision Group help you use the tool more effectively?

11. Do you notice your care receiver growing in faith, trust, and obedience to God through your caring relationship? If so, what is the nature of that growth? If not, what might be some reasons for the lack of growth?

12. How are you growing in faith, trust, and obedience to God through your caring relationship?

13. What Focus Question Set and Focus Questions might your Supervision Group use to discuss your caring relationship?

Questions for Regular Supervision Group Evaluation

Answer these questions quickly and then give this questionnaire to your Supervision Group Facilitator. If you don't have answers for any of the questions, simply mark them "NA."

Evaluating the Overall Supervision Group Process

1. How did you feel about today's Supervision Group session?

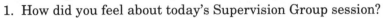

Terrible   Okay   Great

2. Rate the distinctively Christian nature of this Supervision Group session.

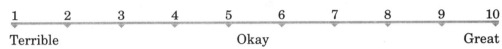

Not at all   Completely
centered on Christ   centered on Christ

3. How well focused was your Supervision Group during this session?

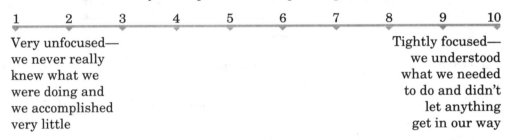

Very unfocused—   Tightly focused—
we never really   we understood
knew what we   what we needed
were doing and   to do and didn't
we accomplished   let anything
very little   get in our way

4. How do you rate the tempo of this Supervision Group session?

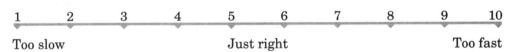

Too slow   Just right   Too fast

5. List any other comments or specific suggestions you'd like to make regarding the Supervision Group:

Evaluating Your Participation in the Supervision Group Session

6. How actively did you participate in this Supervision Group session?

Not at all actively   Very actively

7. Did you find yourself wanting to say things, but not saying them?   ❑ yes   ❑ no
   What do you think was the reason?

Questions for Periodic Supervision Group Evaluation

This evaluation of your Supervision Group is designed to help you:

▶ examine your own Supervision Group participation;

▶ gauge the quality of interaction among Supervision Group members;

▶ monitor the effectiveness of your Supervision Group experience; and

▶ discover areas of growth for you and the Supervision Group.

I. Evaluating Myself

A. My Feelings about My Participation in the Supervision Group

| 1 | 2 | 3 | 4 | 5 |

I feel uncomfortable
in the group

I feel at ease
in the group

Please be prepared to talk about your evaluation. What specifically makes you feel at ease or uncomfortable in the group? Here are some ideas to prompt your thinking (you may indicate any that apply):

I'm uncomfortable because . . .	I'm at ease because . . .
"I feel left out of the group."	"I feel welcome and included in the group."
"I'm not sure I feel completely accepted by the group."	"I feel accepted as I am."
"I wonder whether group members respect me."	"I feel respected by group members."

Thoughts to share with your Supervision Group:

(continued on the next page)

B. My Level of Participation in the Supervision Group

1	2	3	4	5
My level of participation in the group is very low				My level of participation in the group is very high

Please be prepared to talk about your evaluation. Why do you think your participation in the group is very high or very low? Here are some ideas to prompt your thinking (you may indicate any that apply):

I don't participate much because . . .	I participate because . . .
"Sometimes I have a hard time trusting people."	"I am very trusting."
"Sometimes I have a hard time empathizing with people."	"I can really empathize with people."
"I sometimes find myself being critical of others' ideas and opinions."	"I tend to accept others' ideas and opinions unconditionally."
"I have a hard time praising and complimenting others."	"I willingly praise and compliment others."
"Sometimes it is hard for me to be warm and affectionate."	"I freely express warmth and affection."
"I sometimes have trouble paying attention to what others are saying."	"I'm a great listener."
"I find it difficult to express myself in a group setting."	"I enjoy sharing my thoughts and ideas in a group."
"I don't like it when other people make suggestions about what I should do."	"I take others' suggestions and comments seriously."
"I like the way I am and don't see why I need to grow."	"I'm flexible and open to change and growth."

Thoughts to share with your Supervision Group:

(continued on the next page)

II. Evaluating My Supervision Group

A. How Well the Supervision Group Works Together

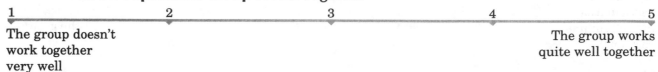

| 1 | 2 | 3 | 4 | 5 |

The group doesn't
work together
very well

The group works
quite well together

Please be prepared to talk about your evaluation. Why do you think the group is working well together or not working well together? Here are some ideas to prompt your thinking (you may indicate any that apply):

The group doesn't work well because . . .	The group works well because . . .
"A few tend to dominate the group."	"Everyone participates equally."
"We have a hard time with listening and sometimes fail to understand one another."	"We listen carefully and understand one another's ideas."
"We're uncomfortable with feelings and often withhold and ignore them."	"We share, recognize, and accept one another's feelings."
"We're more critical than affirming of another's feelings."	"We often affirm one another."
"We tend to wear masks, hiding our real selves."	"We are open and honest about ourselves."
"We really don't trust one another very much yet."	"We have a climate of mutual trust."
"We tend to be more competitive than supportive."	"We support one another."
"We aren't always willing to protect confidentiality."	"We keep confidences."
"Our conversation often wanders, and we lose our focus on our task."	"We keep on track and remain focused on our task."
"We waste time in our Supervision Group."	"We use time wisely."

Thoughts to share with your Supervision Group:

(continued on the next page)

B. How Well the Supervision Group Accomplishes Its Goal

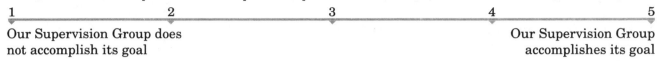

1   2   3   4   5

Our Supervision Group does   Our Supervision Group
not accomplish its goal   accomplishes its goal

Please be prepared to talk about your evaluation. In what ways does our Supervision Group accomplish or not accomplish its goal?

Rate your group using the following question and scales: How much does our Supervision Group help me provide quality care to my care receiver in the following areas? (Rate only those areas that apply to you.)

	Not Very Helpful				Very Helpful
Remaining process-oriented	1	2	3	4	5
Listening	1	2	3	4	5
Helping my care receiver deal with feelings	1	2	3	4	5
Maintaining confidentiality	1	2	3	4	5
Understanding my care receiver's needs	1	2	3	4	5
Using distinctively Christian caring tools appropriately and confidently	1	2	3	4	5
Relating assertively	1	2	3	4	5
Maintaining boundaries	1	2	3	4	5
Making recommendations for other care, as necessary	1	2	3	4	5
Caring for my care receiver's unique needs	1	2	3	4	5
Bringing my caring relationship to a close	1	2	3	4	5
Experiencing and expressing compassion	1	2	3	4	5
Trusting God as I care	1	2	3	4	5
Remaining full of faith	1	2	3	4	5
Growing in caring skills	1	2	3	4	5
Remaining worthy of my care receiver's trust	1	2	3	4	5

Thoughts to share with your Supervision Group:

(continued on the next page)

III. Where Do We Go from Here?

A. Identify one major area in which our Supervision Group needs to grow.

B. What might we do to help bring about that growth?

Supervision: A Key to Quality Christian Care—Part 1

Outline and Focus Notes

Therefore encourage one another and build up each other, as indeed you are doing.

1 Thessalonians 5:11 NRSV

I. Encourage One Another

FOCUS NOTE 1

Paul's Wherefore

Now concerning the times and the seasons, brothers and sisters, you do not need to have anything written to you. For you yourselves know very well that the day of the Lord will come like a thief in the night. When they say, "There is peace and security," then sudden destruction will come upon them, as labor pains come upon a pregnant woman, and there will be no escape! But you, beloved, are not in darkness, for that day to surprise you like a thief; for you are all children of light and children of the day; we are not of the night or of darkness. So then let us not fall asleep as others do, but let us keep awake and be sober; for those who sleep sleep at night, and those who are drunk get drunk at night. But since we belong to the day, let us be sober, and put on the breastplate of faith and love, and for a helmet the hope of salvation. For God has destined us not for wrath but for obtaining salvation through our Lord Jesus Christ, who died for us, so that whether we are awake or asleep we may live with him. Therefore encourage one another and build up each other, as indeed you are doing.

1 Thessalonians 5:1–11 NRSV

II. How Does Small Group Peer Supervision Work?

A. The Importance of Supervision

B. The Goal of Supervision

> **FOCUS NOTE 2**
>
> ### The Goal of Small Group Peer Supervision
>
> The goal of supervision is for Stephen Ministers to work together in order to enable the best distinctively Christian care possible to benefit their care receivers.

C. The Size of the Supervision Group

D. Meetings

1. Frequency

2. Length and Content

> **FOCUS NOTE 3**
>
> ### Supervision and Continuing Education Meeting Schedule
>
> | Group Size | Time | Activities |
> | --- | --- | --- |
> | Whole Class | 5 minutes | Opening, devotion, song, prayer |
> | Whole Class | 40 minutes | Continuing education (or more supervision) |
> | Whole Class | 15 minutes | Break |
> | Small Group | 90 minutes | Small Group Peer Supervision |
>
> **Total 150 minutes (two and one half hours)**

E. Leadership

III. A Demonstration of Small Group Peer Supervision

FOCUS NOTE 4

While Viewing the Supervision Demonstration . . .

Questions to Think About

1. What are some examples of peer supervision in this video—of group members supervising one another?

2. How does Steve, the Stephen Minister in the spotlight, benefit from the supervision session? How might Steve's care receiver benefit?

Documents to Look At

▶ "Check-In Statement Form" (page 384)

▶ "Stephen Minister's Progress Report" (pages 385–386)

▶ "Questions for Regular Supervision Group Evaluation" (page 389)

IV. Steps in the Supervision Process

FOCUS NOTE 5

What Happens in Supervision?

The Beginning of the Supervision Session

1. The Supervision Group gathers and prays.

2. Every member of the group briefly checks in.

   ▸ Each Stephen Minister passes in a "Contact Record Sheet" to the Supervision Group Facilitator.

   ▸ Stephen Ministers then take turns sharing about their caring relationships using prepared check-in statements.

The Heart of the Supervision Session

1. The Supervision Group Facilitator selects one of the Stephen Ministers who have prepared an in-depth report for this session to present his or her caring relationship for in-depth supervision.

2. Using one of the appropriate tools, that Stephen Minister shares his or her caring relationship with the group.

3. The Supervision Group uses Focus Questions and the resulting discussion to explore the caring relationship.

4. The group offers feedback, support, information, care, and listening ears, and in other ways supervises and supports the Stephen Minister whose caring relationship is in the spotlight.

5. The Supervision Group Facilitator leads the group in a summary of the in-depth discussion of this caring relationship and then concludes the discussion.

6. The Supervision Group Facilitator chooses another Stephen Minister who has prepared an in-depth report to present his or her caring relationship for in-depth supervision, and the process (steps 2 through 5 in The Heart of the Supervision Session) is repeated for the new Stephen Minister in the spotlight.

The End of the Supervision Session

1. Group members evaluate the Supervision Group and the session.

2. Finally, the Supervision Group Facilitator brings the supervision session to a close and assigns those Stephen Ministers whose caring relationships will be in the spotlight at the next supervision meeting.

A. The Beginning of the Supervision Session

1. Gather and Pray

2. Check-In

a. Turn in Your "Contact Record Sheet"

b. Share Your Check-In Statement

Characteristics of an Effective Check-In Statement

Brief

▶ The check-in statement should take one to two minutes. If it takes more time than that, it is too long to be a check-in statement.

Honest

▶ A check-in statement should tell the truth.

▶ If Stephen Ministers are feeling uncomfortable or afraid, angry at their care receivers, or concerned about some aspect of the caring relationship, then they need to say so.

▶ The members of the group cannot provide support and encouragement if they don't know what's really going on.

Confidential

▶ The check-in statement is always presented in a way that preserves confidentiality.

▶ Use no names.

▶ Give no needless details.

Prepared in Advance

▶ Stephen Ministers care enough about their care receivers, themselves, and the other members of the Supervision Group to prepare carefully ahead of time.

A Sample Check-In Statement

1. Describe your care receiver's primary need or problem.
My care receiver is experiencing terrible emotional pain, as she grieves for the death of her child.

2. What does your care receiver need from the caring relationship?
Most of all, my care receiver needs support. She needs someone who will listen to her as she talks about very painful feelings.

3. What are your current process-oriented goals for the caring relationship?
My goal is to have the courage to continue to listen, care, support, and love my care receiver.

4. What is going well in the caring relationship, and what is not going well?

The fact that we get together once a week and also talk over the phone is very positive. What is not going well is that things seem to be getting worse for my care receiver, not better.

5. How can your Supervision Group help you be a better caregiver in this caring relationship, now, or the next time you report in-depth?

Help me find the courage to keep caring. This caring relationship is also very difficult for me emotionally.

FOCUS NOTE 8

Instructions for Writing a Check-In Statement

1. Think of a caring relationship to write about. It might be:

   ▶ a caring relationship in which you have been involved in the past or a current one (be sure to preserve confidentiality);

   ▶ a caring relationship you make up—you may draw elements from real life, or from a story you have read or seen on TV or in a movie; or

   ▶ a caring relationship from a previous module's skill practice. There are descriptions of care receivers in Focus Notes 9, 14, and 15 on pages 365, 367–368, and 368–369 of your *Stephen Ministry Training Manual*.

2. Prepare a check-in statement for that caring relationship using "Check-In Statement Form."

3. Work quickly, because you have only five minutes to complete the "Check-In Statement Form."

B. The Heart of the Supervision Session

1. Choose a Stephen Minister to Give an In-Depth Report

a. Regular Rotation

b. Reasons to Interrupt Regular Rotation

FOCUS NOTE 9

Examples of Urgent Needs for Supervision

▸ The care receiver may be hinting about suicide, homicide, or abuse.

▸ The care receiver may be threatening to bring closure prematurely to the caring relationship.

▸ The care receiver may need a recommendation for other care.

▸ The Stephen Minister seems very upset about some other troubling aspect of the caring relationship.

---

2. Present an In-Depth Report

a. The Importance of Preparation

b. In-Depth Report Tools

c. Demonstration of an In-Depth Report

d. Practice Writing an In-Depth Report

FOCUS NOTE 10

Instructions for Writing an In-Depth Report

1. Use the same caring relationship you chose when you filled out your "Check-In Statement Form."

2. Answer the items on both sides of the "Stephen Minister's Progress Report."

3. Spend most of your time on the second side of the progress report.

---

4. Skip the last question about Focus Questions. You will learn about Focus Questions later.

3. *Explore the Caring Relationship*

a. Begin with Affirmation

FOCUS NOTE 11

Affirmations

▶ "You have been so faithful in your care for your care receiver. You haven't missed a week with him."

▶ "I think you have some real insight into your care receiver's situation."

▶ "I remember when you first started telling us about your care receiver. You two have made a lot of progress."

▶ "You were really there for your care receiver when she needed you. I'll bet she's grateful."

▶ "I am impressed by the way you pray for your care receiver."

▶ "Your care receiver seems to have grown spiritually. God has clearly blessed your ministry in wonderful ways."

---

b. Use Focus Questions

4. *Supervise and Support the Stephen Minister*

5. *End the Discussion of the Caring Relationship*

a. How Long Might the Discussion Last?

b. How Does the Discussion End?

Questions for Wrapping Up the In-Depth Discussion

► What has the Stephen Minister heard from the others in the group?

► What personal insights does the Stephen Minister say he or she has experienced?

► What does the Stephen Minister perceive to be the appropriate next step?

6. Another Round of In-Depth?

C. The End of the Supervision Session

1. Evaluate Small Group Peer Supervision

2. End the Meeting

V. Caregiver's Compass Review

_____

_____

_____

_____   COMPASSIONATE · FULL OF FAITH · SKILLED · TRUSTWORTHY   _____

_____   ☧   _____

_____   _____

_____

_____

_____

_____

VI. Looking Ahead

Prayer Partner Requests and Thanksgivings

My prayer partner is _____

Prayer requests and thanksgivings to share with my prayer partner

_____

_____

Prayer requests and thanksgivings shared by my prayer partner

_____

_____

Supervision: A Key to Quality Christian Care—Part 2

Contents

▶ Support, Encouragement, and Accountability for Caregiving Challenges

Over the next three supervision sessions, Wanda, Seth, Erin, Sam, and Brenda all received in-depth supervision for their caring relationships.

The Supervision Group didn't have answers or magic solutions for Wanda. They listened to Wanda tell about her visit with her care receiver and about her care receiver's sadness and fear at her approaching death. After discussing several Focus Questions to help Wanda talk about her feelings, they prayed with her and promised to pray daily for Wanda and her care receiver. At the end of her in-depth discussion, Wanda said, "Thank you. Now I know I'm not alone in this. You've helped me find the courage to go back and stick with my care receiver, at least until our next supervision session."

When Seth brought up the possibility of closure to his caring relationship, the Supervision Group went to Focus Question Set C. They asked some probing questions: "What's happened that makes you think it's time for closure?" "Are there still issues that your care receiver needs to work through?" By the end of the in-depth discussion, the Supervision Group agreed that Seth should bring up the topic of closure with his care receiver. Seth left the group meeting with a clear plan for how he would do so.

As Erin told her Supervision Group about never praying with her care receiver, they listened carefully. Then they used Focus Questions to understand what the reasons might be. Erin realized that she had never prayed with her care receiver even though her care receiver probably expected that prayer would be part of their caring relationship. The Supervision Group also helped Erin realize that, while she prayed by herself, she was uncomfortable praying aloud with others and so she had avoided doing so with her care receiver. Erin left the supervision session with a plan to take written prayers with her to caring visits and use those to start praying with her care receiver and build her confidence to pray aloud.

As Sam described his care receiver's problems, he seemed very nervous. When his Supervision Group asked him about that, he said, "My care receiver is going downhill. I don't know what to do, and I'm feeling as if I'm not helping him." The Supervision Group asked some Focus Questions to help Sam think about how responsible he was feeling for his care receiver's problems. After a while Sam said, "I'm accustomed to solving problems, not living with them. I suppose I've been a little too results-oriented." A group member told Sam about a job-hunter's support group to recommend to his care receiver. Sam decided that he would suggest the group at his next caring visit, but otherwise let his care receiver take responsibility for his situation.

When Brenda reported to her Supervision Group about her caring relationship, she seemed uninterested. Her "Contact Record Sheet" showed that she had visited with her care receiver only three out of the last five weeks. When her Supervision Group Facilitator asked about that, she said, "I guess we didn't get around to meeting those weeks." The Supervision Group used Focus Questions to ask Brenda about the future of her caring relationship, and she said that she didn't know what her care receiver really needed. Then one person asked, "Are you really committed to caring for her?" At that Brenda started to cry. She said she didn't know if she was. As they talked more, Brenda told the group that she felt very insecure about caring for her care receiver and didn't think she was doing any good. She felt so guilty that she was avoiding her care receiver. The group reminded her that she was just the caregiver and that God was the Curegiver. All Brenda had to do was care faithfully for her care receiver. In fact, that was all she *could* do. Brenda agreed to meet with her care receiver in the two weeks before the next Supervision Group meeting, and the group agreed that she would present an in-depth report again at the next session.

▶ How to Work with This Section on Focus Questions

An important goal of the Preclass Reading for this part of the module on supervision is to help you become familiar with Focus Questions and learn how to use them effectively.

Begin your study by reading An Introduction to Focus Questions in Supervision below. Then, spend some time becoming familiar with the Focus Questions themselves. They are listed in the Focus Question Sets section of this Preclass Reading beginning on page 412. Read through them several times until you begin to see which types of questions go with which Focus Question Sets.

To participate effectively in Small Group Peer Supervision it will be very helpful to become familiar with the Focus Questions, so there is no time like the present to start learning about them and how to use them.

▶ An Introduction to Focus Questions in Supervision

"What do we talk about?" "What do we say to each other?" "What will we do

with 90 minutes in small group supervision?" Sometimes Stephen Ministers wonder about these questions as they begin their involvement in Small Group Peer Supervision.

The most important activity that goes on in Small Group Peer Supervision is in-depth discussion of caring relationships. Focus Questions are the main tool that Stephen Ministers use to make each in-depth discussion as beneficial as possible. This introduction explains the nature of Focus Questions and seven important purposes that they serve in supervision.

The Nature of Focus Questions

It helps to know how Focus Questions were designed and why.

Multifaceted

Focus Questions enable small groups to hold up the caring relationship being supervised like a precious jewel. As the group slowly turns it, group members see the various facets of the caring relationship, how they fit together and interact, and why a Stephen Minister needs to be aware of each of them.

As Stephen Ministers use Focus Questions in Supervision Groups, they will grow in appreciating the value of each of the many dimensions of caring ministry.

Structured

Focus Questions have been carefully structured into sets. Structured questions make possible good *peer* supervision and make the best use of the group's time. When all Supervision Group members use the same structured questions to explore in-depth a caring relationship, they keep the group's conversation headed in the same direction and provide the best help for the reporting Stephen Minister.

Because of extensive training, professional experience, or unique intuitive gifts, a few individuals may be able to guide group discussion without using the Focus Questions. If they don't use the Focus Questions, however, they limit the ability of others who are less experienced or gifted in this way to participate in supervision. Then one or two members are likely to dominate the group, and the others will be less involved, grow less, and be less motivated to attend supervision faithfully.

In order to attain the goal of peer supervision, everyone can exercise their Christian freedom to serve others and submit to the discipline of using Focus Questions. The peer supervision that will result will prove far more beneficial for all Stephen Ministers and through them to their care receivers.

Seven Important Purposes of Focus Questions

Why is it important to use Focus Questions?

1. To Allow God to Be at Work in the Caring Relationship

Stephen Ministers use Focus Questions to help one another see how God is working in the caring relationship. They use Focus Questions to help one another consider ways to reshape or improve the caring relationship and improve their caring skills so that they can be better instruments in God's hands.

2. To Be a Means, Not an End

Focus Questions are a means to an end, not an end in themselves. The end toward which Supervision Groups work in using Focus Questions is providing the best distinctively Christian care for care receivers.

3. To Serve the Needs of Stephen Ministers

The Supervision Group uses Focus Questions to serve Stephen Ministers, who can bring a wide range of needs to supervision. Stephen Ministers may need:

▸ additional information about what their care receivers are going through;

▸ an outsider's perspective to clarify what they are experiencing in their caring relationships;

▸ to express their own feelings and have other Stephen Ministers listen, reflect their feelings, and accept them;

▸ prayer or spiritual support;

▸ encouragement or affirmation; or

▸ to be challenged to stretch or take a risk.

Focus Questions help the Supervision Group identify and explore the Stephen Minister's needs and concerns. Focus Questions are not a way for others in the group to force their own solutions, feelings, or agenda on the Stephen Minister being supervised. Rather, Focus Questions help draw out the Stephen Minister's own feelings, thoughts, and ideas about how to provide the most effective Christian care to his or her care receiver.

Focus Questions also permit others in the group to bring up issues that the

Stephen Minister might not have thought about on his or her own. Group supervision gives Stephen Ministers the benefit of perspectives and ideas other than their own. Each Stephen Minister retains responsibility for deciding what to do and how to do it, but he or she is provided with an array of ideas and options that he or she might not have come up with.

4. To Care for Stephen Ministers

When a Stephen Minister's caring relationship is in the spotlight, the Supervision Group treats that Stephen Minister like a care receiver in many ways. The Supervision Group gives care, support, acceptance, encouragement, and guidance as the Stephen Minister reflects on his or her caring relationship.

Supervision Group members use their caring ministry skills to provide peer supervision. Focus Questions make it possible to identify the needs that Stephen Ministers bring to the Supervision Group, so that the group can direct its care to the right places.

5. To Go Deeper

By nature, groups tend to talk primarily about surface issues. They are less likely to talk about the difficult and painful—or surprising and joyful—aspects at the heart of caring relationships. It's less risky when the conversation remains on the surface, but it's also much less helpful. Focus Questions help the Supervision Group to stay with one aspect of the caring relationship long enough to get past the surface issues and face up to in-depth problems or joys.

For example, by using Focus Questions the group will move past a superficial understanding of the words exchanged between a caregiver and care receiver in order to see the spiritual issues that the care receiver was bringing up.

In another example, the Supervision Group might use Focus Questions to help the Stephen Minister see past his or her feelings of anger toward the care receiver to become aware of how his or her own pain may be entering into the caring relationship.

6. To Focus the Supervision Group's Attention

Supervision Groups use Focus Questions to concentrate on one aspect of the caring relationship at a time. The discussion of any caring relationship could take several valid directions. But if the group tries to discuss them all, they will end up not discussing any aspect of the caring relationship in depth.

Using Focus Questions helps the Supervision Group move intentionally from subject to subject, and to spend enough time with each issue to get beneath the surface. This gives Stephen Ministers support, insight, and encouragement in a specific area so that they can improve their quality Christian care for their care receivers in succeeding visits.

7. To Facilitate the Group's Discussion

Focus Questions are not for Stephen Ministers to use slavishly or by rote. They are not intended to pressure others to think or behave in certain ways. Instead, Focus Questions prime the pump of thinking, analysis, and discussion. They facilitate (meaning "to make easier") the work of the Supervision Group by helping Stephen Ministers express their questions, comments, concerns, and ideas to one another.

How to Use Focus Questions

The Focus Questions are divided into eight Focus Question Sets.

A. Focus on the Caring Relationship

B. Focus on the Spiritual Nature of the Caring Relationship

C. Focus on the Direction of the Caring Relationship

D. Focus on the Caregiver's Feelings about the Caring Process

E. Focus on the Caregiver's Skills

F. Focus on the Caregiver's Personal Growth

G. Focus on the Care Receiver's Situation

H. Focus on a Possible Mental Health Referral

The diagram in Reference Box A illustrates one way to organize the Focus Question Sets.

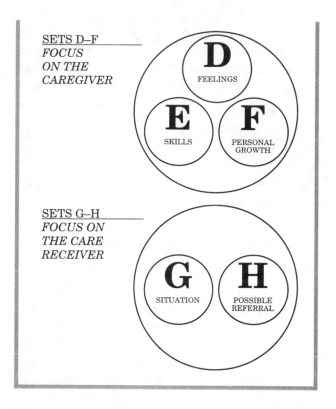

How to Choose Focus Questions

There are many more Focus Questions than the group will ever use in any one supervision session. The steps in Reference Box B tell how a Supervision Group works together to choose Focus Questions.

REFERENCE BOX A

Organize the Focus Question Sets

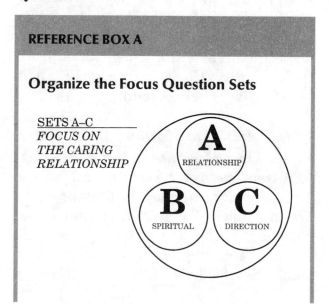

REFERENCE BOX B

How to Choose Focus Questions

Step 1: The Stephen Minister in the spotlight identifies the Focus Question Set and chooses Focus Questions that will best meet his or her needs, and tells them to the Supervision Group as part of his or her in-depth report.

Step 2: Other group members suggest additional possible Focus Question Sets and Focus Questions to concentrate on.

Step 3: The Supervision Group Facilitator helps the group decide on a Focus Question Set with which to start.

Step 4: The group chooses a Focus Question from that set.

Step 5: The group may move to other Focus Questions or Focus Question Sets during the course of the discussion. Whenever a group member suggests moving to a different Focus Question Set, the Supervision Group Facilitator helps the group decide whether they are ready for a new topic and, if so, what that topic should be.

Effectively Using Focus Questions

The large number of Focus Questions offers an advantage and a challenge. The advantage is that the group has a complete tool that they can use effectively with any caring relationship. The challenge is that the number of questions can seem overwhelming.

Several responses to the challenge of Focus Questions may prove helpful.

1. Each member of the Supervision Group can become very familiar with the emphasis in each of the Focus Question Sets. This will give the group a good idea of where to concentrate its search for the right Focus Questions. Move from the caregiver's report on the needs in the caring relationship to the Focus Question Set, and then to specific Focus Questions.

2. Each group member can study the Focus Questions and become very familiar with them.

3. Stephen Ministers can practice using Focus Questions in continuing education exercises.

4. Group members can work together and help one another use Focus Questions more effectively.

5. Don't give up. The group will become more familiar with the Focus Questions over time. The group's tenacity and hard work will be rewarded with high-quality, gratifying supervision sessions and higher quality care.

►Focus Question Sets

Set A: Focus on the Caring Relationship

1. Describe your relationship with your care receiver.
   a. What are the most rewarding aspects?
   b. What are the biggest challenges?

2. What are your feelings when you start your visit? When you conclude your visit?

3. What do you think your care receiver's feelings are when you arrive and when you leave?

4. Does the care receiver trust you enough to share risky thoughts and feelings? If not, why not? What could be done?

5. Evaluate and give examples of the following aspects of the relationship.
   a. *Respect:* Do you both treat one another with respect? Do you tend to consider yourself above your care receiver?
   b. *Genuineness:* Do your verbal and nonverbal messages agree with each other? Do your care receiver's verbal and nonverbal messages agree with each other?
   c. *Warmth:* Do you communicate empathy and acceptance to your care receiver? Does your care receiver sense that?
   d. *Positive Regard:* How do you show that you value your care receiver as loved by God and redeemed by Christ?

6. Do either of you get frustrated because of inappropriate or unrealistic expectations?
   a. Do you place unrealistic expectations on the care receiver or upon yourself?
   b. Does the care receiver place unrealistic expectations on you or on him- or herself?
   c. How do you or your care receiver communicate these expectations?

7. Is your focus on process or results?
   a. Do you offer solutions, give advice, or try to rescue the care receiver? Explain.
   b. Are you pressuring yourself to make your care receiver improve or change?
   c. Do you feel like a failure because your care receiver has not improved or changed?
   d. Do you pressure your care receiver to change?

8. How are you and your care receiver doing with boundary issues?
   a. Is your care receiver becoming too dependent on you? If so, how? Are you becoming dependent upon the relationship with your care receiver? If so, how?
   b. In what ways might you be letting yourself be manipulated by your care receiver?
   c. How might you be enabling your care receiver's unhelpful or inappropriate behavior?

9. Is this caring relationship helping you? If so, how?

When to Use Set A: Focus on the Caring Relationship

Set A Emphasizes the Following Concerns

▸ What is and isn't happening in this caring relationship?

▸ What are the strengths and weaknesses in the caring relationship?

▸ Which vital aspects are, or should be, present in this caring relationship?

Situations in Which the Supervision Group Might Use Questions in Set A

▸ The group wants a beginning look at a caring relationship.

▸ The caregiver needs a refresher course on the basic activities that need to happen in a caring relationship.

▸ The group wants to get a general view of what is going on in the caring relationship.

▸ The relationship between caregiver and care receiver seems to be going sour and the group isn't sure why.

▸ The caregiver needs to value the healing power of the relationship itself apart from any specific results.

▸ The caregiver needs to reflect on how his or her style of relating affects the quality of his or her caregiving.

Set B: Focus on the Spiritual Nature of the Caring Relationship

1. How do you convey Jesus' love through your words and actions? How does your care receiver convey Jesus' love through his or her words and actions?

2. Do you see God at work in you? In your care receiver? In your caring relationship?

   a. Have you encountered Jesus in your care receiver? If so, how?

   b. Is Jesus challenging you through the caring relationship? If so, how?

   c. Has your care receiver encountered Jesus in you? If so, how?

   d. Has your care receiver's faith life blessed you? If so, how?

   e. Are there any other ways God's presence or healing power has been evident in the caring relationship? Describe.

3. What questions about God or God's relationship with people arise in the caring relationship? (For example: What is God really like? Why does God seem so far away? Why does God allow suffering and evil? What is the will of God?) Who raises these questions? In what context? How do you respond when the care receiver raises such questions?

4. What faith issues seem important to your care receiver? (For example: relationship with God, meaning or purpose in life, sense of identity, self-worth, dealing with guilt or fear) How do you know these issues are important? Is this a change?

5. How appropriate and effective is your use of such traditional Christian resources as prayer, Scripture, and sharing a blessing with your care receiver?

6. Does the care receiver need to hear God's words of forgiveness? If so, how will you share forgiveness?

7. What kind of God is your care receiver yearning for? (For example: a God of peace, reconciliation, forgiveness, love; a God who is present in times of crisis)

   a. How have you or might you share those attributes of God?

   b. What biblical story or passage portrays these characteristics of God?

   c. Have you experienced God in these ways? If so, how might you share that experience with your care receiver?

8. How do you pray for yourself, for your care receiver, and for the caring relationship?

9. How does your caring relationship exemplify the idea that "God is the Curegiver; I am the caregiver"?

10. How have you experienced the Holy Spirit's power in ministry with your care receiver? What "fruit of the Spirit" (love, joy, peace, patience, kindness, goodness, faithfulness, gentleness, self-control) are you experiencing and expressing?

When to Use Set B: Focus on the Spiritual Nature of the Caring Relationship

Set B Emphasizes the Following Concerns

► How do you see God at work in this caring relationship?

► What are the care receiver's spiritual concerns? How is the care receiver growing spiritually?

► How effectively has the caregiver communicated and shared God's love?

Situations in Which the Supervision Group Might Use Questions in Set B

► The caregiver needs to see what God is doing in the relationship.

► The caregiver does not see anything constructive happening in the caring relationship.

► The caregiver has lost sight of God's part in the caring relationship. For example, the caregiver is:

▷ emphasizing cure rather than care;

▷ self-centered instead of Christ-centered; or

▷ trying to make everything happen by him- or herself.

► The caregiver needs to look for and respond to the care receiver's less obvious spiritual needs.

Set C: Focus on the Direction of the Caring Relationship

1. Is the caring relationship changing? Since when? How?

2. Where is the relationship going?

3. Are your expectations about the direction of the caring relationship appropriate and realistic?

4. What do you think are your care receiver's expectations for the direction of the caring relationship? How realistic or appropriate are they?

5. How long do you think the caring relationship will last?

6. What were your ministry goals for your previous caring visit? Were they reached?

7. What are your ministry goals for the next visit?

8. How do you set caring ministry goals? Whose needs—yours or your care receiver's—are reflected in your goals?

9. Do your ministry goals seem focused more on process or results?

10. Are you tempted to set goals for the care receiver? If so, how?

11. Do you assist the care receiver to set goals for him- or herself and to establish a sequence of small steps to reach those goals?

12. What will be on your care receiver's mind during your next visit?

13. Are you ready to consider ending the formal caring relationship? If so, what is leading you to consider this?

14. Do you think your care receiver is considering ending the formal caring relationship? What gives you that impression? How have you responded to those signals?

15. Would ending the formal caring relationship at this time be premature? If so, what explains why you or your care receiver would seriously be considering this?

16. If you and your Supervision Group consider it best to end the formal caring relationship, how will you bring this up to your care receiver? What process will you use in your ministry through the closure period?

When to Use Set C: Focus on the Direction of the Caring Relationship

Set C Emphasizes the Following Concerns

▶ What do you think is the future of this caring relationship?

▶ What are the caregiver's and care receiver's expectations and goals?

▶ Do you see signs that it's time to end the caring relationship?

▶ How has the relationship changed?

Situations in Which the Supervision Group Might Use Questions in Set C

▶ The caregiver expresses confusion about what is happening, or what should be happening, in the caregiving relationship.

▶ The caregiver or care receiver wonders whether it's time to bring closure to the caring relationship.

▶ The group is wondering whether it would be appropriate to bring closure to the caring relationship.

▶ The caring relationship seems to have lost its purpose or direction.

▶ The group wants to look ahead in the caring relationship to what might be coming.

▶ The caregiver, or the care receiver, doesn't feel as if progress has been made in the caring relationship.

Set D: Focus on the Caregiver's Feelings about the Caring Process

1. How did you feel when:

   a. you first called your care receiver on the phone?

   b. you got to the care receiver's door?

   c. your visit was over?

   d. the care receiver said . . . ? *[add relevant situation]*

2. How are you doing as a caregiver? What feelings go along with your self-assessment?

3. Evaluate your emotional ties to your care receiver.

   a. Are you becoming too emotionally involved to be an objective, effective caregiver? If so, explore your emotional involvement.

   b. Are you detaching and becoming too distant from your care receiver? If so, why?

4. What are your thoughts about the progress of your caring relationship? What feelings go along with your assessment?

5. How do you feel about the process of caring for this person?

6. Do you feel strong emotions with your care receiver?

   a. What emotion(s)?

   b. When?

   c. What issues may your emotions be inviting you to consider?

7. Do the values or beliefs, or does the lifestyle of your care receiver irritate or frustrate you? If so, how?

8. Do you own responsibility for your feelings in the caring relationship?

9. Are you able to express your feelings about the care receiver and the caring relationship appropriately with the care receiver? With your Supervision Group?

10. How are your feelings helping or hindering your caregiving?

When to Use Set D: Focus on the Caregiver's Feelings about the Caring Process

Set D Emphasizes the Following Concerns

▶ How do the caregiver's feelings affect the caring relationship?

▶ How can the Supervision Group care for the caregiver and explore the caregiver's feelings?

Situations in Which the Supervision Group Might Use Questions in Set D

▶ The caregiver needs to let off steam about the caring relationship.

▶ The caregiver is having difficulty with the caring relationship.

▶ The caregiver feels vague dissatisfaction with the caring relationship.

▶ The caregiver's emotions are too intense or not intense enough.

▶ The caregiver shows signs of boredom in the caring relationship.

▶ The caregiver seems to be relating with sympathy or overidentification instead of empathy.

Set E: Focus on the Caregiver's Skills

1. In your last visit, what went well?

2. In your last visit, what do you wish you had said or done differently?

3. In general, what caring skills do you do well?

4. In general, what caring skills do you need to work on?

5. How well do you listen to and observe the care receiver? Give some examples.

6. Are you, your thoughts, and your emotions coming through to the care receiver? How do you know?

7. Are you being directive? How often? To what degree? In what ways?

8. Do you get into the care receiver's world and view it as he or she does? Explain. Does your care receiver's world seem foreign or familiar? How does this affect your ability to relate to him or her?

9. How well do you lead the care receiver to a better understanding of his or her feelings through reflective listening, summarizing, or interpreting? Give some examples.

10. How accepting are you of facts and feelings the care receiver shares?

11. How do you create a comfortable environment in which your care receiver can share?

12. Are you avoiding clichés with your care receiver? (For example, "Keep your chin up." "I know just how you feel.")

13. Are you assertive with the care receiver when you need to be? Give examples. If not, what aspect(s) of assertiveness do you need to work on? Practice or role-play these situations in your Supervision Group.

14. How are you maintaining confidentiality in the caring relationship?

15. Do you use telecare with your care receiver? If so, in what situations? Describe the effectiveness of your telephone ministry.

16. Is the quality of your caring diminished because some of your basic skills have gotten rusty? How can you polish them?

17. If your care receiver is experiencing a problem that is described in one of the training topics that deal with specific crises (such as dying, hospitalization, grief, or divorce), what special needs does he or she have? Assess the quality of your ministry in this situation and give examples.

When to Use Set E: Focus on the Caregiver's Skills

Set E Emphasizes the Following Concerns

▶ How well is the Stephen Minister using major caregiving skills: listening, reflecting feelings, empathy, confidentiality, and assertiveness?

▶ How well is the caregiver meeting the care receiver's special needs?

Situations in Which the Supervision Group Might Use Questions in Set E

▶ The group wants to affirm the caregiver for using good caring skills.

▶ The group suspects that the caregiver is not using needed skills, or that he or she needs to develop certain skills.

▶ The group wants to look in depth at one visit between the caregiver and the care receiver.

▶ The group wants to determine what kinds of help, growth, or continuing education would most benefit the caregiver.

▶ The caregiver needs to use caring skills more effectively to improve the caring relationship.

Set F: Focus on the Caregiver's Personal Growth

1. How are you growing, changing, or being challenged in this relationship?

2. Is this ministry situation challenging you to acknowledge, express, and confront attitudes or feelings? If so, which ones? (This does not include attitudes and feelings about the caring relationship or the caring process. This refers to your own attitudes and feelings about such aspects of life as aging, disability, death, the use of drugs, pain, dependency, debilitation, or values and lifestyles different from your own.)

   a. Do any of these attitudes or feelings impede your ministry? (That is, do they make it difficult for you really to understand your care receiver or to see life as your care receiver sees it?)

   b. How are you doing at facing these attitudes and feelings, accepting them, and dealing with them? What help do you need to deal with them better?

3. What insights are you gaining about yourself, about other people, about the human condition, about God?

4. Is your understanding of the purpose, goals, and techniques of caring ministry changing? If so, how?

5. Is your understanding of what it means for you to be a Stephen Minister changing? If so, how?

6. Is God renewing or transforming you or your care receiver through this ministry? If so, how?

7. Is your trust and dependence upon God growing through this ministry? If so, how? How do you express heightened trust and dependence on God?

8. How are you learning to value your ministry for what it is rather than what it does?

When to Use Set F: Focus on the Caregiver's Personal Growth

Set F Emphasizes the Following Concerns

▶ Is the caregiver growing in his or her attitudes, values, self-understanding, self-esteem, and relationship with God?

▶ How is the caregiver's growth affecting the caring relationship?

Situations in Which the Supervision Group Might Use Questions in Set F

▶ The caregiver needs to look at how the kind of person he or she is affects his or her caregiving.

▶ The caregiver needs to see how his or her relationship with God affects his or her caregiving.

▶ The caregiver is facing a crisis of personal growth. (The Supervision Group can recognize signs of anxiety, frustration, or anger in the caregiver and can then provide him or her with the opportunity to recognize and deal with the personal growth crisis.)

Set G: Focus on the Care Receiver's Situation

1. What are your care receiver's problems? What does your care receiver think his or her needs or problems are?

2. Do you and your care receiver differ in the way you understand your care receiver's problems? If so, how is that affecting your ministry?

3. How has your care receiver's background contributed to his or her present situation?

4. What's confusing about your care receiver or his or her situation?

5. Have your views of your care receiver or his or her situation changed over recent visits? If so, how?

6. What words or actions of your care receiver seem to give you the greatest insight into him or her?

7. Do any aspects of your care receiver's situation seem too great for you to handle? If so, which ones? How do you plan to address these needs?

8. If the caregiver is considering referring the care receiver to a community resource:

   a. What need prompted you to consider referring the care receiver to a community resource?

   b. Are you or your care receiver tempted to see a referral to a community resource as a quick fix for your care receiver's need?

   c. Which community resources might be the most relevant for the care receiver's situation? (If you are considering a referral to a mental health professional, see Focus Question Set H.)

   d. How would a referral to a community resource affect your relationship with the care receiver?

When to Use Set G: Focus on the Care Receiver's Situation

Set G Emphasizes the Following Concerns

▶ How does the caregiver understand the care receiver's situation, needs, and perceptions?

▶ How appropriate is Stephen Ministry for the care receiver's needs?

Situations in Which the Supervision Group Might Use Questions in Set G

▶ The caregiver does not understand everything that is going on in the caring relationship.

▶ The group detects conflict between the caregiver and the care receiver.

▶ The caregiver believes it may be necessary to refer the care receiver to a community resource.

▶ There is an emergency situation in the care receiver's life.

▶ The group is unsure whether or not this caregiver is the correct caregiver for this care receiver.

▶ The caregiver is feeling overwhelmed, scared, or worried about the caring relationship.

▶ The group suspects there may be multiple needs and priorities for caring ministry in the care receiver's life and that the most obvious needs are not necessarily the most important needs.

▶ There are contradictions between what the care receiver says and what he or she does.

Set H: Focus on a Possible Mental Health Referral

1. What has prompted you to consider referring your care receiver to a mental health professional?

2. Have you noticed any of the following behaviors?

   a. Reduced ability to cope with life

   b. Symptoms of severe depression, such as uncontrollable crying, hopelessness, or inability to get out of bed

   c. Suicidal behaviors or the expression of suicidal thoughts

   d. Physical or sexual abuse to or by the care receiver

   e. Extreme withdrawal

   f. Hallucinations

   g. Significant weight loss or gain

   h. Abusing alcohol or other drugs or chemical dependency

3. Based on the "Referral Form" you received from the Referrals Coordinator, would you have expected your care receiver to be doing better by now?

4. Which type of mental health resource might be appropriate in this situation? (Refer, as necessary, to types and descriptions of mental health professionals in chapter 4 of *When and How to Use Mental Health Resources*.)

5. How do you think the care receiver will respond to your suggestion of a mental health referral?

6. What effect would a referral to a mental health resource have on your relationship with the care receiver?

7. What are some ways in which you could present the idea of a mental health referral positively?

8. If your care receiver refuses to seek help from a mental health professional, what will your next step be?

When to Use Set H: Focus on a Possible Mental Health Referral

Set H Emphasizes a Single Concern

Does this care receiver need to be referred to a mental health professional?

Situations in Which the Supervision Group Might Use Questions in Set H

▸ The care receiver shows signs of being severely depressed.

▸ The care receiver seems increasingly unable to cope with life.

▸ The caregiver wonders whether the care receiver might be suicidal.

▸ The caregiver is considering referring the care receiver to a mental health professional.

▶ Getting Ready for the In-Class Session

In the In-Class Session you will participate in a practice Small Group Peer Supervision session. In order to get ready, review your notes and the Focus Notes about the "Steps in the Supervision Process" on pages 397–403.

Supervision: A Key to Quality Christian Care—Part 2

With this in mind, we constantly pray for you, that our God may count you worthy of his calling, and that by his power he may fulfill every good purpose of yours and every act prompted by your faith. We pray this so that the name of our Lord Jesus may be glorified in you, and you in him, according to the grace of our God and the Lord Jesus Christ.

2 Thessalonians 1:11–12

I. Christ Caring for People through People

II. Using Focus Questions

A. Choosing Focus Questions

FOCUS NOTE 1

How to Choose Focus Questions

Step 1: The Stephen Minister in the spotlight identifies the Focus Question Set and Focus Questions that will best meet his or her needs, and tells them to the Supervision Group as part of his or her in-depth report.

Step 2: Other group members suggest additional possible Focus Question Sets and Focus Questions to concentrate on.

Step 3: The Supervision Group Facilitator helps the group decide on a Focus Question Set to start with.

Step 4: The group chooses a Focus Question from that set.

Step 5: The group may move to other Focus Questions or Focus Question Sets during the course of the discussion. When a group

---

member suggests moving to a different set, the Supervision Group Facilitator helps the group decide whether they are ready for a new topic and, if so, what that topic should be.

B. Practice Choosing Focus Questions

FOCUS NOTE 2

Instructions for the Focus Questions Exercise

1. Read the first situation description from Focus Note 3.

2. Working with "Focus Question Sets" (pages 412–427), discuss and decide on a Focus Question Set that would be appropriate for the caring relationship described in the situation.

3. Then choose a Focus Question that would be a good one to begin with from the Focus Question Set your group chose.

4. Read the next situation description in Focus Note 3 and repeat steps 2 and 3.

5. In this way, decide Focus Question Sets and Focus Questions for the rest of the situation descriptions in ten minutes.

FOCUS NOTE 3

Focus Questions Exercise Situation Descriptions

1. "I don't know where to go next with my care receiver. We seem to have settled a lot of the problems she started off with, but I don't think it's time to bring closure to the relationship. It seems as if there's still more to talk about."

2. "I'm very frustrated with my care receiver. I can't put my finger on why, but every time I get ready to go visit him, I just start feeling angry inside."

3. "The last time I visited my care receiver, she was so depressed she could hardly talk. Her home is usually very neat, but that day it was quite messy. I wonder if she needs more help than I'm giving her."

4. "This is supposed to be Christian ministry, but I don't see what part God has in what I'm doing. All I do is listen. We never pray or read the Bible. I think my care receiver's life should be more victorious."

C. Using Focus Questions

III. Maintaining Confidentiality in Supervision

A. Walking a Tightrope: Balancing Confidentiality and Specificity

1. Maintaining Confidentiality

FOCUS NOTE 4

How to Maintain Confidentiality in Supervision

1. Don't tell the Supervision Group the care receiver's name or the names of family members.

2. Don't tell the Supervision Group something the care receiver very specifically asked you to tell no one. (If this is an issue you need help with, talk to your Stephen Leader in private.)

3. Don't share intimate details of the care receiver's life that have no bearing on the caring relationship.

4. Keep confidential everything that is discussed in your Supervision Group.

5. If your care receiver has shared something that possibly could be very damaging if you were to share it in your Supervision Group, request individual supervision with your Stephen Leader or pastor.

---

2. Providing Enough Information

B. The Hierarchy of Concentration

The Hierarchy of Concentration

1. Most of all, concentrate on the caring relationship.

2. Some of the time, concentrate on the caregiver in the caring relationship.

3. Only as necessary, concentrate on the care receiver's situations and needs.

1. Concentrate on the Caring Relationship

Examples That Concentrate on the Caring Relationship (Focus Question Sets A, B, and C)

▶ How would you describe the caring relationship?

▶ What is going well and what is going poorly in the relationship?

▶ Is the relationship meeting the care receiver's needs?

▶ What is the spiritual nature of the caring relationship?

▶ What are the Stephen Minister's goals for the caring relationship?

▶ What is the future direction of the caring relationship?

▶ Is it time to bring closure to the caring relationship?

2. Concentrate on the Caregiver in the Caring Relationship

Examples That Concentrate on the Caregiver (Focus Question Sets D, E, and F)

▶ What are the Stephen Minister's feelings about the care receiver?

▶ What are the Stephen Minister's feelings about him- or herself as a caregiver?

▶ How well is the Stephen Minister exercising caring skills?

▶ How congruent are the Stephen Minister's words and actions?

▶ How is the Stephen Minister changing and growing through the caring relationship?

3. Concentrate on the Care Receiver's Situation and Needs

FOCUS NOTE 8

Examples That Concentrate on the Care Receiver (Focus Question Sets G and H)

▶ What are the care receiver's needs, and is the Stephen Minister accurately perceiving them?

▶ Is the care receiver somehow in danger? For example, is he or she in a situation of suicide, homicide, or abuse?

▶ Is the care receiver in need of a referral to a mental health professional or a community resource?

C. Trust Your Supervision Group

FOCUS NOTE 9

Do's and Don'ts When You Figure Out a Care Receiver's Identity

Do:

▶ Keep it to yourself

▶ Forget about it as soon as possible

▶ Continue to provide the best supervision possible to the Stephen Minister

Don't:

▶ Tell the Stephen Minister, or anyone else, that you have figured out who the care receiver is

▶ Let on to the care receiver or a member of his or her family that you know who his or her Stephen Minister is

▶ Take pride in the fact that you've figured out who the care receiver is and dwell on your accomplishment

▶ Go to your Stephen Leader and ask to be transferred to a different Supervision Group because you have figured out the identity of a care receiver

---

- ▸ Refuse to participate in supervision
- ▸ Communicate in any other way that you know who the care receiver is
- ▸ Use names, ever

D. Avoid Extreme Rigidity

E. Ways to Be Both Specific and Confidential

FOCUS NOTE 10

How to Be Specific and Maintain Confidentiality

- ▸ Trust the others in your small group. They are all as committed to confidentiality as you are.
- ▸ Be open and truthful, especially about your own feelings, struggles, and doubts in the caring relationship.
- ▸ Plan ahead for your presentation about your caring relationship. Keep the Hierarchy of Concentration in mind as you prepare.
- ▸ Share details with a purpose in mind. Be sure to share what you need to share in order to receive the supervision you need. Do not share details that have little to do with maintaining quality in the caring relationship.
- ▸ Always have highest quality care for the care receiver as your top priority.

IV. Practice Supervision Session

Supervision Skill Practice Instructions

During the beginning of the supervision session:

10 minutes

Share the check-in statements you prepared in part one of this module.

During the heart of the supervision session:

35 minutes

1. Choose a Stephen Minister to present the in-depth report he or she prepared in part one of this module.

2. Listen to the in-depth report.

3. Begin with affirmation.

4. Quickly choose Focus Questions and explore the caring relationship using "Focus Question Sets" on pages 412–427.

5. Offer feedback, support, information, care, and listening ears to supervise and support the Stephen Minister reporting in depth.

6. Before the end of 35 minutes (including the in-depth report), the Supervision Group Facilitator should help the group end the in-depth discussion, including a summary of what the reporting Stephen Minister gained and what he or she would do next.

During the end of the supervision session:

5 minutes

The Supervision Group Facilitator should pass out copies of "Questions for Regular Supervision Group Evaluation," and Supervision Group members fill them out and turn them in.

V. Caregiver's Compass Review

_____

_____

_____

_____   _____

_____   _____

_____   _____

COMPASSIONATE · FULL OF FAITH · SKILLED · TRUSTWORTHY

_____

_____

_____

_____

VI. Looking Ahead

Prayer Partner Requests and Thanksgivings

My prayer partner is _____

Prayer requests and thanksgivings to share with my prayer partner

_____

_____

Prayer requests and thanksgivings shared by my prayer partner

_____

_____

How to Make a First Caring Visit

Contents

▶ "I Think There's Hope"

Cynthia had a message on her answering machine from Richard, her Stephen Leader, when she got home from work. When she called him, he said he had a caring ministry assignment for her and asked if he could come over for a few minutes to give her the "Referral Form" and answer any questions. Cynthia's heart started pounding. She had just been commissioned as a Stephen Minister, and this was her first caring ministry assignment. She said yes to Richard, and he said he'd be right over.

The "Referral Form" said that Cynthia's new care receiver, Miriam, had just had

baby and was feeling overwhelmed. Cynthia thought back to when her own two children had been born and nodded knowingly.

"Is this her first child?" she asked.

He nodded and said, "It was a difficult pregnancy. Miriam had to spend the last month in bed."

Cynthia called Miriam as soon as Richard left. She noticed that Miriam sounded tired as she answered the telephone. They agreed that Cynthia would come over the next day at 7:00 P.M.

When Cynthia arrived, three-week-old Jimmy was making more noise than someone that size should have been capable of. Miriam looked as if she were about ready to cry. There was too much noise to talk, so Cynthia took Jimmy and started walking around the living room with him. Miriam looked relieved and said she would go make some tea. By some miracle, Jimmy fell asleep minutes after Cynthia took him. Miriam put him to bed, and she and Cynthia sat at the dining room table with their tea.

They chatted about babies. Cynthia told Miriam about the time when Claire, Cynthia's youngest, had suffered from colic and cried for a month straight.

"This isn't very encouraging," Miriam said with a laugh.

"I know what you mean," Cynthia said, "but now I look back at that as just one part of my relationship with Claire. I love her so much, and I'm glad I had a chance to take care of her when she needed me. But that's just me, and I'm not saying you should feel the same way. How do you feel about what's going on?"

Miriam started to cry as she told about getting little sleep, feeling overwhelmed by Jimmy's unending demands, and feeling worried about how she and Manny, her husband, were getting along. Cynthia listened and asked whether some specific event had caused Miriam to ask for help. Miriam told her about a fight she'd had with Manny, and how terrible she had felt afterward. Cynthia asked about Miriam's pregnancy. She started to see a bigger picture of months of changes and challenges Miriam had been through and how Miriam felt out of control of her own life.

Cynthia thought to herself, "I can help here. I understand what she's going through, and I'm willing to listen to her and go through this with her as she works it out."

An hour was up before they knew it. Cynthia asked Miriam whether there was anything else she needed to talk about that evening.

Miriam said, "No, thanks. It's really helped just to be able to talk about it. I think I'll see if I can sneak in a nap before Jimmy wakes up again."

Cynthia suggested that they meet at the same time the next week, and Miriam agreed. Once she got home, Cynthia wrote on her "Contact Record Sheet": *Good visit. She's exhausted, but I think there's hope.*

▶ Nuts-and-Bolts Questions and Answers about Caring Relationships

Getting started in a caring relationship can bring up a lot of questions. Reference Box A lists 15 nuts-and-bolts questions about how to begin and conduct a caring relationship, questions you will find answers to in this section.

REFERENCE BOX A

15 Questions about Caring Relationships

1. How often will you meet with your care receiver?

2. Where will you meet with your care receiver?

3. Once your caring relationship has begun, who may initiate a caring visit?

---

4. How long should a caring visit last?

5. How many visits will you have with your care receiver?

6. What records will you keep about your caring relationship?

7. How will you keep those records confidential?

8. When should you be available to your care receiver?

9. What should you do if your care receiver has an emergency?

10. Are there kinds of care that you should not provide?

11. What if you or your care receiver needs to cancel a caring visit?

12. What about communicating with your care receiver by cards, letters, phone calls, and e-mail?

13. What if you discover that your care receiver's family member or friend needs a Stephen Minister?

14. What if you have a question about your caring relationship that is so pressing it can't wait until the next supervision meeting?

15. What if your care receiver offers you a gift?

1. How often will you meet with your care receiver?

Stephen Ministers typically meet with their care receivers once a week. In addition, you may talk on the phone with your care receiver between caring visits.

There are some possible exceptions. If your care receiver is in the midst of a crisis, such as being in the hospital or having just lost a loved one, you may spend much more time with your care receiver for a week or two, assuming that you can. On the other hand, if you are tapering off your caring relationship as you move toward closure, you may meet less frequently than once a week.

2. Where will you meet with your care receiver?

Frequently caring visits take place in the care receiver's home, but that is not always the case.

Advantages to meeting in the care receiver's home might include one or more of the following.

▶ The care receiver's home is the most convenient place for him or her to meet with you.

▶ The care receiver feels comfortable and safe there.

▶ The care receiver doesn't have to travel to get to the caring visit.

▶ You will understand more about your care receiver if you see the person in his or her home.

Your care receiver might not be comfortable meeting in his or her home, however. Other family members may be present, or the care receiver may feel uncomfortable meeting in the home for some other reason. If that is the case, you might meet:

▶ at church;

▶ in a restaurant or coffee shop; or

▶ at some other public place, like a library.

In any of these public places, make sure you can hear each other and not be overheard. Also, make sure your care receiver doesn't mind possibly being seen meeting with you.

3. Once your caring relationship has begun, who may initiate a caring visit?

Either you or your care receiver may request a caring visit.

Typically you will set up your next caring visit at the end of the current one. It is also typical to establish a schedule where you meet at the same time each week. Even if you have a regular schedule, it is a good idea to verify the next visit by saying something like, "We'll be meeting again next Wednesday, right?"

If your care receiver has a special need to meet, he or she may call you and request a caring visit. You will need to negotiate a time that works for both of you. If you need to meet with your care receiver at an unscheduled time, you also may call and negotiate a meeting time.

4. How long should a caring visit last?

Caring visits usually last about an hour. This seems to be a good amount of time to discuss a care receiver's concerns. In a routine caring visit, you probably don't want to meet a lot more or a lot less than an hour.

Sometimes, however, the caring visit may be longer or shorter. If your care receiver is in the midst of a crisis, you may choose to meet longer with him or her. For example, if your care receiver's child is missing, you might stay with him or her until the situation is resolved, if you are able to do so. If your care receiver is in the hospital and feeling very bad, you might limit your visit to 10 or 15 minutes because that may be all that he or she has energy for.

5. How many visits will you have with your care receiver?

While the total number of caring visits can vary widely, in most cases it is more likely to be 40, 60, or 100 than it is to be 4, 6, or 10. The number of caring visits depends on what the care receiver needs. If your care receiver is grieving the loss of a loved one, you may meet with him or her for a year and a half or more. If your care receiver recently moved into your area and is feeling down, you may only meet for three to six months before bringing closure.

6. What records will you keep about your caring relationship?

There are three forms you use in your caring relationships.

You will receive the "Referral Form" when you begin a caring relationship. A sample is on page 470. Your Stephen Leader will explain the form further in this module's In-Class Session.

You will maintain a "Contact Record Sheet" throughout your caring relationship. A sample is on pages 471–472. Your Stephen Leader will further explain the form in this module's In-Class Session.

You learned about the "Wrap-Up Form" when you studied module 15, "Bringing the Caring Relationship to a Close."

7. How will you keep those records confidential?

Never leave your records lying around or in a place where someone else might happen upon them. You may want to keep a file folder for these forms.

8. When should you be available to your care receiver?

It is typical to tell your care receiver that he or she may call you whenever he or she needs to. In an emergency he or she may even call you in the middle of the night. The idea is to be available to your care receiver at any time if he or she really needs you.

You may need to put some limits on your availability. For example, you may not be able to take phone calls from your care receiver at work except in emergencies. If you have an answering machine at home, you might invite your care receiver to leave a message at home during the workday and assure him or her that you will call back as soon as possible.

9. What should you do if your care receiver has an emergency?

If your care receiver has an emergency—such as having to go to the hospital, a loved one's going to the hospital, a family member or friend's dying, or a child's running away—you may want to go and be with him or her. If you can't be there, try to be available over the telephone and assure your care receiver that you will pray for him or her.

You will also want to inform your pastor, with your care receiver's permission and if your care receiver has not already done so. Be sure to ask your care receiver whether your pastor knows yet and, if not, whether you may inform him or her.

10. Are there kinds of care that you should not provide?

There certainly are.

You learned about when and how to refer care receivers for professional care in module 11, "Using Mental Health Professionals and Other Community Resources." You also know that if your care receiver is depressed or suicidal, you should refer him or her to a professional caregiver as soon as possible.

Situations could also arise in which care receivers ask you to provide care that is outside what Stephen Ministers do. For example, your care receiver might ask you to drive him or her to the store every day or even to do his or her shopping. In such a case you need to maintain clear boundaries. You will certainly provide wholistic care for your care receiver. This may include occasionally stopping at the store to pick something up for a homebound care receiver. Primarily, however, you will be a caring Christian friend who listens, prays, and walks with your care receiver through difficult times.

If you believe your care receiver is asking you to provide care that takes advantage of you, ask yourself if you're stepping over your care receiver's boundaries or if he or she is stepping over yours. Discuss the situation with your Supervision Group. You might decide to help your care receiver figure out how he or she can get to and from the store instead of offering to provide transportation yourself.

11. What if you or your care receiver needs to cancel a caring visit?

If you cannot keep an appointment, let your care receiver know as soon as possible and reschedule. Remember, however, that your caring visits need to take very high priority. Don't cancel a caring visit for something like an invitation to go out with a friend or to do something that you could do just as well at another time.

Your care receiver should do the same: call and let you know as soon as possible and reschedule. If your care receiver takes advantage of you by regularly canceling caring visits, you need to bring that up assertively when you meet with him or her. Try to find out why he or she cancels caring visits and address those reasons. Also discuss it with your Supervision Group.

12. What about communicating with your care receiver by cards, letters, phone calls, and e-mail?

All are fine and can be very considerate acts. Just make sure you never think that any of those ways of communicating with your care receiver can replace your regular face-to-face contact. Also, be sure to maintain confidentiality, and get your care receiver's permission before sending e-mail messages or leaving messages on an answering machine.

13. What if you discover that your care receiver's family member or friend needs a Stephen Minister?

While you might be tempted to try to be a Stephen Minister for a family member or friend, you need to focus on your assigned care receiver. Therefore, get the person's permission to let your Stephen Leaders know about his or her need. Your Referrals Coordinator will assign a Stephen Minister if it is possible and appropriate to do so.

On occasion you may have caring conversations with family members or friends, using your Stephen Minister skills as you would with a care receiver. If the person seems to need such conversations regularly, however, ask his or her permission to tell your Stephen Leader, who will see if it would be appropriate to assign a Stephen Minister to the family member or friend.

14. What if you have a question about your caring relationship that is so pressing it can't wait until the next supervision meeting?

If you have a question that affects your care for your care receiver and it can't wait until your supervision meeting, then call your Supervision Group Facilitator, your Stephen Leader, or your pastor.

15. What if your care receiver offers you a gift?

The "Stephen Minister's Covenant to Care," which you learned about in module 7, "Maintaining Boundaries in Caregiving," states that you will never receive any compensation for your caregiving. If a care receiver's gift were so valuable as to be a "payment for your services," you would have to refuse it.

What about smaller gifts, however, such as a piece of cake or a handmade Christmas gift? Read "The Grace to Receive" in appendix A, pages 459–460, for an answer.

▶ How to Conduct a First Caring Visit

The rest of this Preclass Reading will show you how to set up, conduct, and end a first caring visit. Many of these questions and considerations will continue to be important throughout your caring relationship.

As you read about all the steps in the first caring visit, be sure not to lose sight of all you have learned about caregiving up to now. First and foremost, your job in the first caring visit and in every subsequent visit is to listen and to be a caregiver who is compassionate, full of faith, skilled, trustworthy, and Christ-centered.

Before You Set Up a First Caring Visit

Before you set up a first caring visit, you will receive an assignment from the Stephen Leader who serves as your Referrals Coordinator. Reference Box B shows the sequence of events that will take place.

REFERENCE BOX B

The Sequence of Events Leading Up to a First Caring Visit

1. The Referrals Coordinator finds out about a person who may need Stephen Ministry.

2. The Referrals Coordinator or another Stephen Leader meets with the potential care receiver, assesses his or her need for Stephen Ministry, and explains Stephen Ministry.

3. The Referrals Coordinator or another Stephen Leader offers Stephen Ministry to the care receiver.

4. The Referrals Coordinator or another Stephen Leader explains about confidentiality and supervision.

5. The Referrals Coordinator or another Stephen Leader tells the care receiver that a Stephen Minister will call him or her in the next day or so.

6. The Referrals Coordinator or another Stephen Leader fills out a "Stephen Ministry Referral Form" and gives it to you.

7. You have the chance to ask any questions you have about the new ministry assignment.

8. You call the care receiver and set up a first appointment.

Your Stephen Leaders will explain the details of this process in your In-Class Session.

How to Set Up a First Caring Visit

Since your care receiver will be expecting your telephone call, you need to make that call as soon as possible after you learn about your new relationship.

Waiting too long to make this first call may start your caring relationship off on the wrong foot.

Reference Box C lists the five steps in setting up a first visit.

REFERENCE BOX C

The Five Steps in Setting Up a First Caring Visit

1. Pray first.

2. Encourage an early meeting.

---

3. Respond if your care receiver is reluctant to schedule a first caring visit.

4. Respond if your care receiver refuses to meet.

5. Be sure to set a specific time and place, if possible.

Hopefully the third and fourth items in the list will not occur, but you need to know about them in case they do.

Pray First

Before you call your care receiver, be sure to pray. Reference Box D suggests one way that you might word your prayer.

REFERENCE BOX D

Sample Prayer

Caring God, thank you for the opportunity to serve you by bringing your care to *[name]*. Please bless and be with *[him/her]* and let *[him/her]* know that you are near. Use our caring relationship to bring your saving, healing love to *[name]*, and also to me. Equip me, dear God, with the gifts and attitudes I need to bring *[name]* in touch with you. Help me to remember all I have learned and to use my skills sensitively and well. I praise you for all the wonderful things you are going to do through this caring relationship. Amen.

Encourage an Early Meeting

If possible, arrange your first caring visit for the next day or two. You definitely want to meet with your care receiver before a week has gone by. Reference Box E contains a good example of what to say.

REFERENCE BOX E

Calling to Set Up the First Visit

"Hello, *[name of care receiver]*, this is *[your name]*, and I'm a Stephen Minister at *[name of church]* Church. *[Name of Stephen Leader]* called me and said that *[he/she]* talked with you and told you that I would be getting in touch with you. I'm calling to set up a time when we can get together. I thought we could try to find a time tomorrow or the next day when I could drop by your home."

In the preparation interview, your Stephen Leader will ask your care receiver's permission to assign a Stephen Minister to him or her and won't proceed unless he or she agrees. Since your care receiver has already agreed to your ministry, don't feel as if you are intruding when you call. Actually your new care receiver is probably eager to talk to you.

Be assertive when you call. Although your care receiver is probably ready and willing to set up a first visit, avoid making statements that could give the care receiver a chance to change his or her mind and back out. Reference Box F gives some examples of what not to say and what to say.

REFERENCE BOX F

How to Propose a Visit
Don't say:

"Can we get together?"

"Would you like to get together?"

Do say:

"I'd like to set up a time when I could meet you this week."

(After some prior conversation:) "When would be a good time for us to get together?" *(And you might add:)* "I'd like to do it sometime within the next few days, if that's convenient for you."

Respond If Your Care Receiver Is Reluctant to Schedule a First Caring Visit

On rare occasions care receivers may have second thoughts after agreeing to receive Stephen Ministry. They may feel very nervous about beginning a caring relationship, or they may decide they should be able to handle their problems on their own. Another possibility is that someone has tried to talk them out of receiving Stephen Ministry.

Whatever the reason, the best response to such second thoughts is to get your care receiver to talk about them and for you to listen. Use your listening skills to draw out your care receiver and find out why he or she is reluctant to meet.

Once you understand your care receiver's reasons, you can respond. Sometimes a simple clarification about what Stephen Ministry is and how it works will be enough to encourage your care receiver to meet with you.

Be very assertive in your response. Your care receiver will really benefit from Stephen Ministry, and you will want to do everything you can to convince him or her to take advantage of it. Do remain process-oriented, however. Don't try to force or bully a care receiver into receiving Stephen Ministry. Reference Box

G contains some examples of assertive statements you might make to encourage your care receiver to meet with you.

REFERENCE BOX G

Statements to Encourage Your Care Receiver to Meet with You

▶ "I'd really like to meet and talk with you at least once. Then we can go on from there."

▶ "I'd like to talk with you about what's been going on in your life. I know that it is sometimes hard to talk about these things, but that's why I would like to meet with you."

▶ "I can understand that you might be reluctant to meet with me for the first time. It might be pretty scary to talk with someone else about things that are concerning you. But why don't we agree to meet just one time? If things work out, we'll go on from there. If they don't, then we'll just leave it at that."

Respond If Your Care Receiver Refuses to Meet

Very infrequently, a care receiver may refuse to meet with you at all, even after you have assertively emphasized your desire to meet at least once. In such a situation, Reference Box H gives an example of what you might say.

REFERENCE BOX H

When the Care Receiver Says No to a First Visit

"All right, perhaps sometime in the future we might be able to get together. If you would like to call me, here is my phone number."

Afterward, contact the Stephen Leader who serves as your Referrals Coordinator and explain the situation. Then you and the Referrals Coordinator can decide where to go from there.

Be Sure to Set a Specific Time and Place, If Possible

Your telephone call should not end until you and your care receiver agree on a specific time and place for your first meeting.

Getting the First Caring Visit Started

The five parts of a first caring visit are listed in Reference Box I.

REFERENCE BOX I

The Five Parts of a First Caring Visit

1. Get Started
2. Explore
3. Clarify
4. Provide Wholistic Care, If Necessary
5. End the Visit

Each of these parts is divided into a number of steps.

Getting started means making a good beginning to the visit and the entire caring relationship and moving the conversation to talking about the troubling issues facing the care receiver. The seven steps in getting started are listed in Reference Box J.

REFERENCE BOX J

The Seven Steps in *Get Started*

1. Deal with nervousness.
2. Make introductions.
3. Be yourself.
4. Engage in small talk.
5. Mention confidentiality and supervision.
6. Bridge the gap.
7. Listen.

---

1. Deal with Nervousness

Recognize and accept the fact that you will probably be somewhat nervous as you begin each of your caring relationships. Don't feel ashamed about that. Even experienced professionals occasionally have some nervousness when they deal with first caring visits. Such nervousness is not a sign of incompetence or lack of confidence. It is probably a sign of your concern for your care receiver and your hope for all that God will do through the caring relationship.

What do you do about nervousness when you experience it? Before you go up to knock on the door, take a moment to pray. Review your notes. Believe that God will be with you, and trust that you are well prepared for this moment.

2. Make Introductions

When you first meet your care receiver and greet him or her, simply introduce yourself. You don't need to jump immediately into an explanation of what you are there to do or to start taking care of business right away. Instead, spend some time getting to know your care receiver. Reference Box K shows a very simple way in which you might begin.

REFERENCE BOX K

A Possible Beginning

"Hello, I'm *[your name]*. We talked on the phone earlier. I'm really glad that I now have the opportunity to meet you in person."

---

3. Be Yourself

You don't have to become someone else in order to be a caregiver. Reference Box L contains some words from your first Stephen Minister training module, "The Person of the Caregiver." Reread these words and remember that you can be yourself—the person God created, has loved, saved, and blessed—the first time you visit your care receiver and every time.

REFERENCE BOX L

Some Words from "The Person of the Caregiver"

This first module is called "The Person of the Caregiver" because it focuses on you, the person you are and the person you will become, as God equips you to serve as a Stephen Minister. As important as all your skills will be when you enter into your caring relationships, the most important caring tool you will bring is yourself. Let me say that again. You—who you are, how you relate to others, how you care for and accept your care receiver, your trust in God—are the most important elements you bring to the caring relationship. God will use you

---

to bring Christ's healing to your care receivers.

---

4. Engage in Small Talk

Your first caring visit and all subsequent visits will probably begin with some small talk. Small talk is a social lubricant. It makes forward motion possible in relationships. Be aware, however, that small talk can also be a way to avoid hard work. It can result from not knowing what to do. It also can occur because of fear.

No rule tells you what the proper amount of small talk is, because it varies from individual to individual and from situation to situation. You will have to judge for yourself. If you are visiting a person who is homebound, you may spend 15 minutes or even more in chitchat. If you are visiting a person in the midst of a serious crisis, however, you will likely spend little or no time in casual conversation, but will begin at once to get down to the problem.

5. Mention Confidentiality and Supervision

In module 9, "Confidentiality," you learned that during the first caring visit you will mention confidentiality and supervision. Your Stephen Leader will have already told your care receiver about these topics in the preparation interview, but it will be important for you to mention them again just to make sure your care receiver understands.

Reference Box M repeats a Focus Note from the "Confidentiality" In-Class Session. It shows how to explain confidentiality during the first caring visit. Reference Box N contains the example from the same module that shows how to explain supervision. As you read these, remember that you will probably rephrase these to fit your care receiver's needs and your style. If your care receiver doesn't have any questions about confidentiality and supervision, then quickly move on to the next step in the first caring visit. If he or she does have questions, listen and address his or her concerns.

REFERENCE BOX M

Explaining Confidentiality to Your Care Receiver

"I know that *[name of Stephen Leader]* explained confidentiality to you, but I want to share what it means to me. What happens in our relationship is just between the two of us. You and I may talk about some very personal matters in our caring visits, and I want you to be assured that what we talk about will remain confidential."

REFERENCE BOX N

Explaining Supervision

"*[Name of Stephen Leader]* told you that I am required to participate in Small Group Peer Supervision to help me provide the best possible care for you. At those meetings we talk about our caring relationships but never use names or identifying details that would break confidentiality."

It is not likely to happen, but what if your care receiver said he or she could not accept your participating in Small Group Peer Supervision? If that were to happen, explain that you need to talk with your Stephen Leaders about this since you are required to work in a Supervision Group. Then politely end the visit and tell your care receiver that someone would be contacting him or her in the next day or so. Then you and your Stephen Leaders would figure out what to do next.

6. *Bridge the Gap*

After you and your care receiver have engaged in small talk and you have mentioned confidentiality and supervision, you need to "bridge the gap" and move into a more purposeful discussion of the concerns or challenges that your care receiver is facing. Sometimes the care receiver him- or herself will bridge the gap, and sometimes you will need to.

Care Receiver Initiates

If your care receiver brings up the concern or challenge on his or her own, that's great. Then you and the care receiver are well on your way to getting started with the caring relationship.

Stephen Minister Initiates

Otherwise, you will need to bridge the gap, leading the discussion to your care receiver's concerns or challenges. One way to do so is by sharing some basic information about your role as a Stephen Minister. Reference Box O gives an example of what you might say.

REFERENCE BOX O

Bridging the Gap by Describing Your Role

"As a Stephen Minister I have the privilege of sharing other people's diffi-

---

cult times, listening to them, sharing their challenges and pain, and praying for them. I'm not here to try to solve your problems or to tell you what to do. I believe that God will care for you and guide you. I want to walk alongside you as a caring Christian friend.

"You've had some concerns in your life recently. Would you mind telling me about what has been going on for you? That's a good way for us to get started."

Reference Box P contains some other "bridging the gap" statements that you can make in order to make a smooth transition from small talk to discussion of the care receiver's concerns.

REFERENCE BOX P

Bridging the Gap Statements

"*[Name of Stephen Leader]* told me a little bit about what's happening in your life. It sounds as if it's been hard for you recently. I'm wondering if you could tell me more about it."

"I know you're having surgery tomorrow, and I'm wondering how you're feeling about it."

"You've been divorced now for about two months, and often people who have gone through a divorce find a lot of strong feelings surfacing. I'm wondering how you're doing. What feelings have you had to deal with lately?"

The statements in Reference Box P are assertive and matter-of-fact. You and your care receiver both know why you are there. After you spend some time getting acquainted, your care receiver may appreciate your assertively helping

the conversation move into talking about his or her issues.

7. Listen

From this point on, you will want to let the care receiver do most of the talking. You may remember from module 3, "The Art of Listening," that care receivers should do a very high percentage of the talking in a caring visit. Exercise your listening skills; pay attention, show that you are listening, reflect, and ask open-ended questions in order to encourage your care receiver to say more.

Explore

Next you explore your care receiver's concerns or challenges to learn more about what the person needs and to help him or her see the issues more clearly. You will do five steps as you explore. These steps may last well beyond your first caring visit. They are listed in Reference Box Q.

REFERENCE BOX Q

The Five Steps in *Explore*

1. Focus on the precipitating cause.
2. Find out about a larger problem, if there is one.
3. Find out how the care receiver has tried to solve the problem.
4. Discuss other current help, if any.
5. Determine whether this is a forced referral.

The way you accomplish these steps is by using your Stephen Minister skills of listening, exploring feelings, asking open-ended questions, relating assertively, and remaining process-oriented.

1. Focus on the Precipitating Cause

The precipitating cause is the specific event that caused your care receiver to ask for help. The event might be obvious, such as the death of a loved one, or it may be hidden, such as when a care receiver finally realizes that her pregnancy is not an altogether happy event for her. The way the care receiver seeks help will often be to talk to the pastor, but it could also be to talk to a friend who suggests Stephen Ministry or to call the church office and request a Stephen Minister.

Once you know what the precipitating cause is for your care receiver, make that the focus of your conversation. That is most likely what your care receiver wants to talk about. Don't be surprised, however, if you soon start talking about other issues that are important to your care receiver. Start with the precipitating cause, but follow wherever your care receiver leads.

How do you find out what the precipitating cause is? If it is obvious, you will know; for example, Harry's wife just went in the hospital and they learned that she has inoperable cancer. The "Referral Form" will include information about the circumstances prompting the referral, which may tell you what the precipitating cause is.

Other times the precipitating cause may not be obvious. You may need to ask some questions to discover what it is. Reference Box R lists some examples of the kind of questions you might ask.

REFERENCE BOX R

Inquiring about Precipitating Causes

▶ "What happened that led you to talk to Pastor *[name of pastor or the person who made the referral]* about this?"

▶ "How is it that you and Pastor *[name of pastor or the person who made the referral]* decided that you needed a Stephen Minister at this time?"

▶ "Pastor *[name of pastor]* told me that Thursday afternoon you called him feeling very upset and wanting to talk with someone. What was going on in your life at that time?"

These questions are certainly assertive, and caringly so. You may need to ask several times in several different ways to get your care receiver to share what led him or her to seek care at this time.

2. Find Out about a Larger Problem, If There Is One

Your care receiver's precipitating cause may be a part of a larger concern or challenge. For example, personal doubts about his or her faith may be part of a larger pattern of being only nominally active in the congregation for many years.

As you start talking about the precipitating cause, you may find that it is related to a larger problem. This may be a problem that has been around for a long time, but has finally become painful enough to cause the care receiver to seek help.

If there is a larger problem, find out more about it, including:

- how it started;
- how long it has been going on; and
- who else may be involved.

You won't find out everything about a larger problem in your first caring visit, but you can begin to explore it, using your listening skills to encourage your care receiver to say more about it.

3. Find Out How the Care Receiver Has Tried to Solve the Problem

If you discover that there is a larger problem, find out what your care receiver has done to try to solve it. This will help you understand the problem better and help you avoid suggesting ways of addressing the problem that the care receiver has already tried.

For example, a care receiver might have been praying about his or her child's unemployment for many months and arrived at the conclusion that God is not going to help with that problem. If you don't know that, you may encounter some strong feelings when you bring up prayer and you may not understand where the strong feelings came from. Knowing about this attempted solution, you may stay away from suggesting prayer for a while.

4. Discuss Other Current Help, If Any

Try to get an idea of what other help or care your care receiver is receiving. For example, he or she might be seeing a physician for a physical problem, a financial counselor, a support group for job seekers, or a professional counselor for his or her emotional issues.

When you know what other help your care receiver is receiving, you can un-

derstand better the overall scope of his or her concern or challenge. This knowledge may help you avoid duplicating, interfering with, or competing with other efforts. If the care receiver is working with a professional counselor, for example, sometimes the counselor will insist that the care receiver not be working with anyone else. On the other hand, some counselors welcome other caregiving efforts. You will need to encourage the care receiver to check this out.

5. Determine Whether This Is a Forced Referral

Most of the time care receivers welcome the caring relationship and have requested it themselves. Sometimes, however, someone forces a care receiver to meet with a caregiver or Stephen Minister. If you suspect your care receiver was forced to meet with you, explore your suspicions and find out whether he or she really wants to receive care. Reference Box S contains a suggestion of one way to proceed.

REFERENCE BOX S

If You Think the Care Receiver Has Been Forced to Meet

"As we've been talking, it sounds as if someone has talked you into this and you haven't had much say in the matter. Even if that's the case, however, it's still my opinion that it would really be good for us to continue to meet periodically. I certainly am willing to and want to. What do you think?"

If the care receiver is unsure about whether to accept your ministry, talk further. Explore his or her feelings about the caring relationship. Help your care receiver decide whether to continue. Without the care receiver's own commitment to receive care and to work on whatever problem or life situation he or she is experiencing, he or she might give up the process when it becomes difficult, or blame you for forcing unwanted care.

Clarify

Once you have explored the care receiver's concern or challenge, continue listening, reflecting, and asking open-ended questions in order to clarify what your care receiver's issues are—both for your understanding and also for your care receiver's. Reference Box T contains the four steps in Clarify.

REFERENCE BOX T

The Four Steps in *Clarify*

1. Recognize the tip of the iceberg.

2. Develop preliminary hypotheses.

3. Focus on the problem and possible solutions.

4. Find out about desired changes.

---

1. *Recognize the Tip of the Iceberg*

Keep in mind that what you learn about your care receiver in the first caring visit might be only the tip of the iceberg. The problems your care receiver first talks about may be the least threatening ones to reveal. Your care receiver may be testing the water to see if he or she can trust you.

There is no fast way to get to the whole iceberg. Perhaps you've heard the old riddle: *How do you eat an elephant? One bite at a time.* Don't worry about moving quickly. As a trusting relationship builds in subsequent sessions, your care receiver will be open to sharing more of his or her concerns, and deeper concerns, with you. It just takes time.

Consider this example. A man who is out of work complains to you, his caregiver, that there just are not any good jobs available. This might be very true. He might also be troubled, however, by deeper concerns related to his ability to provide for his family, his worries about aging, his inadequacies in obtaining a job, and possible strained relations at home. As trust develops and the rapport between you strengthens, your care receiver will be more willing to reveal more of the iceberg.

2. *Develop Preliminary Hypotheses*

As the two of you talk during this first visit, you will want to begin forming some preliminary hypotheses about the care receiver—what has happened, what is happening now, what needs to happen.

Consider this example.

▶ *What has happened?* The care receiver has been in shock over the death of his or her spouse.

▶ *What is happening?* The care receiver is showing signs of anger and sadness as he or she begins to admit to the reality of the loss.

▶ *What needs to happen?* This care receiver will need many caring visits in which to recognize, accept, and express his or her feelings of grief.

Here's another example of constructing a hypothesis.

- *What has happened?* The care receiver recently lost his or her job and is having trouble finding a new one.
- *What is happening?* He or she is feeling frustrated about the difficult job search and is also feeling guilty about not providing for his or her family.
- *What needs to happen?* The care receiver may need some help from a career counselor, and he or she also needs someone to listen as he or she deals with painful feelings.

Never lose track of the fact that your hypotheses are preliminary and tentative. Always be ready to change or drop your initial hypotheses as you gather more information and gain new perspectives on your care receiver. Some caregivers make the mistake of being biased by their initial conclusions, a phenomenon that is called the *primacy effect*. The primacy effect is a matter of letting your initial ideas become so firmly entrenched in your mind that no new data will ever dislodge those erroneous conclusions. Your openness to new information will help you avoid the primacy effect.

3. Focus on the Problem and Possible Solutions

As your visit continues, help your care receiver clarify and specify what the problem is. Help him or her sift through what might have caused the problem, and what the care receiver might do to overcome the problem.

Regardless of whether your care receiver discovers new insights or solutions, the process of digging into the problem can be quite therapeutic. Your care receiver may come away with a sense that the situation is not as hopeless as it had seemed. You will also build trust between the two of you as you work together.

4. Find Out about Desired Changes

After you have explored, developed, and discussed the care receiver's situation, you may want to find out what kind of changes your care receiver desires. If he or she doesn't know what changes he or she wants, that is okay. You will have many visits to talk about his or her desires and plans. Care receivers may have unrealistic expectations, too. That's okay. You need not rush to instruct. Often, as the relationship flourishes, their ideas about what is reasonable and possible will change.

You do not have responsibility for bringing about the changes your care receiver wants. Your responsibility is to work the caregiving process and leave the results to God. You might give your care receiver's morale a boost, however, just by suggesting that the two of you will be exploring alternatives and possibilities for change. You will have accomplished a great deal in the first visit if your care receiver starts thinking about the possibility of positive change.

Provide Wholistic Care, If Necessary

Wholistic care means caring for the whole person—for his or her spiritual, emotional, physical, psychological, and social needs. As you develop your relationship with your care receiver, watch for the wholistic needs he or she might be experiencing.

While Stephen Ministry is primarily listening, caring, and praying, sometimes you may help meet physical or social needs, for example, by running an occasional errand or helping your care receiver become involved in a group or a club. Often you will help provide wholistic care by recommending that your care receiver take advantage of other kinds of care, as you learned in module 11, "Using Mental Health Professionals and Other Community Resources." How much you try to meet wholistic needs will depend on the nature of your care receiver's needs and your capability—your talents, training, time, and energy to respond to those needs. Your Supervision Group can help you decide what to do for your care receiver and how best to help him or her get his or her own needs met.

In the first caring visit you might discover a need for some kind of wholistic care, beyond your ministry of listening and caring. For example, your care receiver may need to contact a social service agency in order to begin receiving food stamps or some other assistance. If your care receiver needs help with such an issue, work with the individual to decide what he or she can do to get these needs met. Don't rush in, in a results-oriented manner, to solve the problem yourself. Rather, follow a process of helping your care receiver learn to meet his or her own needs, if possible.

End the Visit

After an hour or so, you will need to bring the caring visit to a good conclusion. The six steps to take are listed in Reference Box U.

REFERENCE BOX U

The Six Steps in *End the Visit*

1. Ask about further pressing problems.

2. Postpone new material.

3. Summarize.

4. Offer a prayer or blessing.

5. Set up the next caring visit.

6. End the caring visit.

---

1. Ask about Further Pressing Problems

When it's about time to end the visit, find out whether the two of you need to discuss any other immediate and pressing problems. Reference Box V shows a simple way to ask.

REFERENCE BOX V

Probing for Further Pressing Problems

"Is there anything else that is pressing that we haven't talked about?"

If your care receiver has problems that simply can't wait, discuss them at this time. Otherwise, save them for your next caring visit. You aren't going to get to everything in the first caring visit. This will be true for subsequent visits also. You will probably end every caring visit with some topics left undiscussed.

2. Postpone New Material

If your care receiver does raise a new problem or situation that could be picked up at a later time, go ahead and postpone the discussion of it until your next visit. Reference Box W shows something you might say.

3. Summarize

As you bring your caring visit to a close, you may find it helpful to summarize what the two of you have discussed. You can see one example of how this summary might go in Reference Box X.

4. Offer a Prayer or Blessing

The process of summarizing may lead naturally to a time for praying together or saying a blessing. As with all distinctively Christian caring tools, use prayer if it will meet your care receiver's needs and feel comfortable for him or her.

If it is appropriate to pray, try to gather your care receiver's concerns into your prayer or blessing. Help him or her see that God is concerned and present and that he or she can count on God's help and care.

5. Set Up the Next Caring Visit

Be sure to set up a second visit with your care receiver. Before you leave, always have an appointment established for the next visit. Never leave it hanging on the assumption that one or the other of you will arrange something later.

Being definite about the next time you are to get together is part of your caring. The care receiver knows then that the two of you will continue working together. That means further growth and change are possible. The care receiver's thoughts may go like this: "Although we really don't know yet what we're going to do, it's hopeful to know that we're going to do something."

As you plan your second meeting, possibly you will want to establish a regular basis for getting together—every week at a certain time, for instance. You may also want to give the person your telephone number and explain that you are available if he or she needs to call.

6. End the Caring Visit

Reference Box Y shows some ways to end the first visit.

► Getting Ready for the In-Class Session

In your In-Class Session, you will be practicing the first caring visit. Since there is a lot to remember, go over the steps in the first caring visit several times so you will remember what each entails. You don't have to have all these steps memorized for the skill practice, but it will help a lot if you are very familiar with them.

► Overview of the First Caring Visit

The chart on page 457 shows all of the parts and steps in the first caring visit.

Overview of the First Caring Visit

Before You Set Up the Visit	**The Referrals Coordinator will:** 1. Find out about a person who needs Stephen Ministry. 2. Meet with the potential care receiver. 3. Offer Stephen Ministry. 4. Explain confidentiality and supervision. 5. Tell the care receiver that a Stephen Minister will call in the next day or two. 6. Give you a completed "Referral Form."
Set Up the First Caring Visit	**You will:** 1. Pray first. 2. Encourage an early meeting. 3. Respond to any reluctance to meet. 4. Respond to a refusal to meet. 5. Set a specific place and time.

Conduct the Caring Visit

Part 1: Get Started	1. Deal with nervousness. 2. Make introductions. 3. Be yourself. 4. Engage in small talk. 5. Mention confidentiality and supervision. 6. Bridge the gap. 7. Listen.
Part 2: Explore	1. Focus on the precipitating cause. 2. Find out about any larger problem. 3. Find out how the care receiver has tried to solve the problem. 4. Discuss any other current help. 5. Determine if the referral was forced.
Part 3: Clarify	1. Recognize the tip of the iceberg. 2. Develop preliminary hypotheses. 3. Focus on the problem and on any possible solutions. 4. Find out about desired changes.

Part 4: Provide Wholistic Care, If Necessary

Part 5: End the Visit	1. Ask about further pressing problems. 2. Postpone new material. 3. Summarize. 4. Offer a prayer or blessing. 5. Set up the next caring visit. 6. End the caring visit.

Appendix A

The Grace to Receive

by Kenneth C. Haugk

Tommy was in third grade at the church's school when I first met him. He was depressed, angry at himself and the world, and confused by many hurts in his life. On his teacher's recommendation, Tommy agreed to meet with me once a week to talk about his problems. At the beginning of one early session, Tommy walked in, handed me a nickel, and said, "This is for you." He wanted to give me the nickel, he explained, because he liked me and I was helping him with his problems.

As I stared at the nickel Tommy had given me, I struggled to make a quick but important decision. I knew Tommy's family didn't have much money and that a nickel was probably important to him. And although I charge for my private counseling practice, I never charge for counseling individuals and families at the church and school. Besides, I was already getting a salary for the work I did at the congregation.

But finally, it was precisely because I knew the nickel was meaningful to Tommy—and because he wanted to do something meaningful for me—that I decided to accept the gift. Just to make sure he didn't feel compelled to pay me, I said, "You know that you don't have to give this to me."

His answer settled the matter: "Yes, I know; but I want to give it to you." I

thanked him, took the nickel, and we proceeded as usual with the counseling session.

Counselors, teachers, ministers, parents, friends—all of us often find it difficult to receive gifts from others. Oh, we find it relatively easy to help others—to give money to them, to spend time with them when they're sick, to visit them when they are in need of a visit, and so on. But when it comes time for us to be on the receiving end, we often fidget, squirm, make excuses, and even refuse—for their own good, of course! We employ clichés like "Better to give than to receive" to support our one-sided way of relating to people.

But when we refuse a gift from someone, are we really doing so out of concern for them? Or are we rather avoiding feelings of discomfort and indebtedness? Could our refusal be a good way to keep the upper hand in the relationship? Do we refuse gifts in order to avoid community and intimacy with that person or those persons?

Strange that we Christians should find it difficult to be gracious receivers when we confess that our entire lives—physical and spiritual—are gifts of God's Spirit. And although the Bible stresses *giving,* it also gives us examples of *receiving.*

Christ showed us how to be gracious receivers when He allowed the sinful woman to anoint Him. In fact, I think Jesus rather enjoyed receiving this gift. He had forgiven and accepted the woman, and she wished to demonstrate

Reprinted with permission from "The Grace to Receive" by Kenneth C. Haugk in *Interaction* 16:10 (1975), pp.15–18.

her faith and gratitude. Jesus and the woman shared an act of community that would not have been possible had He refused her ministrations.

The Apostle Paul had a similar give-and-take relationship with the people of Philippi (Philippians 4:10–20). Paul gave to them; they gave to him: they both received from each other. Paul highly valued self-sufficiency, but he could graciously receive gifts when in need. Both giving *and* receiving were important to Paul and he participated comfortably in both.

It is a general psychological and theological truth that individuals have difficulty giving to others unless they have first received. Scripture emphasizes this most clearly. The first letter of John (1 John 4:7–21) stresses that we are able to love others only because we have first received love from Jesus Christ. In 2 Corinthians 1:4 Paul tells us that we are able to comfort and help others only because Jesus has first comforted us.

It is this divine love and concern that we have experienced that expands and becomes a source for our acts of love and concern for others. When Christians, then, give love and concern to others, they are sharing the love of Christ active within them. And when we receive gifts of love from our brothers and sisters in Christ, we are in a real sense also receiving Christ.

The parable of the last judgment in Matthew 25:31–46 instructs us to feed people, give them something to drink, welcome strangers, clothe people, take care of sick persons, and visit prisoners. And, Jesus takes time to emphasize, when we do this we are not only helping other people, we are also ministering to *Jesus Christ Himself*. ("Truly I tell you, just as you did it to one of the least of these who are members of my family, you did it to Me.") So Christ is present in both the giver and the receiver, in both the act of giving and the act of receiving.

In the interaction between Tommy and me there was such a give and take. It is obvious that I was in Christian ministry to him as I counseled with him about his problems. Perhaps less obvious but just as real, Tommy—by his words of affection and his gift of the nickel—was just as involved in sharing Jesus Christ *with me*. Had I refused his gift, I could have destroyed a part of the Christian community which was growing between us. . . .

We all probably agree that we could improve our acts of giving. But perhaps we also need to brush up our receiving actions and attitudes as well.

How to Make a First Caring Visit

The people were amazed at his teaching, because he taught them as one who had authority, not as the teachers of the law.

Mark 1:22

I. Your Authority to Care

II. How Referrals Work

A. Finding, Preparing, and Connecting Care Receivers

1. Finding Care Receivers

2. Preparing Care Receivers

3. Connecting Care Receivers with Stephen Ministers

III. Practice the First Caring Visit

FOCUS NOTE 1

Care Receiver's Instructions for Skill Practice 1

Spend five minutes studying the information in this Focus Note and preparing to play your role.

Your situation:

Your name is Pat Carlton. You have been an active member of your congregation for six years. Since your spouse, Casey, went in the hospital two weeks ago, no one from church has visited him or her in the hospital, had any prayers in church, or even showed that they knew what was going on. You are angry at the church. You are thinking about

---

not going to church for many years, and feeling guilty about these thoughts and feelings.

Your congregation's new pastor, Pastor Nancy, called on you yesterday. You told her about your worries about your spouse and shared some feelings of anger at the church. Your pastor recommended that you meet with a Stephen Minister to talk about your feelings, and you agreed. The pastor explained what Stephen Ministry is and how it works and said a Stephen Minister would be calling you in the next day or so.

The precipitating cause for you was your pastor's visit. The pastor's visit was a pleasant surprise, and you suspect that God knew what you needed and sent the pastor over to visit you.

You have tried talking yourself out of your anger, but it doesn't work.

The change you would like would be not to feel angry at the church anymore, but you don't see how that could happen.

You are interested in gardening, and you have a large flowerbed in front of the house with many different kinds of flowers.

Think about additional details you could add to make this character more real and one that you will feel comfortable playing.

Steps in your skill practice:

1. The skill practice will begin with your Stephen Minister calling you to set up a first caring visit. Be somewhat reluctant to make an appointment for your first caring visit, but agree as you discuss it with your Stephen Minister.

2. Be slightly uncomfortable at the beginning of the first caring visit. Become friendlier and more comfortable when you start engaging in small talk.

3. Wait for your Stephen Minister to bridge the gap before you start talking about your concerns.

4. Be a little embarrassed about your concerns and reluctant to say a lot about your feelings about church and God. Make the Stephen Minister ask lots of questions and draw you out.

5. Don't share your precipitating cause until the Stephen Minister asks you to.

6. As your Stephen Minister asks questions, reflects, and listens, slowly reveal small parts of your story, such as what you have done to solve the problem and the change you would like to see.

7. End the skill practice at the end of ten minutes.

Observer's Instructions for Skill Practice 1

Read the care receiver's instructions in Focus Note 1 on pages 461–462, and review the Overview of the First Caring Visit on page 457. Also review the discussion questions in Focus Note 3 to prepare to lead the discussion after the skill practice.

Discussion Questions for Skill Practice 1

1. How did the care receiver feel about the visit?

2. How did the Stephen Minister feel about the visit?

3. What went well, and what would you do differently in the phone call to set up the first caring visit?

4. What did the Stephen Minister do to bridge the gap? How well did it work?

5. How would the Stephen Minister summarize the care receiver's concern or challenge? Does the care receiver agree that this is accurate?

IV. Practice the First Caring Visit (cont.)

Observer's Instructions for Skill Practice 2

Read the care receiver's instructions in Focus Note 5 and review the Overview of the First Caring Visit on page 457. Also review the discussion questions in Focus Note 6 on page 465 to prepare to lead the discussion after the skill practice.

Care Receiver's Instructions for Skill Practice 2

Spend five minutes studying the information in this Focus Note and preparing to play your role.

Your situation:

Your name is Pat Baggio. You recently finalized a divorce from your spouse of 12 years. You have two sons, Robert and Dean, ages nine and six. Your ex-spouse, Casey, has custody of the children. You agreed to that because you thought it would be better for the children, whom you love deeply. Your ex-spouse was extremely demanding in the divorce proceedings, but you didn't want to make a lot of waves. As a result you ended up with all the debt, and your spouse ended up with the house and most of the other resources. Now you have to live in a cramped apartment because that is all you can afford.

You maintained your positive attitude throughout the divorce proceedings, but now your ex-spouse is making it very difficult for you to see your children. You cannot afford to go back to court, and when you demand your rights, your ex-spouse punishes your children and makes their lives miserable. You feel trapped and deeply hurt. After you bent over backwards to make the divorce as smooth and easy as possible—for the sake of your children—your ex-spouse is now taking advantage of you and treating you disrespectfully. While you are normally an easygoing person, you are starting to feel very angry. As you admit to your angry feelings about the visitation issues, you find that a lot of other feelings of anger, sadness, and hurt, which you had been ignoring, are now coming to the surface.

You needed someone to talk to, so you made an appointment with Pastor Klinsmann. After listening to you, sharing some Scripture passages, and praying with you, he recommended that you start meeting with a Stephen Minister. You agreed eagerly because you have realized that you don't want to go through this crisis alone.

The precipitating cause of your visit to your pastor was what happened last weekend. It was your weekend to have the boys, and you had bought tickets to see the circus as a special surprise. You had to skip some meals to afford the tickets, but you really wanted to do this for your children. You went to pick up the children at the regular, mutually agreed-upon time on Friday, but they were not home. You waited for three hours and then went home. You left messages on your ex-spouse's answering machine but did not receive a call back until Monday evening, when your ex-spouse said, "We received a last-minute invitation to go to the lake with my parents. You may have the children two weekends in a row."

The change you would like is to be able to stand up to your ex-spouse, find a way to protect your children from the fallout of the divorce, and be treated with more respect.

Think about additional details you could add to make this character more real and one that you will feel comfortable playing.

Steps in your skill practice:

1. You have already set up the first meeting over the phone. Your skill practice will start with the arrival of the Stephen Minister for the first caring visit.

2. You are anxious to start talking about what has been troubling you. You have been thinking about the situation with your ex-spouse all the time, and you really want to tell someone else about it. Therefore you aren't very interested in small talk, and you will move the conversation quickly into talking about your children and how much you miss them.

3. Share your precipitating cause if your Stephen Minister asks about it.

4. Share your desired change if your Stephen Minister asks about it.

5. End the skill practice at the end of ten minutes.

FOCUS NOTE 6

Discussion Questions for Skill Practice 2

1. How did the care receiver feel about the visit?

2. How did the Stephen Minister feel about the visit?

3. What did the Stephen Minister do to bridge the gap? How well did it work?

4. What hypothesis did the Stephen Minister develop? Did anything in the caring visit support or contradict the hypothesis?

5. What do you think needs to happen in the next few caring visits of this caring relationship?

Care Receiver's Instructions for Skill Practice 3

Spend five minutes studying the information in this Focus Note and preparing to play your role.

Your situation:

Your name is Casey Keller. You are 72 years old, and you fell and broke your hip a month ago. Up until then you had lived on your own in your own home. Your spouse died ten years ago, and you have lived alone since then. When you broke your hip, you decided that you needed to move into a retirement facility. You just moved into your own apartment, and the facility can provide more and more care as you need it, including a bed in a nursing home, if that ever becomes necessary.

You have been in your new apartment for a week, and you are feeling terribly lonely. You miss your friends in your old neighborhood, and you miss your home. You feel terribly sad about all you have lost in the last month—your home, your friends, and your mobility. A recent visit from Berti Vogts, a friend from the old neighborhood, really reminded you of how sad and lonely you are. You have been wondering if this is the beginning of the end of your life, which also makes you feel very sad. You know you will be able to snap out of it eventually, but right now life is pretty painful.

The worst part for you is not having anyone to talk to. You are a shy person and don't make new friends easily. You were very happy when your pastor called to say that he was coming over to visit, and you welcomed his suggestion of a Stephen Minister. You have been looking forward to having company, and you arranged for someone to buy some cookies so you could serve them to your Stephen Minister.

You need to talk about spiritual issues, such as your future, the fact that you are going to die, your anger at God for letting all this happen, and the fact that you have been having trouble praying recently. You want someone to share some Bible passages with you and pray with you. In your mind you have set aside the entire Saturday afternoon for a long visit with your new Stephen Minister.

Your precipitating cause is Berti's visit, which brought to a head how you miss the old neighborhood.

The change you would like is to feel more comfortable making new friends in your new home.

Think about additional details you could add to make this character more real and one that you will feel comfortable playing.

Steps in your skill practice:

1. You will begin the skill practice almost an hour into the first caring visit. You have already set up the appointment, started the visit with delightful small talk, served the cookies, and moved into talking about your spiritual concerns.

2. Tell your Stephen Minister about the concerns you have been having about your relationship with God.

3. When your Stephen Minister suggests that you end your first caring visit, you will be surprised and unhappy. You will say that you haven't had time to talk about the most important issue you've been thinking about, which is how to start making new friends. Say that you were expecting to visit much longer than this.

4. When your skill practice is almost over, agree to end the visit and to make an appointment for another visit.

5. End the skill practice at the end of ten minutes.

FOCUS NOTE 8

Observer's Instructions for Skill Practice 3

Read the care receiver's instructions in Focus Note 7 and review the Overview of the First Caring Visit on page 457. Also review the discussion questions in Focus Note 9 on page 467 to prepare to lead the discussion after the skill practice.

FOCUS NOTE 9

Discussion Questions for Skill Practice 3

1. How did the care receiver feel about the visit?

2. How did the Stephen Minister feel about the visit?

3. How did trying to end the visit go? What might the Stephen Minister do differently next time?

4. What do you think needs to happen in the next few caring visits of this caring relationship?

V. Looking Forward to Your First Caring Visit

VI. Caregiver's Compass Review

VII. Looking Ahead

Prayer Partner Requests and Thanksgivings

My prayer partner is _____

Prayer requests and thanksgivings to share with my prayer partner

_____

_____

Prayer requests and thanksgivings shared by my prayer partner

_____

_____

Referral Form

CONFIDENTIAL

Stephen Ministry® Form

Date _____

Person in Need of Care

Name _____

Address _____

Phone _____ Approximate age ____ Gender _____ Marital status _____

Occupation _____

Place of work _____ Work phone _____

Best time to contact _____

Church affiliation _____ Currently active? ❑ Yes ❑ No ❑ Uncertain

Who initially identified the care receiver? _____

Circumstances Prompting Referral

Other Persons Caring for the Care Receiver (e.g., family or professional caregivers)

Name _____ Relationship to care receiver _____

Name _____ Relationship to care receiver _____

Name _____ Relationship to care receiver _____

Person to Contact in Case of Emergency

Name _____

Address _____

Phone _____ Relationship to care receiver _____

❑ Check here if the care receiver 1) has been prepared for Stephen Ministry, and 2) has consented to the care of a Stephen Minister (necessary before first caring visit is made).

Form completed by _____

Stephen Minister assigned _____

Additional Information or Comment

Appendix B

Contact Record Sheet

Stephen Ministry® Form

Stephen Minister _____

Contact Number	Date	Initiated by	Type of Contact	Length of Contact	Notes

(continued on the next page)

Explanation of Categories

Contact Number
Beginning with your first contact, all encounters with your care receiver should appear on this sheet regardless of their nature (phone, in person, or correspondence, for example).

Date
Date of contact

Initiated by
Note whether the Stephen Minister, the care receiver, or a third party initiated the contact. Be sure not to use the care receiver's name or initials.

Type of Contact
Phone call, visit, correspondence, happenstance encounter, or other

Length of Contact
Amount of time taken for the encounter in minutes

Notes
Record here, very briefly, notes for future reference. They can serve also as a "memory jogger" for your preparation of check-in statements and in-depth reports on the caring relationship. You might include such matters as these:

▶ The primary impression you received from the contact
▶ The location of the visit
▶ Anything special that took place during the contact
▶ A special need, concern, question, or issue that was raised
▶ An intense feeling you or the care receiver experienced
▶ The reason for the contact
▶ Any follow-up activities that are necessary
▶ Any change in the care receiver's situation, attitude, feeling, or behavior

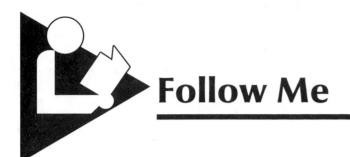

Follow Me

Contents

▶ The End of the Beginning

This module marks the end of the beginning. You have faithfully participated in 19 sessions of initial training and have learned much of what you need to know in order to serve as a Stephen Minister. Now it is time to bring the initial phase of your Stephen Ministry training to a close by reviewing and celebrating all that God has done so far. It is also time to get ready for the next phase of your service as a Stephen Minister by preparing for your commissioning and beginning to work with your Supervision Group.

In this Preclass Reading you will review the answer to a very important question: What does it mean to be a Stephen Minister? You will not only read answers to that question, you will also reflect on your own answers and have a chance to renew your commitment to all that is involved in being a Stephen Minister.

▶ What Does It Mean to Be a Stephen Minister?

You are almost ready to be commissioned as a Stephen Minister. This, therefore, is an excellent time to ask a key question: What does it mean to be a

Stephen Minister? You have already learned the shape of the answer to this question, but some review and some further ideas now will add color and dimension.

Once you have finished your initial training and have been commissioned, you have come not to the end of what you do in order to be a Stephen Minister, but only to the end of the beginning.

Being a Stephen Minister is not just a matter of what you have done; it is also a matter of what you are doing. Stephen Ministers are people who are actively involved in a caring relationship, who participate faithfully in Small Group Peer Supervision and continuing education, who remain connected to Jesus, and who do all this as a member of a larger team. Being trained and commissioned is the starting point—you can't be a Stephen Minister without those steps. From then on, you are a Stephen Minister as long as you continue to do the activities that Stephen Ministers do.

Reference Box A contains a definition of a Stephen Minister.

REFERENCE BOX A

Definition of a Stephen Minister

A Stephen Minister is someone who:

1. participates in extensive initial training;

2. receives commissioning;

3. cares for a care receiver;

4. participates faithfully in supervision and continuing education;

5. stays connected to Jesus; and

6. serves as part of a larger team.

Read on for more about each of the six elements of this definition.

A Stephen Minister Participates in Training

As you have participated in initial training, you have come to see even more clearly the value and the necessity of training. Christian caregiving requires skills and knowledge that go beyond what most people pick up in their daily lives. From listening skills and dealing with feelings, through confidentiality and crisis theory, to caring for people who are grieving or depressed, you need to know how to care and you need to practice those caring skills in order to refine them.

The caregiving you will do as a Stephen Minister will go beyond the ad hoc caring that all Christians do at one time or another. You will enter into a formal caring relationship with someone who has requested care. Your care receiver, as well as your congregation, will count on you to provide care faithfully and skillfully. The training you have received will help you do that.

It's important to remember that your training doesn't end when you are commissioned. Your initial training provides a solid foundation for your service as a Stephen Minister, but you will continue to learn for as long as you serve. Perhaps you have received professional training or job training, or maybe you have taken a class, read a book, or watched a video to learn a certain skill. If so, you may have noticed that even though you learned a lot in your training, you learned even more from using your skills. The same will be true as you serve as a Stephen Minister. Skills and insights that you learned about in training will gain a whole new meaning as you put them to use. Then, when you and the others in your Supervision Group discuss your caregiving, you will come to understand much more deeply what it means to care. You will also participate in continuing education for as long as you are a Stephen Minister. Be sure to let your Stephen Leaders know if there are skills you need to learn or refine, or areas of caring that you need to understand better. Your Stephen Leaders want to make continuing education very responsive to your needs as a caregiver.

A Stephen Minister Receives Commissioning

Read the passage in Reference Box B.

REFERENCE BOX B

An Example of Commissioning

In those days when the number of disciples was increasing, the Grecian Jews among them complained against the Hebraic Jews because their widows were being overlooked in the daily distribution of food. So the Twelve gathered all the disciples together and said, "It would not be right for us to neglect the ministry of the word of God in order to wait on tables. Brothers, choose seven men from among you who are known to be full of the Spirit and wisdom. We will turn this responsibility over to them and will give our attention to prayer and the ministry of the word."

This proposal pleased the whole group. They chose Stephen, a man full of faith and of the Holy Spirit; also Philip, Procorus, Nicanor, Timon, Parmenas, and Nicolas from Antioch, a convert to Judaism. They presented these men to the apostles, who prayed and laid their hands on them.

Acts 6:1–6

This is an example of a biblical practice that can be called commissioning. When God called people to a special ministry, others in the community would lay hands on them, pray for them, and send them out to do their ministry. Through this commissioning, they asked for God's blessing on the ministry and the Holy Spirit's power and wisdom for the ministers. They also assured the ministers of their prayers and support. The commissioning clearly communicated that the church supported this ministry and those who did it.

At the same time the ministers who were commissioned publicly stated their commitment to the ministry and their willingness to serve God and the church in this way. By receiving the prayers and the blessings of their congregation, these ministers showed that they accepted God's call to ministry and that they would serve in partnership with their fellow Christians.

When you are commissioned, you will receive and make similar commitments. Your congregation will ask God's blessings on your ministry and promise to support you in it. You will also be asked to state publicly your promises to serve God, your care receivers, and your congregation. Your commissioning will formalize and solemnize your call to serve as a Stephen Minister. It will mark the turning point between being a trainee and a Stephen Minister.

In the upcoming In-Class Session your Stephen Leaders will tell you some of the details about your commissioning, if they haven't already done so. Many Stephen Ministers have found their commissioning to be a joyous experience of affirmation and commitment. May you experience the Holy Spirit's joyful presence as you are commissioned.

A Stephen Minister Cares for a Care Receiver

You have spent many hours of training and study learning to care for the care receiver to whom you will be assigned. Perhaps you have thought about what it will be like and felt excited, nervous, or happy about your upcoming assignment. Throughout your training you have heard and read that Jesus will be with you as you care. He cares for your care receiver even more than you will, and he will provide the healing, comfort, and growth that God wants for your care receiver.

Take a moment to remember what you have learned about caring for a care receiver. When you care, you will listen and focus on feelings. You will carefully begin the caring relationship and trust God throughout. You will be the caregiver and allow God to be the cure giver. You will do your best to understand empathetically what your care receiver is going through and use your best skills to provide the care he or she needs. You will walk with your care receiver through his or her pain and be there for him or her through thick and thin.

After you have been trained and commissioned *to be* a Stephen Minister, caring for your care receiver is the most important part of *being* a Stephen Minister. It is, however, not the only part.

A Stephen Minister Participates Faithfully in Supervision and Continuing Education

At times people who have been trained and commissioned as Stephen Ministers have thought they could be Stephen Ministers on their own, without giving and receiving Small Group Peer Supervision or taking part in continuing education. They were wrong. Anyone who is not participating faithfully in Small Group Peer Supervision and continuing education is not a Stephen Minister.

You have learned that the goal of supervision is to provide the best distinctively Christian care possible. The fact is that no one can provide the best care possible without participating regularly and actively in Small Group Peer Supervision. God works through your sisters and brothers in Christ to support you, guide you, inspire you, and hold you accountable. God will give others insights into how you can care best for your care receiver, and he will work through them to give you the wisdom you need. He will also use you to work in their lives and support their ministries. Supervision is your main way to receive and give God's help for Stephen Ministry. Without taking part in your Supervision Group regularly, preparing well, and participating fully in it, you are not a Stephen Minister.

As complete as your initial training has been, it is not enough. You have much more to learn about being a Stephen Minister. You have probably noticed in your *Stephen Ministry Training Manual* that there are still many training modules to come. In continuing education you will learn about vital areas of ministry, including ministry to people who are dying and to their families and friends, ministry to people during and after hospitalization, and ministry to those who are divorcing. Even if you never care for a person in these situations, you will learn a lot about caring for *your* care receiver as you consider how to apply your caring skills to people in various situations. In addition, your Stephen Leaders will provide other continuing education that will help you shore up your basic Stephen Minister skills, address needs you see as you actively care, and reveal new horizons of caregiving and understanding others' needs. Stephen Ministers are sufficiently humbled by the challenges of caring for another person that they welcome additional training.

A Stephen Minister Stays Connected to Jesus

Read the Bible passage in Reference Box C.

REFERENCE BOX C

Connected to Jesus

Abide in me as I abide in you. Just as the branch cannot bear fruit by itself unless it abides in the vine, neither can you unless you abide in me. I am the vine, you are the branches. Those who abide in me and I in them bear much fruit, because apart from me you can do nothing.

John 15:4–5 NRSV

Your central concern as a Stephen Minister is to pay constant attention to your relationship with Jesus Christ. You do this always trusting that Jesus created that relationship and will maintain it. The clear and central focus of your energies and efforts must be upon Jesus. As long as you keep in constant touch with Jesus, the Holy Spirit will be able to use your training, knowledge, faith, love, and skills to God's glory and to accomplish what is best in the life of your care receiver.

If you take your eyes off Jesus, however, your caring will not be ministry that God can use. Even if everything that you do in your caregiving is technically right, Jesus' power will not flow through it. Without a close, continuous connection with Jesus, the caring relationship can sink into trouble as Peter sank when he took his eyes off Jesus and began to look at the size of the waves around him.

Consider how the following Bible passage in Reference Box D relates to your ministry as a Christian caregiver.

REFERENCE BOX D

Keep Your Eyes on Jesus

During the fourth watch of the night Jesus went out to them, walking on the lake. When the disciples saw him walking on the lake, they were terrified.

> "It's a ghost," they said, and cried out in fear.
>
> But Jesus immediately said to them: "Take courage! It is I. Don't be afraid."
>
> "Lord, if it's you," Peter replied, "tell me to come to you on the water."
>
> "Come," he said.
>
> Then Peter got down out of the boat, walked on the water and came toward Jesus. But when he saw the wind, he was afraid and, beginning to sink, cried out, "Lord, save me!"
>
> Immediately Jesus reached out his hand and caught him. "You of little faith," he said, "why did you doubt?"
>
> Matthew 14:25–31

Keeping your concentration on Jesus is important, because if God does not dominate your life and your caregiving, other forces jostle one another in their eagerness to occupy first place in your life. Once Peter took his eyes off Jesus, for example, his fear took over. If God does not rule your life, then your human concerns may dominate, and empathy can too easily degenerate into sympathy or escalate into overidentification. If you are not leaning on God, then the weight of responsibility you carry can overburden or even crush you. If God's Spirit doesn't control you, you will be driven by other thoughts, desires, and feelings that can easily enslave you and rob you of your glorious freedom as God's child. If you do not delight in God, you will try to please yourself or your care receiver, and in the end you will fall into the trap of shortsighted, results-oriented caregiving. If you attempt this ministry by relying on your own strength and wis-

dom, these will ultimately fail you, and your ministry will seem empty and worthless. You will eventually lose proper perspective, feel drained, and even become depressed or resentful—burned out, in short.

Your most important need as a caregiver, therefore, is to maintain your focus on Jesus, that is, to "be with Jesus," to "abide in Jesus," the true vine. How can you do that?

Two Important Tools

God has given two important tools to help you abide in Jesus and maintain your focus on Jesus and his sustaining Spirit. These tools are prayer and Scripture. Certainly there are other useful tools, but these two are a good way to begin. By using them you open yourself to God; you make it possible for God to work in your life and ministry.

Prayer

When Jesus reached crucial times in his ministry, he spent intensive time in prayer. As you look forward to beginning your work as a Stephen Minister, make these next days and weeks a time when you allow yourself quiet contemplation and conversation with God. Open yourself to God's presence, let God speak to your heart, and then pour out your heart's desire to God.

Where do you begin? Some of you may be experienced in the rich traditions of prayer and meditation. By all means continue them. But if you don't know where to start, here are a couple of suggestions.

1. The book of Psalms is the Scriptures' own prayer book; make this your

prayer book also. Pray at least one psalm per day. The psalms cover the full range of human emotion and experience. Praying the psalms puts you in touch with the deep parts of human nature as well as with the God who touches those depths with grace and truth.

2. Pray the Lord's Prayer, petition by petition, slowly, meditatively, and thoughtfully. Let the words of Jesus' own prayer sink deeply into your conscious and unconscious being.

Perhaps during continuing education your group will cover additional resources for deepening your prayer life.

Scripture

The words of Scripture were frequently on Jesus' lips. Even more, the words of Scripture were planted deep within his heart. Paul reminds Christians to "Let the word of Christ dwell in you richly" (Colossians 3:16). As you regularly read the Gospels and other parts of the Old and New Testaments, ask yourself the questions that follow.

What is God:
▸ giving you?
▸ requiring of you?
▸ asking of you?
▸ promising you?
▸ empowering you to do?

Select a particularly meaningful passage of Scripture and memorize it, meditate on it, regularly recall and recite it. Let God speak to your heart as well as your head. Let the richness of God's love embedded in the Scripture soak deeply into you. You may learn many other ways of studying and medi-

tating on Scripture as time goes on, but these are some good ways to get started.

Make these and other spiritual disciplines part of your daily life in Christ. If you have not committed yourself to using these tools faithfully during your initial training, do so now as you begin ministry. Covenant with your prayer partner or with another Stephen Minister to pray for one another, to meet together for Scripture study, or to encourage and support one another in your spiritual growth. These are the ways God has given us to remain focused and to maintain a lively, growing, and exciting relationship with Jesus.

A Stephen Minister Serves as Part of a Larger Team

To be a Stephen Minister is to be part of a ministry team. Every Christian related to Jesus Christ by faith is connected to every other person who also trusts in Jesus. Paul goes to great lengths in 1 Corinthians 12 and 13 to state the crucial interdependence Christians have with one another. Those chapters are worth rereading and applying to yourself and to every person involved in your congregation's Stephen Ministry. Christians are not "independent operators," but by virtue of their union with Christ are joined to a living body, a whole community with many different members. Neither are Stephen Ministers independent operators. Your caring ministry can be sustained only if it remains united with the Christian community that gave it birth—your congregation's Stephen Ministry.

Each Stephen Minister needs every other Stephen Minister to fulfill his or her ministry effectively. As sometimes happens in close relationships, at times you may think you can function better without someone to help and support you. But this is one of Satan's deceptive lies. When Satan isolates people and gets them alone, they become much more vulnerable to Satan's attacks and subtle sabotage of ministry. Even with all the failures and defects that other Stephen Ministers may have, we all need one another. If you are open to it, God will show you how graciously others receive and love you with all your faults and weaknesses!

In addition—and this applies especially to supervision—Stephen Leaders and Stephen Ministers cannot learn and grow without one another. You need the disciplines of meeting regularly, reflecting on your caring ministry, remaining accountable and responsible to one another, and supporting and encouraging one another. You need not only to receive help from others for your caring relationships, but also to give others the help they need in theirs. That is why your faithful attendance at supervision and continuing education is not just a matter of following a rule or keeping a promise; it is a statement of care for your other Stephen Ministers and Stephen Leaders. To come and actively participate is to say, "You matter to me!" Not to come or to participate halfheartedly is to say, "I don't care"—and such a statement is incompatible with being a Stephen Minister.

If yours is the first class of Stephen Ministers in your congregation, you have a special responsibility. You are blazing the trail and setting the standard for all Stephen Ministers who will follow you. How straight or twisted a path will you create for others? What kind of standard will you set? Will it be the "path of least resistance" or the standard of "my utmost for God's highest"? It is especially important that from the very beginning you do Stephen Ministry right. Performing your ministry haphazardly not only reflects on yourself, but will have negative consequences for your care receivers, those Stephen Ministers who come after you, and Stephen Ministry in your congregation. You can either help to establish a positive vision and direction for this ministry for the future, or you can sow the seeds for its ruin. And if the Stephen Ministry program in your congregation ceases to exist, the tragedy will be that people will not receive the quality of care that they need in Jesus' name. The first class of Stephen Ministers in a congregation holds a unique position and bears a special responsibility.

If your class is the second or later in a succession of classes in your congregation's Stephen Ministry, you also have a singular responsibility: to learn from and to lift up those who have gone before you. For peer supervision you will likely be integrated into small groups with previously commissioned Stephen Ministers. They have much to teach you, and you also have much to give them. They may need your energy and enthusiasm; they may benefit by being reminded of key principles or skills fresh from your more recent training; and they will certainly grow because of the unique perspective and personal gifts that you bring to your group. You can also learn from them. As they share their experience of Stephen Ministry and offer suggestions that have worked for them and may also work for you, they share a valuable and hard-earned gift.

Also consider that there would be no Stephen Ministry in your congregation without your Stephen Leader(s). Have you given any thought as to how you personally or as one of a class will affirm and express your gratitude to your Stephen Leader(s)? Your Stephen Leaders went away to be trained at a Leader's Training Course and have spent many hours preparing and teaching, sharing and caring for you. They will continue to guide you in supervision and train you through continuing education. Offer your respect, support, prayers, and concern to these key members of your congregation's caring ministry team. Thank God for them. Appreciate them. Love them. Pray for them.

All Stephen Ministers are responsible to their congregation for the ministry they perform. It is important to realize that Stephen Ministry was begun by the congregation, is conducted for the sake of the people of the congregation and its community, and is accountable to the congregation. When a person is identified as a Stephen Minister, what he or she does and how he or she does it matters. Your behavior now reflects not only on you, but also on your whole Stephen Ministry and your congregation, which you represent. Remember, your congregation does not exist for Stephen Ministry; Stephen Ministry exists in order to help your congregation fulfill its mission.

Your pastors are also key members of your Stephen Ministry Team, whether or not they are trained as Stephen Leaders. The final responsibility for providing care for the congregation lies with the pastors, and you are sharing in their ministry. Find ways to support and honor your pastors. Tell them "thank you" for all the care they provide and for how they equip you for your Christian life and for ministry week after week. As part of your prayer discipline, pray for your pastors. As you serve in Stephen Ministry, you may get a small taste of the special demands and pressures that pastors experience every day. Use your insights to be a caregiver for your pastors in ways that they need and welcome.

And finally, there would be no Stephen Ministry without Stephen Ministries St. Louis. Since 1975 Stephen Ministries St. Louis has worked with many thousands of congregations in more than 90 denominations to begin and maintain Stephen Ministry. The staff developed and publishes the material you and your Stephen Leaders use in Stephen Ministry training and implementation. Stephen Ministries St. Louis works and prays daily for enrolled congregations and facilitates your ministry. Remember to pray for them and perhaps find other ways to support Stephen Ministries St. Louis in order to make it possible for more and more congregations to have Stephen Ministry.

As a Stephen Minister, you are part of a large family of trained and supervised lay caring ministers who provide care to others. Did you know that hundreds of thousands of people have been trained as Stephen Ministers? Just think of all the care that God has brought about using the compassion, faith, skills, and trustworthiness of uncounted people like you.

The picture is pretty clear, isn't it? Stephen Ministry is team ministry. We need one another! Thanks to God, we have been given to one another in Christ! Welcome to the team. Thanks be to God for you and your commitment to care in Jesus' name. Your completion of initial training and commissioning as a Stephen Minister is the first step along a new path of caring discipleship. Jesus calls you, saying, "Follow me." And because Jesus has promised to be with you every step of the way, the best is yet to come!

▶ Getting Ready for the In-Class Session and Beyond

Be sure to bring both volumes of your *Stephen Ministry Training Manual* to class.

Since you will soon be commissioned and begin serving as a Stephen Minister, this Preclass Reading concludes with some activities you can do to get ready not only for the In-Class Session but also for your commissioning and your service as a Stephen Minister.

Prepare for the "Stephen Ministry Emblem" Exercise

During the In-Class Session you will do an exercise in which you make a "Stephen Ministry Emblem," which shows what being a Stephen Minister means to you. In order to prepare for this exercise, do the following.

1. Take a few moments to reflect on what Stephen Ministry means to you.

Serving
accepting
loving
listening

In a few words or sentences, write your thoughts and feelings below.

2. Select a Bible passage or story that you would like to use as your "Motto of Stephen Ministry" or your "Picture of What Stephen Ministry Means."

   ▶ Write the Scripture reference for your passage or story here. (If it is brief, write it out completely.)

   ▶ Briefly note here why this passage or story exemplifies Stephen Ministry for you. Be prepared to share this with others in your training class.

Statement of Readiness to Be Commissioned as a Stephen Minister

Knowing what it means to be a Stephen Minister, use the Statement of Readiness on page 484 to indicate your readiness to make the necessary commitment and be commissioned as a Stephen Minister. Study it, pray about it, and then, when you are ready to make the commitment, sign it. At the In-Class Session you will receive another copy of the Statement of Readiness to sign and turn in as part of one of the In-Class activities.

Prayer before Commissioning

Jesus made time to be alone and pray before major milestones in his ministry. Consider setting aside some significant quiet time, at least 30 to 60 minutes, to be alone with God in prayer. Enjoy God's presence. Take your joys, concerns, thanksgivings, and requests about serving as a Stephen Minister to him. Make this a time of maintaining your connection to Jesus.

Statement of Readiness
to Be Commissioned as a Stephen Minister

Having prayerfully considered what it means to be a Stephen Minister, I hereby state my promise to fulfill the commitments of a Stephen Minister and my readiness to be commissioned as a Stephen Minister.

1. I will complete the initial training.

2. I will receive commissioning as a Stephen Minister at one or more worship services.

3. I will care for the care receiver assigned to me to the best of my ability, meeting with him or her regularly and praying for him or her daily.

4. I will participate faithfully in Small Group Peer Supervision and continuing education, coming prepared to every supervision session unless illness, emergency, or unavoidably being out of town make it impossible for me to be present.

5. I will do all I can to stay connected to Jesus, trusting that he will stay connected to me.

6. I will serve as part of a larger team, honoring and praying for my fellow Stephen Ministers, Stephen Leaders, and pastors, and for Stephen Ministries St. Louis.

7. I will receive ministry assignments from my Stephen Leaders and serve under their direction as well as the direction of my pastors.

I pray that God will give me the faith and love I need to fulfill this commitment.

Signature _____

Date _____

Follow Me

Outline and Focus Notes

"Whoever serves me must follow me; and where I am, my servant also will be. My Father will honor the one who serves me."

John 12:26

I. Following Jesus

FOCUS NOTE 1

Following Jesus into Servanthood

Let the same mind be in you that was in Christ Jesus, who, though he was in the form of God, did not regard equality with God as something to be exploited, but emptied himself, taking the form of a slave, being born in human likeness. And being found in human form, he humbled himself and became obedient to the point of death—even death on a cross.

Philippians 2:5–8 NRSV

FOCUS NOTE 2

Following Jesus into Death

Very truly, I tell you, unless a grain of wheat falls into the earth and dies, it remains just a single grain; but if it dies, it bears much fruit. Those who love their life lose it, and those who hate their life in this world will keep it for eternal life. Whoever serves me must follow me, and where I am, there will my servant be also. Whoever serves me, the Father will honor.

John 12:24–26 NRSV

TM-18 OFN Follow Me.doc C: 1/1/2000 R:

II. The Caregiver's Compass Revisited

> **FOCUS NOTE 4**
>
> ### The Caregiver's Compass

A. Revisit Your Ratings

> **FOCUS NOTE 5**
>
> ### Self-Evaluation Exercise
>
> For each of the five characteristics of a caregiver, mark on the scale where you believe you are right now. Note that both ends of the scale are extreme positions; most people probably will be more toward the middle. Mark the scale to show where you see yourself now. Then write under each scale one way in which you know you need to grow in that particular characteristic.

1. Compassionate

10   9   8   ⑦   6   5   4   3   2   1

I thoroughly understand
and am willing to share
others' pain.

I never know what
others are feeling and
I'm scared to find out.

find out why's in gentle ways

One way I can grow in compassion is: *to listen*
stay process oriented

2. Full of faith

10   9   8   7   ⑥   5   4   3   2   1

I have unshakable faith in
Jesus, pray without ceasing,
and always hope in God.

I don't know what I
believe, I don't know
how to pray, and I'm
not very hopeful.

One way I can grow in being full of faith is: *continue to pray for God's*
help and read bible daily.

3. Skilled

10   9   8   ⑦   6   5   4   3   2   1

I am completely competent
in all caregiving skills.

I have very few
caregiving skills at
this time.

One way I can grow in caregiving skills is: *attend supervision*
sessions — continuing ed.
review

4. Trustworthy

10   9   ⑧   7   6   5   4   3   2   1

I am 100% reliable, and
committed to serving
as a Stephen Minister.

I still have doubts
about whether I want
to make the necessary
commitment.

One way I can grow as a trustworthy caregiver is: *just do it — don't*
think so much.

5. Christ-centered

10   9   8   7   (6)   5   4   3   2   1

I keep Christ at the center of all I do as a Christian and a caregiver.

Christ is at the periphery of what I do as a Christian and a caregiver.

One way I can grow as a Christ-centered caregiver is: *remember & say out loud that Christ is caregiver. Pray before care giving sessions*

B. You Have Become Even More Compassionate

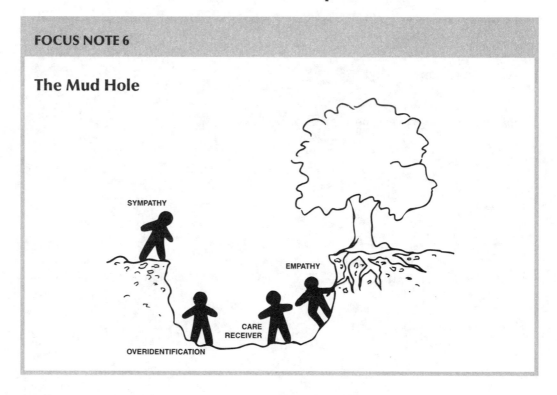

FOCUS NOTE 6

The Mud Hole

C. You Have Become Even More Faith-Full

D. You Have Become Even More Skilled as Caregivers

E. You Have Become Even Worthier of Trust

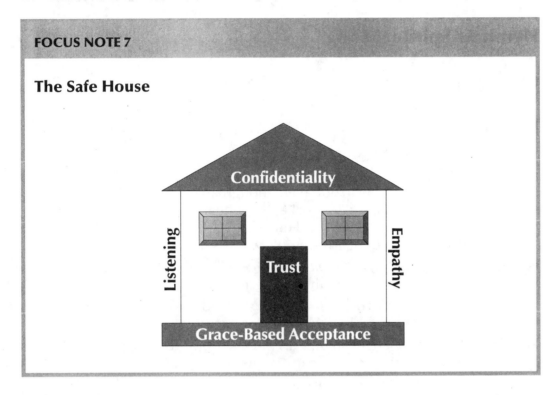

FOCUS NOTE 7

The Safe House

Confidentiality

Listening

Empathy

Trust

Grace-Based Acceptance

F. You Have Become Even More Christ-Centered

III. What Stephen Ministry Means to Me

IV. *Follow Me:* a Message from Dr. Kenneth Haugk

V. Nuts and Bolts

VI. Give Thanks to God

Service of Thanksgiving and Commitment

Hymn or Spiritual Song

The Psalm

Psalm 46 NRSV

Leader: God is our refuge and strength,
a very present help in trouble.

All: Therefore we will not fear, though the earth should change,
though the mountains shake in the heart of the sea;
though its waters roar and foam,
though the mountains tremble with its tumult. *Selah*

Women: There is a river whose streams make glad the city of God,
the holy habitation of the Most High.

Men: God is in the midst of the city; it shall not be moved;
God will help it when the morning dawns.

Leader: The nations are in an uproar, the kingdoms totter;
he utters his voice, the earth melts.

All: The LORD of hosts is with us;
the God of Jacob is our refuge. *Selah*

Women: Come, behold the works of the LORD;
see what desolations he has brought on the earth.

Men: He makes wars cease to the end of the earth;
he breaks the bow, and shatters the spear;
he burns the shields with fire.

Leader: "Be still, and know that I am God!
I am exalted among the nations,
I am exalted in the earth."

All: The LORD of hosts is with us;
the God of Jacob is our refuge. *Selah*

Scripture Readings

Colossians 1:3–6, 9–14 NRSV

In our prayers for you we always thank God, the Father of our Lord Jesus Christ, for we have heard of your faith in Christ Jesus and of the love that you have for all the saints, because of the hope laid up for you in heaven. You have heard of this hope before in the word of the truth, the gospel that has come to you. Just as it is bearing fruit and growing in the whole world, so it has been bearing fruit among yourselves from the day you heard it and truly comprehended the grace of God. . . .

For this reason, since the day we heard it, we have not ceased praying for you and asking that you may be filled with the knowledge of God's will in all spiritual wisdom and understanding, so that you may lead lives worthy of the Lord, fully pleasing to him, as you bear fruit in every good work and as you grow in the knowledge of God. May you be made strong with all the strength that comes from his glorious power, and may you be prepared to endure everything with patience, while joyfully giving thanks to the Father, who has enabled you to share in the inheritance of the saints in the light. He has rescued us from the power of darkness and transferred us into the kingdom of his beloved Son, in whom we have redemption, the forgiveness of sins.

Luke 4:14–21

Jesus returned to Galilee in the power of the Spirit, and news about him spread through the whole countryside. He taught in their synagogues, and everyone praised him.

He went to Nazareth, where he had been brought up, and on the Sabbath day he went into the synagogue, as was his custom. And he stood up to read. The scroll of the prophet Isaiah was handed to him. Unrolling it, he found the place where it is written:

"The Spirit of the Lord is on me,
   because he has anointed me
   to preach good news to the poor.
He has sent me to proclaim freedom for the prisoners
   and recovery of sight for the blind,
to release the oppressed,
   to proclaim the year of the Lord's favor."

Then he rolled up the scroll, gave it back to the attendant and sat down. The eyes of everyone in the synagogue were fastened on him, and he began by saying to them, "Today this scripture is fulfilled in your hearing."

Prayers

Leader: Heavenly Father, we give you thanks for loving us, for giving your Son to die and rise for us, and for calling and equipping us for this ministry. Bless us now at the end of our training and give us your Holy Spirit to guide and strengthen us for the ministry you have given us. Lord, in your mercy,

All: Hear our prayer.

Leader: We ask your blessings on our congregation and its leaders. Strengthen, encourage, and inspire our pastor(s). Give [him/her/them] your vision for this congregation's current and future ministry, and use [him/her/them] to lead us into the future that you have in store for us. Bless all the other staff and lay leaders here. Use them to provide the support and the leadership we need. Lord, in your mercy,

All: Hear our prayer.

Leader: Thank you for this class of Stephen Ministers, for their love, their commitment, and their compassion. You have gifted them in many different ways and now they offer their gifts back to you. Use them to carry your good news of healing, freedom, recovery, and release to a hurting world. Lord, in your mercy,

All: Hear our prayer.

Leader: We ask your blessings on our care receivers, whoever they may be. Strengthen and comfort them during their times of sadness and crisis. Use us to bring your love and hope to them. Lord, in your mercy,

All: Hear our prayer.

Leader: Thank you for our Stephen Leaders. You have given them gifts to teach and lead us, and you have blessed us greatly through them. Give our Stephen Leaders the satisfaction that comes from serving you and grant that they will hear you say, "Well done, good and faithful servant." Lord, in your mercy,

All: Hear our prayer.

Leader: Lord, we give you thanks for Stephen Ministries St. Louis. You have used that organization to equip us and give us the tools we need to do Stephen Ministry here. Continue to work in and through Stephen Ministries' staff to bring the blessings of equipping and care to more and more congregations. Lord, in your mercy,

All: Hear our prayer.

Leader: Holy God, you are the source of all mercy and giver of all good gifts. Thank you for all the gifts you have given us and for this opportunity to serve you. Receive our offering of ourselves as our loving response to your great mercies.

All: Amen.

Offering

Sign your Statements of Readiness, bring them forward, and place them on the altar.

Prayer

Leader: Heavenly Father, you have been with us, blessed us, and equipped us for ministry. As we begin this new path in our ministry journey, give us your Holy Spirit to guide us, empower us, and give us faith always to follow Jesus, in whose name we pray.

All: Amen

Hymn or Spiritual Song

Prayer Partner Requests and Thanksgivings

My prayer partner is _____

Prayer requests and thanksgivings to share with my prayer partner

_____

_____

Prayer requests and thanksgivings shared by my prayer partner

_____

_____

Ministry to the Dying and Their Family and Friends

Contents

▶ Mike's Story

When Mike found out he was going to die, he simply didn't believe it. He had made his reputation by solving problems, not by giving in to them. He told his wife Sylvie, "Don't you worry. I'm not going to let this lick me."

The next day Mike was in the library researching his disease. He leaped into researching alternative treatments. He knew he had a good doctor, but Dr. Kramer was pretty traditional and might not know about cutting-edge treatments.

Mike started taking an assortment of vitamins and pills to promote general good health. He knew he needed to be strong to fight the cancer.

When Mike asked Dr. Kramer to prescribe an experimental medicine he had read about, Dr. Kramer refused. He said, "It won't do any good, Mike. They just want your money." Mike traveled to Mexico to buy the drugs he wanted and determined his own daily dosage.

To save money, Sylvie wanted to cancel the vacation they had planned. She was scared that she wouldn't have enough when Mike was gone. Mike refused to cancel the vacation. "That would be giving in," he said.

Two weeks after his cancer was discovered, Mike had surgery for bowel obstruction. After the surgery Dr. Kramer told Mike, "We took out several feet of your intestines, but it's just a matter of time before the cancer spreads throughout your system."

At that point Mike became angry at everyone. He fought with his business partner, Peter, until Peter threatened to sell out and dissolve the partnership. Mike terrorized the hospital staff, developing a reputation as the meanest patient in the hospital. He even yelled at Sylvie for years of cooking all the wrong foods for him, which left her trembling and in tears.

A week later Mike was back in high spirits. He met with the hospital's director of development and promised that if they could cure him he would help raise a million dollars for their cancer treatment ward. "I know they won't be able to resist an offer like that," Mike told his Stephen Minister, Arthur Lee.

As Mike got sicker, his energy dwindled. He had always been abundantly energetic. Now he had tried to do too much, which made him sicker, and put him back in the hospital. When he tried to leave the hospital before he had regained his strength, he passed out, and his fall put a big gash in his head. At that point Mike became very depressed. He refused to get out of bed and he wouldn't talk to anyone except Sylvie, Dr. Kramer, and occasionally Arthur Lee. He lay in bed for days just staring at the ceiling. He lost a lot of weight and was rarely able to sleep more than an hour.

Mike moved home, and a nurse came for a couple of hours a day to help care for him. Finally, one day Mike gestured weakly to Sylvie to come close to hear him.

"I fought as hard as I could, but I lost. I don't like leaving, but there's nothing I can do about it. You'll have enough money; I've seen to that. Arthur Lee says I can look forward to being with Jesus, and the more I think about that, the better it sounds. I'm going to die tomorrow, so ask Arthur Lee to come by one more time, please, and see if Pastor Juvenus will come by. I love you."

By that time the next day Mike had died. Sylvie sat beside him and wept.

****

Do you think much about death? Many people don't. Maybe they will when they see a gruesome death on the evening news, or worse, when someone close to them is terminally ill or dies. For most people, most of the time, however, death is not something they usually think or talk about.

If it is true that you seldom think about death, this module will change your thought patterns, at least for a while. This Preclass Reading and the In-Class Session will give you a chance to think and learn about what it is like for people to die. As a result you will be able to care for people who are dying and those who love them. As an added benefit, you will have the chance to think about yourself as a person who will die someday and to consider how you want to live between now and then.

This module focuses on the specific needs you can meet as a Stephen Minister. First, this module focuses on the emotional reaction that people have to their own death and on how people react to the death of a loved one. Then it teaches you more about how to care emotionally and spiritually for people who are dying. Module 12, "Ministering to Those Experiencing Grief," provided a good foundation for ministry to the dying and their family and friends. Ministering to the dying and to their family and friends is caring for people who face a terrible loss. You'll find that the stages of coming to terms with death are similar to the stages of grief.

When you care for a dying person, you will be a member of a team of caregivers. The team might include the person's family, medical personnel, your pastor, the hospice staff, people who provide respite care for the family, an attorney, a hospital's financial counselor, and others. You will not have responsibility for all the care that a dying person requires, but your Stephen Min-

istry will meet specific and definite needs for him or her.

▶ Five Reactions to Dying

Just as there are stages in the grief journey, there are also reactions that people may go through when they realize they will soon die. In a book titled *On Death and Dying,*[1] Elisabeth Kübler-Ross identified five reactions that she learned through her research with hundreds of terminally ill people and family members. People close to a dying person may also have these reactions, which are in Reference Box A.

REFERENCE BOX A

The Five Reactions to Dying

1. Denial
2. Anger
3. Bargaining
4. Depression
5. Acceptance

How people experience these stages can vary greatly. Those possible differences are in Reference Box B.

REFERENCE BOX B

Differences in the Five Reactions to Dying

▶ People may or may not experience the reactions in order.

▶ People may repeat reactions. For example, they may experience denial,

---

1 Elisabeth Kübler-Ross, M.D., *On Death and Dying* (New York: Macmillan Publishing Company, Inc., 1969).

move to bargaining, and then return to denial again.

- ▶ People may experience more than one reaction at the same time.
- ▶ People may not experience all five of the reactions, and it is okay if they don't. For example, some people never experience acceptance.
- ▶ No one—not the dying person or anyone else—can control which reaction a dying person experiences or when he or she experiences it.
- ▶ Family and friends may experience these reactions, but they may not go through them in the same order or at the same time as the dying person or as other family or friends.

Reaction 1: Denial

When people encounter a painful truth, they often deny it. This is true with grief, it is also true with learning about one's imminent death.

Terminally ill persons may try to convince themselves and others that their condition is not really serious. Those who are dying may say, "This isn't happening to me," or, "My physician is wrong. I'll find another who will give an accurate diagnosis!" Family members and friends may support these kinds of statements.

Sometimes people admit the truth in one breath and revert to denial in the next. They may say something like, "There's nothing more the doctors can do for me; nobody can help me now." This sentence is immediately followed by, "I guess I'll just have to lie here and take it easy until I'm all better again." The person you care for may assure you that he or she is "better and better

every day," when it is obvious at a glance that the opposite is true.

Reaction 2: Anger

People feel angry when they believe they are treated unjustly. What could seem more unjust than learning that you will soon die? The anger of the dying person may also have another source. "This patient makes sure that he is not forgotten. He will raise his voice, he will make demands, he will complain and ask to be given attention, perhaps as the last loud cry, 'I am alive, don't forget that. You can hear my voice, I am not dead yet!'"[2]

Dying people may be short-tempered and inclined to find fault with everything and everybody. Enraged by their helplessness to change their situation, dying persons might express anger toward God, family, friends, medical personnel, or their Stephen Ministers.

Those who love the dying person may also feel angry. They may be angry at God for allowing this to happen, at the physician for not being able to do anything, or even at the dying person.

Those who receive this anger usually don't deserve it. Dying people and their family and friends can be so full of helpless anger that they spill it on anyone they meet.

Reaction 3: Bargaining

In bargaining, the care receiver begins to acknowledge that he or she is dying.

---

2 Kübler-Ross, *On Death and Dying*, p. 46.

Realizing that, it is natural to request an extension of time.

Some bargains involve practical matters. People may ask God to postpone death until they draw up a will, conclude an important business deal, or attend a child's graduation. Dying people sometimes keep generating just one more "last request" for God or someone else to grant. Other bargains involve promising to do something specific for God in exchange for extending one's life.

Often people try to bargain with God. Sometimes, however, they may try to bargain with medical personnel, you, or others. Kübler-Ross gives an example of a difficult patient who promised to cooperate with the medical staff if she was permitted to leave the hospital for a day to attend her favorite son's wedding. When she returned to the hospital she said, "Now don't forget I have another son!"[3]

Usually patients don't keep these promises, even if they do get well. What's important is that the person has begun to face the fact that his or her death is a real possibility. This is not true of the denial or anger reactions, in which the individual either completely refuses to acknowledge the likelihood of death or displaces rage about the situation onto others.

As people begin to understand that their bargaining is not going to work, they may become depressed.

Reaction 4: Depression

"When the terminally ill patient can no longer deny his illness, when he is forced to undergo more surgery or hospitalization, when he begins to have more symptoms or becomes weaker and thinner, he cannot smile it off anymore. His numbness or stoicism, his anger and rage will soon be replaced with a sense of great loss."[4]

Depression is one reaction to a crisis or loss, whether that loss has already happened or lies in the imagined future. (See module 13, "Dealing with Depression: The Stephen Minister's Role," for more information.) Any loss, no matter how large or small, can cause at least mild depression.

Dying people can experience deep depression because they face so many losses at once. In addition to losing their life, they are losing their family and friends. They have lost their hopes for the future. Dying people lose their image of themselves as healthy, whole, productive people. Physical losses, disfigurement, or significant weight loss attack the dying person's self-esteem and invite depression as well. As care receivers notice their lives trickling away, they may begin to feel very sad and low.

One way that dying people deal with their depression is gradually to detach themselves from the world. They may say good-bye to friends, to relatives, and finally to close family members. Near the end, they may want to be with one

---

3 Kübler-Ross, *On Death and Dying*, p. 73.

4 Kübler-Ross, *On Death and Dying*, p. 75.

or two people who do nothing more than stay quietly at their side.

Reaction 5: Acceptance

Some dying people reach a point where they accept that they are going to die. They no longer fight death, and they have grieved their own death to where the thought of dying no longer depresses them.

When dying people react with acceptance, they may speak frankly and unemotionally about their death. They may want to put affairs in order, talk to the pastor about funeral arrangements, or label possessions to be given to certain people. These may be signs that the person is letting go.

Acceptance may not be permanent. A dying person may react with acceptance one day, and with denial, anger, or bargaining the next. You may even find acceptance competing with denial in the same day, as a person seemingly accepts his or her death and at the same time talks about getting well and going home.

Eventually with some people, however, acceptance will come to stay. Usually this occurs when they are near death. Kübler-Ross writes, "Acceptance should not be mistaken for a happy stage. It is almost void of feelings. It is as if the pain had gone, the struggle is over, and there comes a time for 'the final rest before the long journey' as one patient phrased it. . . . While the dying patient has found some peace and acceptance, his circle of interest diminishes. He wishes to be left alone or at least not stirred up by news and problems of the outside world. Visitors are often not desired and if they come, the patient is no longer in a talkative mood."[5]

▶ Caring for Dying People

In many ways your care for dying people is similar to the care you give in any situation. One general guideline is not to try to move a person from one reaction to another. Accept the person in whatever stage he or she is, listen, and provide whatever other care he or she requests. Some people get stuck in a reaction and others move through all five. Neither course is better than the other.

Caring for Someone Reacting with Denial

A person in denial needs time to come to terms with the situation and will probably accept reality sooner or later. Think of denial statements as wishes rather than statements of fact. Reference Box C contains a couple examples of how you might do this.

REFERENCE BOX C

Responding to Statements of Denial

Care receiver: I know that someone got the test results mixed up. That's the only logical explanation for it.

Caregiver: It sure would be great if you found out that they've made a mistake.

[or]

Care receiver: This can't be happening to me. I'm only forty years old. I've got

---

5 Kübler-Ross, *On Death and Dying*, p. 100.

a lot more years left in me.

Caregiver: A person doesn't expect news like this when she's still in her prime.

In both examples, the caregiver did not contradict the care receiver nor lie to him or her. Instead, the caregiver reflected the dying person's own feelings and concerns. The examples illustrate that while it is not helpful to try forcing someone out of denial, it is equally unhelpful to agree with denial statements.

Caring for Someone Reacting with Anger

When caregivers realize where the anger comes from, they know not to take it personally. Instead they help the person recognize, accept, and express his or her angry feelings, discussing the sense of being helpless and out of control that can cause the anger. "A patient who is respected and understood, who is given attention and a little time, will soon lower his voice and reduce his angry demands. He will know that he is a valuable human being, cared for, allowed to function at the highest possible level as long as he can. He will be listened to without the need for a temper tantrum. . . ."[6]

Anger Directed at You

The sample dialogue in Reference Box D shows an inappropriate way and an appropriate way to respond to a care receiver's expressing anger at you.

---

6 Kübler-Ross, *On Death and Dying,* p. 46.

REFERENCE BOX D

Responding to an Expression of Anger

Care receiver: Why do you bother coming here every week? I don't need to see you. And I'm fed up with all these get-well cards and flowers you bring.

Don't say: I go to a lot of trouble to come here to see you. If you don't appreciate it, I'll just leave.

Do say: You're pretty angry and fed up with the situation you're in. It must be a very difficult time for you right now.

In the *Do say* response the caregiver reflected the care receiver's feeling of anger and understood that the anger was not really directed at him or her, but at the care receiver's situation. The *Don't say* response probably would have reinforced the care receiver's frustration and anger.

What if you feel angry with your care receiver? Your Small Group Peer Supervision session provides a chance to express and process your own anger. Your fellow Stephen Ministers will understand and care for you.

Anger Directed at God

Expect some dying people to express anger at God. Remember that you don't have to be insulted for God, nor do you have to defend him. God can take it; he has heard such expressions of anger many times. You don't have to go along with the anger, but don't argue with your care receiver. Reference Box E shows possible responses.

Both of these responses recognize the care receiver's pain and encourage him or her to say more about his or her feelings about God. Even though it may be difficult to hear those feelings, it is a gift to listen as care receivers express them. Your listening grants care receivers a chance to get their feelings in the open instead of holding them inside. That may be what the care receiver needs to move past his or her anger at God.

After listening and allowing your care receiver to share his or her feelings about God, you might witness to your care receiver about what you believe and offer hope. Reference Box F contains an example.

Be sure you listen to your care receiver and reflect his or her feelings before offering this kind of response. Don't use a witnessing response to cut off your care receiver's sharing.

Often people who react to dying with anger are also asking, "Why me, and why now?" Generally speaking, the best response—perhaps the only response is, "I don't know."

Let care receivers express their feelings of anger, resentment, and rage no matter how unpleasant these feelings are for you to hear. If you are accepting and supportive at this point, dying persons will have a much better chance of working through their feelings, perhaps even to reach a peace.

Caring for Someone Who Is Bargaining for Longer Life

Bargains are often aimed at God, and because you are a Christian caregiver, you may be one of the people who hears the bargain. This gives you yet another opportunity to care.

Since a bargain is a kind of denial, it does not help to debunk it. As with denial, it also doesn't help to condone the care receiver's bargain, as if you thought it would work. Instead, encourage your care receiver to talk about what is underneath his or her denial, as Reference Box G shows.

REFERENCE BOX G

Responding to a Bargain

Care receiver: I have been talking to God about my illness, and I told him that I need more time and that, if he will let me live until my children graduate from high school, I will go to church every week and read the Bible every day.

Don't say: That's five years from now. Don't you think that's a pretty unrealistic bargain with God?

Do say: It sounds as if you are concerned about your children making it through high school.

Another possible reason for bargaining is guilt. If you detect feelings of guilt, explore and minister with reflective listening and by using Christian caring resources. The dialogue in Reference Box H demonstrates one approach to ministering to guilt.

REFERENCE BOX H

Ministering to Guilt

Care receiver: I have been talking to God about my illness, and I told him that I need more time and that, if he will let me live until my children graduate from high school, I will go to church every week and read the Bible every day.

Caregiver: How are you feeling about God these days?

Care receiver: I don't think God is real happy with me. I haven't been a very religious person.

Caregiver: It sounds as if you're feeling guilty.

Care receiver: I suppose you could put it that way.

Caregiver: And you want to make up for your past by going to church regularly?

Care receiver: I'd better do something. I don't want to die with God mad at me.

Caregiver: May I share with you what I believe about that?

Care receiver: Sure.

Caregiver: I believe that God loves us and forgives us because of Jesus. The Bible says: "For God so loved the world that he gave his one and only Son, that whoever believes in him shall not perish but have eternal life. For God did not send his Son into the world to condemn the world, but to save the world through him. Whoever believes in him is not condemned."

Care receiver: Do you think God forgives me?

Caregiver: Do you want him to?

Care receiver: Yes, I do.

Caregiver: I believe God does forgive you.

Notice in this dialogue that the caregiver gave the care receiver several chances to talk about his or her guilt. (As a matter of fact, in real life the caregiver would allow many more opportunities for the care receiver to talk about his or her guilt feelings.) Then the caregiver witnessed about what he or she believed and shared a Bible passage in order to tell the care receiver about God's free gift of forgiveness.

By ministering to a bargaining person with the resources of Scripture and the Christian gospel, you help the person rely less on bargaining and more on God's mercy, no matter what course his or her illness eventually takes.

Caring for Someone Who Is Experiencing Depression

Since depression grows out of losses, encourage the care receiver to talk about his or her losses. This may be difficult, because talking about the losses can make the pain worse for a while. You may need to sit with your care receiver through long periods of silence or little conversation. Doing so shows your concern and lets your care receiver know that you will stick with him or her during the toughest times.

Pay special attention to the losses that haven't happened yet. A dying person may feel deep sadness over the loss of family, future, and hopes—over losing his or her life. Watch for opportunities to talk about such future losses, as Reference Box I illustrates.

REFERENCE BOX I

Talking about Future Losses

Care receiver (*slowly and sadly*): Frieda and I were going to join the Peace Corps when we retired. We knew some people who went to South America and said it was very rewarding.

Caregiver: But now that's not going to happen.

Care receiver: No, it won't. That's too bad. I wanted to give something back.

Caregiver: I imagine you had lots of plans.

Care receiver: I suppose everybody does.

Caregiver: How do you feel when you think about those plans?

Care receiver (*tears come to his eyes*): I just feel really sad and let down. I worked hard so we could have some fun when we retired, but now it's all gone.

Depressed care receivers may want to cry. Reassure them that crying is a natural way to express feelings. You as the caregiver may also cry.

Avoid the temptation to cheer up the depressed person. There are several reasons why cheering the person up is not a good idea.

▶ It is not likely to work for long.

▶ It may distract the person from dealing with deep and painful feelings.

▶ It may communicate that you are less willing to talk with him or her when he or she is depressed.

▶ It may, therefore, get in the way of your Stephen Ministry by discouraging the person from sharing his or her real fears, sadness, and frustrations.

A person can feel depressed because he or she feels caught between competing demands. For example, a young mother about to come to terms with her death may feel unable to do so because of her obligation to care for her children. She may not believe that her children will be well cared for after she dies. Her Stephen Minister might help her plan to share her concerns with her husband or others. When she feels confident that her children will be well cared for, she may be free to release them and accept her upcoming death.

Caring for Someone Who Is Accepting Death

When the care receiver reacts with acceptance, receive his or her reaction without trying to change it. The dialogue in Reference Box J shows one example of such acceptance.

REFERENCE BOX J

Responding to Acceptance

Caregiver: Hello, Mr. Jones. How are you today?

Care receiver: Oh, I'm okay. I had another one of those radiation treatments today. Did I tell you that they're moving me back home on Tuesday?

Caregiver: No, you didn't. Are they going to continue the treatments when you get home?

Care receiver: Oh, no. That wouldn't do any good. There's too much cancer in me. It's just a matter of time now. One thing that's been on my mind lately is that I need to find a nursing home for my wife. Her health has been bad for a long time. She can't look after herself anymore.

Caregiver: That sounds like a good idea. Do you have any particular place in mind?

Care receiver: I sure do. There's a good place where the waiting list isn't too long.

If a dying person asks you to help arrange his or her personal affairs, do what you can. The request itself may mean that the care receiver has reached a point of acceptance.

Kübler-Ross identified the two barriers that most often keep dying people from reaching acceptance. One is medical staff unnecessarily intervening to prolong a person's life when he or she is clearly going to die and is ready. The other, which is more frequent, is the dying person's family and friends hanging on and not letting go. It is difficult for a person to relax and accept the inevitable when a loved one continues to react with anger, anguish, and anxiety.

If such a barrier prevents your care receiver from resigning him- or herself to death, you might seek opportunities to talk about his or her reactions and how he or she feels about others' inability to accept his or her death.

As a person gets closer to death, he or she may react with more and more acceptance. As he or she becomes less and less talkative and turns increasingly inward, your way of caring may change also. You may just sit with the person, squeeze his or her hand now and then, and say very little. Your care receiver may communicate through very few words, or just through gesture or facial expressions. Even though nothing is said, your silent presence communicates volumes—that you still care, that you will stick with the person until the end, that he or she will not be abandoned now that he or she is resigned to death.

▶ Caring for Family Members and Friends

Stephen Ministers may find many opportunities to care for family or friends of dying persons.

Formal and Informal Care

You may provide formal or informal care for a family member or a friend of a dying person. A family member or friend may be assigned to you as your formal care receiver. In fact, one family could have three or more Stephen Ministers assigned, one to the dying person and others to family members.

When your formal care receiver is a dying person, you will probably have opportunities to care informally for one or more of your care receiver's family members or friends. For example, you may step out of the hospital room so the medical staff can work and listen to or pray with a family member or friend who is also visiting. Such informal, ad hoc care is an important and appropriate part of your Stephen Ministry. If you find, however, that you are regularly caring for someone other than your official care receiver, perhaps that person needs his or her own Stephen Minister. Check with your Stephen Leader and suggest that the other person also have a Stephen Minister.

Similar to Grief Care

Before the terminally ill person dies, friends and family begin grieving. Some family and friends may do quite a bit of their grief work before the loved one actually dies. They may come to terms with the reality that their loved one will soon be gone and go a long way toward learning to live without him or her. By the time the loved one dies, they may almost be ready for the rebuilding stage of the grief journey. No matter how much grieving people have already done, however, a fresh sense of loss and pain will probably surge over them when the loved one dies.

Specific Care for Family and Friends in the Five Reactions

There are specific needs families and friends have as they experience each of the five reactions and specific ways to care for them in each.

Caring for Family and Friends during the Denial Stage

Family and friends may long deny that their loved one is going to die. They may deny much longer than the dying person does because they don't have a dying body convincing them that the news is true.

Denial can take many forms. Family and friends may try to convince the medical personnel, the dying person, and other family and friends that the situation isn't that bad. They may hustle the dying person from physician to physician hoping to hear a diagnosis and prognosis they can accept. They may research the dying person's disease and recommend new treatments they believe will surely cure the disease. They may enlist faith healers to pray for their loved one and then insist that the person will get better if everyone will only believe that he or she has already been healed.

A family member's or friend's denial can become painful for the dying person and for other family and friends, especially if it lasts long after others have moved beyond denial. At times one individual's denial can hinder the dying person from working through his or her own feelings.

Family and friends can also worry about a dying person's denial that continues after others have moved past that reaction. They may worry if a dying person postpones or refuses care that could prolong his or her life.

Don't try to stop a care receiver's denying. Care for him or her in the state he or she is in.

If your care receiver's denial causes problems for others, talk about how the others have reacted to your care receiver's actions. You might also ask your care receiver how he or she believes his or her actions are affecting others. This provides an opportunity for your care receiver to talk about the pain and fear he or she feels, which may be what is prolonging his or her denial.

If your care receiver is concerned or hurt by the dying person's denial, give him or her the chance to talk about such feelings and concerns. You might also help your care receiver understand that it is natural for people to deny when they learn of a major loss.

Caring for Family and Friends during the Anger Stage

Sometimes a dying person lashes out in anger at family or friends. If this hap-

pens to your care receiver, listen as he or she tells about the incident and how it made him or her feel. You might explain that such anger is a natural part of dying. Even though the anger was expressed at them, it is not necessarily anger with them.

Your care receiver may also become angry for the same reasons that the dying person does: There's no good reason why the loved one has to die, and your care receiver is powerless to stop it. Family and friends may lash out at others, including the dying person, God, and you. As when caring for a dying person who is angry, allow your care receiver to express feelings and get them off his or her chest. Understand that the anger is normal and remember where it comes from.

Caring for Bargaining Family and Friends

Family and friends may try to bargain for the dying person's life. They may make a vow, promising God they will keep it if the dying person survives. As with caring for dying persons, accept the bargain instead of trying to debunk it. Don't think you have to agree with the bargain or that it will work. Look for signs of guilt associated with the bargain and minister to that guilt with your caring skills and using God's word of forgiveness.

Caring for Depressed Family and Friends

Deep sadness and depression are a normal part of the grief journey, one of the ways people learn to live without the loved one they have lost. When that loved one is not yet dead, it can be very difficult to detach from him or her, and the family member or friend may feel guilty about already loosening the bonds of their relationship.

Your typical Stephen Ministry practices of listening and caring are the best you can give a depressed care receiver. You might also help him or her work through his or her guilt, separating real from undeserved guilt and offering God's word of forgiveness.

Caring for Family and Friends through the Acceptance Stage

The dying person's acceptance of death may feel like rejection to family and friends, and in a way it is. The dying person's upcoming death is so compelling that it may take his or her attention away from all other people he or she values. It isn't that the dying person doesn't love family and friends anymore, it's just that the person must move on and there's nothing he or she can do about it.

When a dying person is in the acceptance stage, his or her family and friends may actually need more care than does the dying person. Friends and family members may not have reached the acceptance stage. They may be frustrated with the dying person for giving up, for not paying attention to them, and for no longer meeting their needs.

If your care receiver is angry or depressed because the dying person has accepted his or her death and withdrawn, empathize with his or her feelings. It is very painful to face. A time may also come when it is helpful to talk with your care receiver about why the dying person has given up and become so inwardly focused.

When family and friends come to the point where they accept the loved one's death, it may mean they have already progressed quite a ways along their grief journey. They may feel guilty that they have already loosened their bonds of attachment with their loved one before he or she is even dead. They may feel especially guilty if they have come to accept the death, but the dying person has not. Listen a lot and offer forgiveness at the right time—when the care receiver has had a full opportunity to tell about his or her guilt feelings.

▶ Getting Ready for the In-Class Sessions

In preparation for the In-Class Sessions, you might review your thoughts and notes about using distinctively Christian caring resources or reread the chapters in *Christian Caregiving—a Way of Life* on using the Bible, prayer, forgiveness, and a "cup of cold water."

For Further Reading . . .

Yes, Lord
by Dona Hoffman

Yes, Lord charts the journey of Dona Hoffman, poet, wife, and mother, through the struggles that follow her diagnosis of terminal cancer. Through her poems, journal entries, and letters, Dona's faithful "Yes, Lord" takes shape as a cry wrung from the heart as she balances between hope for healing and hope for death, daily trying to entrust herself to God's hands in the midst of her agony, despair, and longing. No plaster saint but a real woman, Dona's courage, love, faith, and humor will charm and encourage both those who suffer and those who care for others.

To learn more or to order a copy, log on to www.stephenministries.org or call Stephen Ministries at (314) 428-2600.

Ministry to the Dying and Their Family and Friends

Outline and Focus Notes

For since death came through a human being, the resurrection of the dead has also come through a human being; for as all die in Adam, so all will be made alive in Christ.

1 Corinthians 15:21–22 NRSV

I. Bad News, Good News

II. LIFE: Thoughts and Feelings about Death

III. What It Is Like to Be Dying

A. Living with a Death Sentence

B. Isolation

1. Social Isolation

2. Physical Isolation

3. *Emotional Isolation*

4. *Spiritual Isolation*

C. The Approach of Death

1. *Symptoms in the Months and Weeks before Death*

a. Pain

b. Changes in Eating and Digestion

c. Fragility

d. Agitation

e. Confusion

f. The Nature of the Decline

2. *When Death Is Close*
a. Difficulty Swallowing

b. Changes in Breathing

c. Changes in Body Temperature

d. Fading Attention to Surroundings

e. Final Moments

IV. Looking Ahead

V. Opening

VI. Caring for People As They Die

A. Caring in Response to Isolation

FOCUS NOTE 1

Reflecting Nonverbal Expressions of Feelings

Caregiver: You just sighed deeply a couple of times, and I see a slight smile on your face. Are you finding some peace in the midst of all this?

[or]

Caregiver: You have been crying for a few minutes. Not everything's settled yet, is it?

[or]

Caregiver: You look very uncomfortable. Are you feeling physical or emotional pain?

B. Helping People Understand the Dying Process

C. Caring during the Last Days and Weeks

D. Caring for Family and Friends

E. Participating in the Funeral

VII. Using Distinctively Christian Caring Resources

FOCUS NOTE 2

Guidelines for Using Distinctively Christian Resources

1. Always listen before you use the resource.

2. Make sure that your reason for using the distinctively Christian resource is to meet your care receiver's need and not your own.

3. Tailor the resource to meet your care receiver's needs.

4. After you use the resource, listen again to find out what your care receiver's reaction is.

FOCUS NOTE 3

Instructions for Distinctively Christian Resources Exercise

1. Choose a convener to lead your group's work and a recorder to write your ideas down and report to the rest of the class.

2. Think of a situation in which it would be appropriate to use your distinctively Christian caring resource with a dying person or a family member or friend. Include what the care receiver's specific need for this caring resource is.

3. Prepare to describe or demonstrate how you would use your resource in your situation. You may perform a brief skit or role play or just tell what you would do.

4. You will have three minutes to share, so keep it simple.

VIII. Looking Ahead

IX. Skill Practice in Caring for the Dying and Their Family and Friends

---

FOCUS NOTE 4

Stephen Minister's Situation Description for Skill Practice 1

You were recently assigned to a care receiver who has been feeling ill. After several weeks of tests, he or she had exploratory surgery. You were visiting your care receiver in the hospital when the physician came to report the results of the surgery. She told your care receiver that they found so much cancer that they could not remove it all. Your care receiver now realizes that he or she will probably die very soon.

The care receiver will begin the skill practice.

FOCUS NOTE 5

Care Receiver's Situation Description for Skill Practice 1

You have been ill for a couple of months. After many tests, you underwent exploratory surgery. Your physician has just told you that many of your organs have been affected by cancer and that there is nothing further medicine can do. You asked if this meant you were going to die. The doctor hung her head and said, "I'm so sorry."

You react with anger at God. You have been praying that you would not become too ill or that God would heal you if you were seriously sick, but now it seems as if God has not heard your prayer. You have three children living at home, and you are angry that you will not be there to help care for them. You wonder why someone much older than you couldn't die instead—someone who has already fulfilled his or her responsibilities for raising children.

Begin the skill practice by saying, "I can't believe God would do this to me." Then for the duration of the skill practice find various ways to express your anger at God.

Discussion Questions for the Skill Practice

1. How did the Stephen Minister feel about caring in this situation?

2. How did the care receiver feel about the care the Stephen Minister provided?

3. What did the Stephen Minister do well in this situation?

4. If you had this to do over again, how might you care differently?

Stephen Minister's Situation Description for Skill Practice 2

Your care receiver's mother is terminally ill. Your care receiver has been caring for her daily, using all his or her free time to do so. Yesterday your care receiver's mother told your care receiver that she really didn't want to fight anymore and that she was ready to die. Furthermore, she felt at peace about her decision.

Your care receiver will begin the skill practice.

Care Receiver's Situation Description for Skill Practice 2

You have been caring for your dying mother for several months. It has been extremely difficult for you to work, tend to your own family, and also care for your mother, but you've made the necessary sacrifices.

Yesterday your mother told you that she didn't want to fight anymore, that she was ready to die, and that she felt happier and more at peace than she had in a long time. Your mother's announcement has made you very angry. You don't want your mother to die, and you believe she could stay alive for many more months or years if she made the effort. You have been working so hard on her behalf that you don't believe she has a right to give up. You want your Stephen Minister to help you figure out how to get your mother to keep fighting.

Begin the skill practice by telling your Stephen Minister what your mother said and how you feel about it. Share your feelings and your reasons. Then ask your Stephen Minister to help you convince your mother to fight for more life.

Stephen Minister's Situation Description for Skill Practice 3

Your care receiver has known for several months that he or she is dying. He or she has been very angry most of that time. At this caring visit, however, he or she is upbeat, excited, and almost happy.

Your care receiver will begin the skill practice.

Care Receiver's Situation Description for Skill Practice 3

When you found out you were going to die, you became very angry. You are too young to die, and you have worked for years to become successful. Now that you are beginning to enjoy the fruit of your success, you find out that you will die.

You have been thinking about your life and feeling bad that you worked so much that you didn't take time for family or for God. Then a plan struck you: You decided that if God would give you ten more years, you would spend them working for the church. You see some real hope in this plan. It would give you a chance to make up for your previous life, and you think it is a good deal for God too. You believe God will take you up on this deal.

Since your Stephen Minister is much better at praying than you are, you want your Stephen Minister to pray for you and propose your plan to God.

Begin the skill practice by telling your Stephen Minister about your plan and then ask him or her to pray for you and propose your bargain to God.

X. Caregiver's Compass Review

_____

_____

_____

_____

_____

_____

_____

_____

_____

_____

_____

_____

XI. Looking Ahead

Prayer Partner Requests and Thanksgivings

My prayer partner is _____

Prayer requests and thanksgivings to share with my prayer partner

_____

_____

Prayer requests and thanksgivings shared by my prayer partner

_____

_____

Caring for People before, during, and after Hospitalization

Contents

► Crises before, during, and after Hospitalization

Given the nature of hospitalization nowadays—when cost-cutting and advanced medical procedures shorten stays more and more—many times a parishioner will enter the hospital and be discharged before a Stephen Minister is ever assigned. Still, you need to know about the hospitalization process to be the best caregiver you can be. You will then be prepared if a person who is already your care receiver has to be involved with a hospital, whether in an emergency, for outpatient treatment, or by being admitted.

The five stories that follow are not exactly typical of hospitalization. They represent worst-case scenarios, but they express the feelings real people have. Your care receivers will not always endure the pain and difficulties mentioned here, but they may. By dealing with these more extreme cases, you will be adequately prepared to minister to your care receiver in a hospital setting.

Rosalie Vendetti

Rosalie Vendetti, 37, looked out the window, watching the children play in the schoolyard across from her home and waited for her husband, Tony, to drive her to the hospital. She was already exhausted. She had hardly slept the night before.

Rosalie sighed. The worst part was not knowing what would happen. The doctor would only discover during surgery how much of her intestine he should remove. She could end up with a colostomy bag. The physicians made it sound so clinical and distant, but it was her body they would change forever, and who knew how much?

She felt jittery about many things: the anesthetic that would put her totally out of control, the uncertainty about the extent of the surgery. She felt so vulnerable. What if she died? How would Tony and the children manage?

Rosalie also felt nervous about coming home after the surgery. How would she feel? What kind of help would she need? Who would take care of the house and family if she couldn't? She would stay in the hospital to recuperate for a couple of days, but it certainly wouldn't be long enough for her to recover fully. With the health insurance company questioning every expense, she imagined she'd be booted out of the hospital before she was ready.

She whispered a short prayer. She didn't know how they would afford their share of the hospitalization expenses. Tony ran their small business, and she had always been his assistant and bookkeeper. They carried a basic major medical plan that covered catastrophic illness or accident, but it would leave them with large debts. The doctor was fairly reassuring about cost containment, but she knew that the past three months was Tony's usual slow time, so their savings were already depleted. How would they make it?

She heard Tony coming down the stairs and her stomach knotted. The drive to the hospital was quiet and tense. Rosalie felt a mounting panic as they drove into the hospital parking lot.

Donald Sarkis

Donald Sarkis, 24, sat nervously in the emergency room waiting area, watching the other patients and wondering what was wrong with them. Watching the long line at the desk as the stony-faced receptionist dealt with every variety of unhappy person. Anything to keep his mind off the accident. No question—it was his fault. He'd been in a hurry to get home to take Kristen out to dinner and a movie. But that was no excuse for running the stop sign. The driver of the white sedan that broadsided him had no reason to expect him not to stop. The driver was really nice, though; he had called the ambulance on his car phone, assured Donald that he himself wasn't hurt, and helped with the police report and the insurance companies. He'd been so nice, which made Donald feel even worse about causing the accident.

Donald's arm throbbed with ferocious pain. The emergency medical technician had told him it was broken, but Donald worried that the doctors would find more wrong—if they got around to treating him. He wondered whether his car could be fixed. Would his insurance company raise his rates? He felt so guilty. If only he had been more careful.

As he watched the others in the waiting room, Donald felt alone and insignificant. If only he had someone to talk to. His mind swirled with painful thoughts. Donald saw that there was not a line at the emergency room desk for the first time in more than an hour. He strode over. "I've been waiting for more than an hour and no one has seen me yet," he said to the receptionist. "My arm hurts. Any idea when I'll be seen?"

The receptionist's gaze froze him. "Please sit down, sir. All the staff members are involved in critical emergencies at the moment. Someone will call you when a staff member becomes available. Thank you."

Donald sat back down, his face flaming. Didn't anyone care that he was in pain? How long would he sit here waiting for treatment? He wouldn't be so annoyed if he knew what was going on and how long it would take. What really bothered him was not knowing anything. Did they even know he was here?

Frederick Ebert

Frederick Ebert, 55, lay on the bed in the emergency room, breathing as deeply as the pain allowed. And the pain was excruciating. Even though the medication was beginning to lessen his physical suffering and dull his thinking, still the pain seemed to crush his chest as it spread into his shoulders, arms, and back. It was so difficult to breathe! He had never experienced such pain. If only they could halt it soon.

Frederick squeezed the nurse's hand. He clenched hard against the pain—and the panic. His father had died of a heart attack, and he hadn't been that much older than Frederick. What was going to happen? The tests and scheduled procedures sounded painful, some downright dangerous. What if the treatments didn't work? What if he died?

He'd always been too busy to worry about what happened after death. Now it seemed uncomfortably relevant. But if God was good, as he'd been taught, how could he have let this happen? Frederick was sure he was too young to die.

He opened his eyes, unwilling to dwell on his thoughts. The nurse said, "Try to be calm, Mr. Ebert, you'll be all right." She was kind. He knew she must have had other tasks to do, but she stayed with him. She was his one comfort.

His thinking was beginning to get fuzzy. He felt alone and wished he could talk to someone he knew, someone who knew him and cared about him as a person, not just as a patient. What if he died without getting to say good-bye to his family?

Juanita Beck

Juanita Beck, 37, gazed wearily through the window. The IV dripped slowly but inexorably. She didn't feel too bad—yet. But it was only the first day for her week of chemotherapy. Tomorrow it would be another story, and she never remembered much of the later part of the week. Probably just as well.

One week on, three weeks off: That had been the schedule for her second round of chemotherapy, after the doctor told her that the first round had not eliminated the cancer. In fact, the cancer had spread. She'd been through two of the four-week cycles already, and she knew what to expect now.

She never felt good anymore. By the time her body had almost stabilized after the chemotherapy—and it took two weeks at least—she had only a few days to feel somewhat better before it started again. Cooking a meal or just setting the table wore her out. She seemed to drag herself around, every step an act of

the will and a horrendous effort. Other people must have felt such fatigue, and she must have known some of them and maybe even spoken with them. How did they endure? Her fatigue followed her like a shadow. She felt as though she could never quite recover from the flu.

She tried not to look in the mirror. Doctor Elias had told her, "Your hair probably will not fall out. That seldom happens anymore." He was right, but so what? She had no strength to fix it, and her face was so gaunt that it was almost cadaverous.

Her children, Emma and Steve, were very supportive. Her mother had stayed with them so they wouldn't be alone. They were all due to visit in about half an hour to sit with her. It helped—she didn't feel quite so desperate then. But it wasn't enough; she knew they couldn't follow where she had to go.

She sighed. What was the point? Here she was, a burden on her family and friends, suffering slow, little tortures beyond her ability to express and for what? A chance she might survive? Who knew how strong a chance? But she was a single parent and her children's only provider. She had to keep fighting the battle, although right now she did not have the slightest idea how.

Henry Vaughn

Henry Vaughn, 60, flipped irritably through the television channels. Wasn't there anything worth watching during the day? Hour after hour of vapid talk shows and soap operas—it was almost enough to make him wish he were back in the hospital! Not that there was much to do there either, but at least people were around. It was too quiet here.

His leg still hurt badly from his extensive surgery. He hated having to stay off it and keep it elevated. He couldn't do a thing for himself. Why send him home if he couldn't even take a shower? And he didn't trust the pain pills they sent with him; they sure didn't work as quickly as the shots in the hospital.

Sending him home this early might have been a good financial decision, but he didn't feel comfortable with it. It put a lot of extra work on his wife, Jane. Every time he wanted or needed anything, he had to call her to get it. She came with the glass of water or sweater—whatever he needed. She brought his meals and sat in the bedroom to eat with him. He knew what an imposition it was and he wondered if she resented it. It disrupted her routine and kept her from getting much done.

The visiting nurse arrived every morning to check on him and give him his bath. When she left, he was nervous, knowing that she wouldn't be back until the next day. What if something happened before then? What if he reacted to the new pain medication? Anything could happen, and in a matter of minutes! If he were in the hospital, he'd have a fighting chance in an emergency. Here, he could die and no one might notice for hours.

Where was Jane? Fixing dinner? Talking on the phone with a friend? Why didn't she spend more time with him? Didn't she care that he was worried and lonely here by himself? People came to visit him in the hospital, but now that he was home, they'd forgotten him. It would be weeks before he could go back to work. Why had they sent him home so early?

▶ The Many Faces of Hospitalization

These stories illustrate several different hospitalization scenarios. In these cost-cutting, profit-driven, less-staff-and-more-productivity times, hospitalization has many different faces, from a long stay for a life-threatening illness, to surgery and recovery, to outpatient surgery and same-day release and then fending for oneself while recovering at home.

Regardless of the face a hospitalization experience presents, concerns and challenges confront care receivers. This Preclass Reading describes those challenges and suggests how Stephen Ministers might care for people experiencing the challenges.

▶ Caring during the Challenges That Surround Hospitalization

Hospitalization almost always involves danger. The danger may be to one's life, health, job, financial well-being, or relationships. A natural human reaction to danger is to feel fear, and sometimes the anxiety, frustration, sadness, and despair that can accompany fear. These feelings may occur before, during, and after hospitalization.

Here are descriptions of the main fears and concerns people may have about hospitalization and ways you can care for those concerns.

The Fear of Death

Not every patient admitted to a hospital will face an immediate threat of death, as do Frederick Ebert, Rosalie Vendetti, and Juanita Beck. Even if death is not imminent, however, any injury or illness requiring hospitalization makes death more of a concern than when life goes on as usual. While Christians believe that God has given them eternal life, they are likely still to fear death. No one knows what exactly to expect after death; it can seem like stepping off a cliff into the unknown. For many Christians facing death, trust mingles with fear.

Providing Care for Care Receivers Who Are Facing Death

Module 19, on ministry to the dying, explains that dying people typically experience five reactions to the process of dying. These reactions are listed in Reference Box A.

REFERENCE BOX A

The Five Reactions to Dying

1. Denial
2. Anger
3. Bargaining
4. Depression
5. Acceptance

Denial

It may be difficult to maintain denial for long if a person is in the hospital surrounded by reminders of his or her con-

dition, but some people steadfastly maintain their disbelief in spite of all evidence to the contrary.

Anger

There can be a lot to be angry about in the hospital: lack of information, lots of time waiting and doing nothing, not being allowed to eat or drink what one wants, being awakened in order to take a sleeping pill, invasion of privacy; the list could go on. A care receiver who is dying may latch on to any of these reasons and rage about them. It may be, however, that he or she is mostly angry about the possibility of dying.

Bargaining

A care receiver may have agreed to enter the hospital as part of his or her bargaining with God, medical personnel, or family. He or she may believe that, because of the bargain, the hospital staff has the ability to cure him or her. This can be another way of denying the terrible truth of impending death.

Depression

Illness and hospitalization can be depressing. Depression usually stems from loss, and people often face many losses in the hospital and after returning home. Care receivers during and after hospitalization may spend many hours alone. They may have abundant time to stew about their troubles and few opportunities to talk about them. When a person fears that he or she will die soon, the depression can became worse.

Acceptance

By the time dying people reach the point of accepting their approaching death, they will often be in the hospital. Some care receivers may want to die at home and thus they will be sad if they have to stay in the hospital.

Any of the five reactions are possible, singly or in combination, with a hospitalized care receiver dealing with the fact that he or she may die soon. You have learned about how to care in all these reactions, and you will apply what you have learned to a care receiver who is or has recently been hospitalized.

Loss of Body Image or Function

Some patients who enter the hospital anticipate changes to their bodies— some drastic, others less severe. Some people, like Rosalie Vendetti, face surgery to remove parts of their body because of cancer or diabetes, or because an organ has failed to function. Some will have scars that mar their appearance; others will lose their hair or endure other changes to their bodies due to the side effects of drugs that they need to stay alive.

Some patients expect a series of losses. Juanita Beck had already been through a painful course of chemotherapy, which subjected her to fatigue and indignities and brought her life to a standstill. Then she had to face those same losses in a second course of chemotherapy. Other examples include diabetics who have a number of amputations, and people with chronic diseases who see their capabilities slip away as their disease progresses.

Providing Care

Such care receivers need reassurance that, although their body image or function may change because of injury or illness, they will still be accepted for the people that they are.

The Ministry of Touch

One of the best ways a caregiver can communicate acceptance is through the ministry of touch. Sometimes people fear that they will become repulsive or untouchable. A gentle touch on the hand or shoulder can give an amazing reassurance, particularly when changes cut deeply into that person's self-image.

Nonjudgmental Listening

It also helps gently to encourage care receivers to talk about their concerns regarding their bodies and to listen nonjudgmentally as they do. Be sensitive to your reactions as you relate to your care receivers' appearance or words. They may look to you for acceptance and encouragement, and if they see that you are shocked or repulsed, they may be deeply hurt.

Pain

Pain is a very realistic fear for most hospitalized care receivers. Often a person's first indication that something is wrong, whether illness or injury, is pain of some sort. Although modern pain control medications have greatly improved, medical treatment itself can still result in pain.

Providing Care

Helping the care receiver put the fear of pain into perspective can give him or her a measure of control over it. Encourage your care receiver to talk about his or her pain. Some care receivers may believe they should suffer in silence. In many cases, however, talking about their pain can help care receivers to bear it. At least they know they are not alone in their suffering.

Changes in Relationships

Hospitalization often signals changes in a person's lifestyle. A person used to providing for his or her family may face a crisis of identity when he or she is suddenly plunged into depending on others for everything, including life itself. A person who sees him- or herself as strong and self-reliant may have difficulty accepting his or her dependency and thus hate being a burden.

Juanita Beck feared that her long-term chemotherapy treatments would ultimately prove too much of a burden for her family and friends. She wondered whether preserving her life was worth the time and expense.

Opportunities for Growth

The crisis of hospitalization may offer opportunities for growth in relationships, however. The care receiver's needs can open the door to deeper closeness among family members, as they recognize how much they value the care receiver and one another. The care receiver may recognize in his or her vulnerability the humbling fact that, no matter how strong people are, they still must depend on the strength of others and upon God. Through the perception of weakness, a care receiver may grow closer to God and to those around him or her.

Changes in the Relationship with the Stephen Minister

If you've been working for months or years with a care receiver who then is hospitalized, your relationship with him or her may change. The care receiver may become more dependent on you than before and may appreciate your care more fully. Or your care receiver may withdraw from you while trying to come to terms with new difficulties.

Providing Care

The crises of changing relationships bring the possibility for danger or opportunity. Try gently to nudge the care receiver toward greater growth and wholeness. You can facilitate this by being trustworthy even when changes strain your relationship with your care receiver. You might also help your care receiver recognize and remember that family members and friends love him or her and will be there for him or her no matter what.

Career Changes

An illness or injury may signal far-reaching changes on the part of the patient. An injury may prevent the patient from doing the work he or she has done for years. A severe back injury, for example, may prevent a mover from continuing to load trucks. A heart attack, as in the case of Frederick Ebert, may demand that the person let go of some of the stresses and responsibilities that have led to the problem.

Providing Care

For many people career changes bring a deep sense of loss and sadness. Care receivers may grieve their former jobs and their old lives. Be aware that you may need to do grief ministry with your care receiver during or after hospitalization as your care receiver comes to terms with a series of losses.

Never try to minimize the losses that people feel. Enter their hurt and reflect their pain. But you are also a representative of Christian hope. As you do not deny their pain, also be sensitive to God's grace that meets them in their new life tasks. Losing the ability to perform certain tasks may even force the care receiver to find a new sense of worth in a new occupation. As the care receiver works through his or her grief and builds a new life, he or she may be surprised to find that, while a change in career direction was wrenching, it was positive too. Your role is not to preach, but to point out how the center of Christ's life—his cross and resurrection—repeats itself in the Christian life. Although the care receiver may earn less, he or she may find greater peace, happiness, security and closeness with family members. Greater physical well-being may result from the shift to less stressful responsibilities at work. It may not be easy, but the career changes that result from hospitalization may grant the care receiver the chance to grow in trust and find new and vital values to replace old ones.

Loss of Economic Stability

For many people hospitalization presents some degree of financial crisis, as it did for Rosalie Vendetti. For some, meeting deductibles and paying the percentage owed by the patient poses a problem. Determining whether an insurance company will cover a given procedure or treatment may cause anxiety. Wrestling with insurance companies over claims that they first refuse and finally pay after the care receiver spends hours waiting on the telephone

to talk to a representative can be maddening and exhausting. Some people have no insurance coverage and must depend on government programs or agencies to provide for their care and treatment.

Many hospitalized patients lose income due to time spent in the hospital. Although some workers accrue sick leave to protect their income when they are ill or injured, many workers do part-time and freelance labor and have no benefits beyond their wages. They face substantial loss of income in addition to the costs of hospitalization.

Providing Care

The care receiver will have many feelings of loss and anger to deal with. Besides your ministry of listening and emotional and spiritual support, you can help put your care receiver in touch with community resources. Most hospitals have a social worker on staff to counsel patients and their families. Such hospital staff can present options for handling hospitalization costs. Your church staff may know of programs through your congregation or denomination that offer short- or long-term assistance. The patient may also seek help from family members. If you research places where your care receiver might go for help, be sure to fill out a "Community Resource Assessment Questionnaire" (get this form from a Stephen Leader) and put it in your congregation's *Community Resources Handbook*.

Being Sent Home Too Early

In this era of managed care, cost containment, and improved surgical techniques, patients are more frequently discharged from the hospital before they feel comfortable going home. Surgeries that once required spending several days or weeks in the hospital are now performed on an outpatient basis. Patients check in early in the morning and are released before the end of the day. People must recuperate at home, even when they don't feel ready or comfortable doing so, as in the stories of Rosalie Vendetti and Henry Vaughn.

Hospital staff work with patients on discharge planning and help them find needed resources. Still, this trend toward convalescence at home rather than in the hospital is alarming for patients who do not have a good support system at home. The possibility of physical complications, the lack of trained nursing care, and the reliance on already overburdened family to care for the patient can make the return home a stressful experience for any patient as well as for his or her family.

Providing Care

While the concerns the care receiver feels are valid, some of the problems can be resolved. Convalescent homes, visiting nurse programs, and similar community resources offer back-up care to recently discharged patients who do not technically need to be in a hospital but who need more professional care than families can provide. You may be able to refer your care receiver to community resources and help him or her think through the many choices.

You can allow your care receiver to express and acknowledge his or her feelings of distress, fear, loneliness, and disorientation. Visiting more frequently than usual after the care receiver has been released from the hospital is important, because often friends stop visiting when the patient has gone home. Until the care receiver is able to return to his or her normal routine or to establish a new one, he or she is likely to feel out of sync with the home environment. Listening to your care receiver talk about his or her new limitations and the feelings that go along with them may help the person accept limitations, temporary or permanent, and make adjustments.

Lack of Information

Hospital patients may need to make decisions, sign forms, or give information without fully understanding the implications. Sometimes a patient doesn't understand information about his or her condition, and the implications of that information, because he or she lacks medical knowledge. Some patients wonder if the hospital staff fails to share adequate information for legal reasons. Some even believe that the staff is more concerned with legal liability than with their rights and needs.

Making decisions without adequate information can be disastrous. A patient may refuse surgery to bypass clogged arteries only to suffer a stroke the following week as a result. A patient who doesn't understand a hospital's requirement to resuscitate—and his or her right to waive that requirement— could end up on expensive life support without hope for recovery. A patient who hasn't been told the pros and cons of a treatment may opt for expensive and invasive therapy that will improve his or her quality of life only marginally. Patients need to know the hows and the whys and all their options in order to make decisions consistent with their best possibility for recovery.

Leaving the patient confused or uncertain is rarely intentional. While most hospital staff are caregivers by nature and profession, nurses and doctors are human. They may be preoccupied with a difficult situation involving another patient. They may be rushed and understaffed, and not realize that the patient needs more information. Doctors or nurses may use medical jargon, not realizing that the patient doesn't understand the information or its implications.

Whatever the reasons for inadequate information, however, patients have the right to know and understand fully the prognosis for their condition and their possible treatments and choices. Patients must persist in asking the questions that will bring answers they understand. Patients can only make intelligent, informed decisions if they understand the risks and benefits of the various treatments and the likelihood of success or failure.

Providing Care When There's Inadequate Information

You might be able to help your care receiver deal with the frustration of inadequate information and get the information he or she needs. By listening and reflecting feelings you can help your care receiver express his or her frustration and other feelings. Your listening can help your care receiver regain the calmness he or she needs to make good decisions about getting needed information. You may also listen as your care receiver sorts out his or her thoughts about difficult decisions.

Some care receivers are intimidated by medical personnel or believe that they should not question a doctor's judgment. You might encourage your care receiver assertively to seek the information he or she needs and listen as he or she figures out how to do so.

If your care receiver is unable to get the information he or she needs, you might ask if the hospital has a patient advocacy service. Offering your care receiver options for getting help may be the best ministry you can do.

The Fear of the Known

Some patients do not fear the unknown as much as they fear what they already know and have experienced. For those like Juanita Beck who have undergone repeated treatments for an illness or injury—chemotherapy or radiation, progressive amputation, repeated angioplasty to open clogged arteries—their fears center on the known and the expected. Their dread is firmly anchored in their prior experiences and is perhaps all the worse because of their certainty of it.

Providing Care

Since fear of known pain is closely tied to his or her discouragement with the situation, allowing the care receiver to speak of that fear lets him or her put limits on the fear and cope more effectively with it. Avoid devaluing the fear, as the care receiver knows well what he or she has experienced, and that fear is grounded in knowledge. The care receiver needs encouragement and the assurance that he or she does not face the experience alone—that God is with us in all the trials and the joys of our lives.

Hold out the promise that you will be with the care receiver through whatever lies ahead and that God will be with him or her too.

▶ Ministering to the Family of the Care Receiver

Hospitalization presents a crisis not only for the person hospitalized, but for his or her family as well. How can you best care for a family member of a hospitalized person if you are the Stephen Minister for that individual?

Helping Family Members Express Their Feelings

Family members, like hospitalized patients, may fear for the safety and well-being of their loved one and feel anxious about an uncertain future. You will not be able to dispel the fear and anxiety—they are grounded in real uncertainties and cannot be resolved until the situation has been worked out. Yet by listening, you can give family members a safe place to express their fears and uncertainties, and help them deal with their feelings in an atmosphere of acceptance and understanding.

Sometimes the feelings that need release may not be rooted in life-and-death questions. They may be just the normal frustrations of dealing with hospital routine, such as the difficulty in getting hospital staff to sit down and talk with the family members.

By listening, a Stephen Minister can provide a safe harbor where family members can put their feelings into perspective and focus on resolving the conflicts and difficulties that lie ahead,

knowing that even in the worst difficulties they are not alone. A Stephen Minister's care reflects the love that Christ has for all God's suffering creatures. In him, we never walk alone.

Helping Family Members Communicate Their Feelings to One Another

During a crisis, family members may neglect to mention difficult topics, sometimes because it doesn't occur to them, sometimes because they are reluctant. For example, the wife of a man who just had prostate surgery may feel confident that she will always value her husband, but she may not tell her husband. She may not realize that her husband worries about changes in their relationship. He knows that when he leaves the hospital he cannot do any strenuous activity for four to six weeks, he is not even able to drive until he sees his doctor again. He is anxious about problems associated with his incontinence and possible impotence, and he needs to hear her say that she will always love and value him. For her, it is not even a question. For him, it is an issue of incredible magnitude. She may wonder why her husband seems to draw farther and farther away, despite her daily visits.

Sometimes, a Stephen Minister will recognize the breakdown of communication and give the care receiver a chance to think and talk about how to reestablish communication. The Stephen Minister can encourage the care receiver to put into words those feelings of love and acceptance that his or her family member so needs to hear.

Helping Family Members Plan for and Adjust to Change

The Stephen Minister can minister to a family member by helping him or her face the future, whether the future involves massive or minor changes. Family members need to plan for the patient's discharge and for the patient's care during his or her recovery. Family members may need to arrange for a visiting nurse or even full-time nursing help. They may need to prepare a room or to get special equipment, like a hospital bed or an oxygen tank. The hospital's discharge staff will most likely assist in arranging for any special needs.

Family members may need to prepare emotionally. Caring for a patient after his or her discharge can be a heavy burden, and family members may feel frustrated and even angry because of the inconvenience. A hospital bed in the living room, the disruption of schedules to make sure someone is always available, dealing with the mood swings of a patient who is mentally ready to return to his or her routine long before he or she is physically able—all these stress a family that is already emotionally overextended. Your ministry to a family member can help him or her name and voice his or her feelings. You can help the family member understand and accept that his or her feelings are real and appropriate. You can assist him or her to plan for the needs of the hospitalized person as well as for the rest of the family.

As time goes on, new crises and problems will arise and new adjustments will need to be made. The patient may recover or may worsen, and either option brings stress to the patient and to the family as well. Throughout, you can provide a caring and listening presence to help the care receiver deal with the new—and old—stresses that arise.

▶ Do's and Don'ts about Ministering to a Hospitalized Care Receiver

The following do's and don'ts are organized into three segments: Before a Hospital Visit, When There Are Others in the Room, and When You Are Alone with Your Care Receiver.

Before a Hospital Visit

▶ **DO** remember that Jesus is the most important person in the caring relationship—for your care receiver and for you. Your care receiver is the second most important, and you, as a compassionate, trustworthy, full of faith, and skilled Stephen Minister, are third. You care, Jesus cures.

▶ **DON'T** visit the care receiver if you are ill. If you have symptoms that suggest you are coming down with a contagious illness, never expose your care receiver. Phone or send a card, but don't visit until you are well.

▶ **DO** arrange your visit ahead of time, if possible. The hospital may allow visiting at other than normal visiting hours, but the care receiver may be out of the room with tests or treatments then. If you arrive during visiting hours, your care receiver may have other visitors. Telephoning in advance can't eliminate interruptions but can reduce the possibility of your coming when the care receiver normally expects family members or has his or her room cleaned. Also, avoid visiting during a meal, unless he or she needs your help eating.

▶ **DO** be self-aware but not self-conscious in your visiting. Hospital visitors can feel anything from mild anxiety to extreme discomfort. Being aware of your feelings and accepting them helps you control them rather than being controlled by them. Being aware of your feelings prepares you to understand and better care for your care receiver's feelings.

▶ **DO** contact the chaplain on your first visit, if possible, and check in at your care receiver's nurses' station. Ask if any precautions are necessary. Alerting the nursing staff to your visit as one "calling from the church" may ensure that your visit is undisturbed. Most hospital staff members value the care offered by Stephen Ministers, pastors, and chaplains and recognize that healing occurs in more than physical ways.

▶ **DO** look for signs indicating special precautions on your care receiver's door, such as a requirement that visitors wear a mask. Knock before entering the room. If you don't hear a response, knock harder and wait—a courtesy the care receiver will appreciate. He or she may need extra moments to get ready for your visit.

▶ **DO** ask the nursing staff if you should awaken your care receiver. If you've phoned ahead and your care receiver is not critically ill, awaken him or her. If your care receiver is seriously ill or you are in doubt, come back later.

When There Are Others in the Room

▶ **DO** assess the place and people immediately upon entering the room. Is there a roommate? Does the roommate have visitors? Are medical or other hospital personnel in the room? Does your care receiver have visitors? Evaluate quickly if this is a potentially good time to visit.

▶ **DO** be sensitive to your care receiver's needs. If the care receiver has visitors when you arrive and is clearly enjoying them, you may join for a while and ascertain what the care receiver wants. If you sense the care receiver wants to speak with you privately, wait, if you can, until the others leave. Take your cue from your care receiver.

▶ **DO** feel free to talk and relate with your care receiver's roommate or the roommate's family. Your ministry to your care receiver may bring peace to the roommate as well. If someone else in the room needs a Stephen Minister, ask permission to talk with one of your Stephen Leaders. If you establish a relationship with a roommate and his or her family, tell them when your "friend" will be discharged and that you will no longer be visiting. This helps ease that person's feelings of loss or abandonment.

▶ **DON'T** promise your care receiver's roommate a Stephen Minister. Referring is the job of the Referrals Coordinator. He or she must be free to decide who does and does not qualify for the care of a limited number of Stephen Ministers.

▶ **DO** deal graciously with interruptions. A nurse may arrive to take the care receiver's vital signs; the doctor may visit; the housekeeping staff may need to clean the room. Promptly and graciously leave the room for the hospital staff and wait outside until invited to return.

▶ **DO** note what the care receiver was saying if you are interrupted, so that when you return you can ask the care receiver to continue.

▶ **DO** carry on your ministry as part of the hospital team. You probably won't be accustomed to your caring visits being interrupted, but remember that all—physicians, nurses, other medical staff, hospital chaplains, other hospital staff, your pastor, and you—are a team, working for your care receiver's good.

When You Are Alone with Your Care Receiver

Even when you are alone with your care receiver, the caring you offer in a hospital will be different.

On Location

▶ **DO** recognize that your care receiver's hospital room is a bedroom and probably a bathroom also. Behave as though you are a guest admitted to these private rooms in the care receiver's home.

▶ **DON'T** sit on the bed. This invades the care receiver's personal space— and invasions of his or her personal space are all too common during hospitalization. Also, your weight on the blankets may be painful to the care receiver.

▶ **DO** bring a chair to the bedside rather than tower over the care receiver— eye-to-eye contact puts the care receiver more at ease. Standing can

make the care receiver think you are poised to leave as soon as possible.

▶ **DO** protect the confidentiality of the caring relationship. If the patient needs to discuss a sensitive matter while a roommate is present, you might find a quiet lounge to talk. If your care receiver is unable to be up, you may be able to draw the curtain and discuss the matter quietly. Try to make this comfortable for your care receiver, but recognize that the roommate has a right to be in the room.

In Relationship

▶ **DO** remain aware of the spiritual dimension of your care. The reason you visit is to communicate Christ's love and concern for your care receiver. Bring Jesus to your care receiver with humility and prayer.

▶ **DO** understand the value of being with your care receiver. Your initiative in planning your time, traveling, parking, and finding your way through the hospital to your care receiver's room makes your presence a strong statement of concern.

▶ **DO** be first and foremost a listener. The hospitalized person or his or her family especially need a trained Stephen Minister's listening skills. Unfamiliar and intense feelings assault both patients and families. The hospital staff provides vital services to a large number of people but they work on a prescribed schedule and do not always have as much time to listen as they or their patients would like. Your primary purpose in visiting is to listen and care in order to bring Christ's care. You visit not to chitchat or be company for the hospitalized person, but to hear the care receiver's feelings and spiritual concerns.

▸ **DO** expect to pray with your care receiver. Never force a prayer or Bible verse on your care receiver, but ask if he or she would like to pray with you. If yes, build a prayer as you learned in *Christian Caregiving—a Way of Life*. Listen well enough to understand what the care receiver's concerns are and then mention those concerns in prayer.

▸ **DO** touch the care receiver, if you both are comfortable with touch. A gentle touch on the hand or shoulder sometimes offers reassurance more tangibly than words. Take care that the touch is appropriate, and that you do not hurt the care receiver. A strong embrace can be painful, but a caring touch helps the care receiver know he or she is valued.

▸ **DON'T** stay longer than thirty minutes. Fifteen minutes is usual. You can ruin your visit's effectiveness if you stay too long. A seriously ill patient or a patient just out of surgery will benefit from daily five-minute visits much more than from half-hour visits twice a week. Take your cue from your care receiver. Judge your care receiver's needs and stamina and stay for a time that truly helps his or her recovery.

▸ ## Getting Ready for the In-Class Sessions

In preparation for the first In-Class Session, remember a time in your adult life when you were, or a family member has been, in the hospital. What were the surprises, the challenges, and the unexpected joys of hospitalization?

Caring for People before, during, and after Hospitalization

Outline and Focus Notes

As soon as they got out of the boat, people recognized Jesus. They ran throughout that whole region and carried the sick on mats to wherever they heard he was. And wherever he went—into villages, towns or country-side—they placed the sick in the marketplaces. They begged him to let them touch even the edge of his cloak, and all who touched him were healed.

Mark 6:54–56

I. His Healing Touch

II. LIFE: Hospitalization Memories

III. Basic Elements of Hospital Ministry

A. Before the Hospitalization

FOCUS NOTE 1

Invitations to Express Feelings and Concerns

"You're going into the hospital next week for the first time in your life. How do you feel about it?"

"How do you feel about hospitals? Have you had experiences that cause you concerns now?"

"I imagine you've thought a lot about going into the hospital. Would you mind sharing your thoughts and feelings?"

"What are your biggest concerns about going into the hospital?"

TM-20 OFN Caring for People before, during, and after Hospitalization.doc C: 1/1/2000 R:

B. Life and Death Decisions

C. Visiting a Care Receiver in the Hospital

1. Prepare for the Visit

2. Reviewing Do's and Don'ts of Hospital Ministry

IV. Looking Ahead

V. Opening

VI. Caring for Those Affected by Hospitalization

A. Before Hospitalization

FOCUS NOTE 2

Discussion Questions
1. What issues was the care receiver wrestling with?
2. How did the Stephen Minister provide care?
3. What was the care receiver's most pressing need?
4. What kinds of care would the Stephen Minister have provided if there had been a full hour for the caring visit?

B. During Hospitalization

C. After Hospitalization

VII. Looking Ahead

VIII. Opening

IX. Learning from Experts about Hospitalization

FOCUS NOTE 3

Panel of Hospital Personnel

Use the space below to take notes on the questions asked of the panel and the responses panel members give.

Question:

Response:

Question:

Response:

Question:

Response:

Question:

Response:

Question:

Response:

X. Caregiver's Compass Review

_____

_____

_____

_____

_____   _____

_____   _____

_____   _____

COMPASSIONATE · FULL OF FAITH · SKILLED · TRUSTWORTHY

_____

_____

_____

XI. Looking Ahead

Prayer Partner Requests and Thanksgivings

My prayer partner is _____

Prayer requests and thanksgivings to share with my prayer partner

_____

_____

Prayer requests and thanksgivings shared by my prayer partner

_____

_____

Ministering to Those Experiencing Losses Related to Aging

Preclass Reading

Contents

▶ I Must Be Getting Old

The day Don turned 65 they held a combination birthday and retirement party for him at work. Don felt a mixture of sadness and exhilaration. He felt sad as he packed up his personal items from his desk and realized that this would soon be someone else's desk. On the other hand, Don had plans. He was looking forward to having enough time to pursue interests he had put off for years. Don had been planning his retirement garden for a couple of years as he looked forward to retirement. He had grown up on a farm and had been longing to make things grow again. He had even thought about keeping some chickens, but his wife, Alice, vetoed that idea. Don also planned to give a lot of time to church. He had just been elected president of the congregation and he had been talking with Rev. Jenkins about some changes that needed to be made. As Don and Alice stood off to the side and watched the party, Don said, "Well, I'm finally retired. I guess this means I must be getting old." They both laughed at the joke.

Alice died when Don was 78. They had been married for 56 years and he felt terribly sad and listless for more than a year. Don learned to cook and clean for himself and still took care of the house. Having that work to do helped keep him going.

Don's son, Harold, was quite worried about his father and spent a lot of time with him. "It isn't just Alice," Don said to Harold one day. "I miss her most of all, but she's just the most recent one to die. We went out with Walt and Francine just about every week for more than 20 years. Walt died two years ago and Francine followed him six months later. I've seen too many people die. I guess I must be getting old."

Harold said, "You still have a lot of life in you."

When Don was 84 he broke his leg getting out of the shower. He lay in pain for three and a half hours and probably would have died there if Harold hadn't dropped by unexpectedly. Don spent three weeks in the hospital. When Harold suggested that his father move into a long-term care facility, Don agreed without a fight.

Don felt as if the injury had taken the fight out of him. He didn't have the energy to live on his own anymore. One beautiful spring day the attendant at the nursing home took Don to walk outside. The dogwood trees were blooming white and pink. Don was so happy to be outside on this lovely day that he tried to walk too far. Soon his legs lost their strength and he was lucky to make it to a bench before they gave out. The attendant had to find someone to go get Don's wheelchair.

As the attendant returned, Don shook his head and said, "I guess I must be getting old."

"It happens to the best of us," the attendant replied.

****

▶ Caring for Older Persons

When is a person old? What, besides mere years, makes the difference between someone who is middle-aged and someone who is old? Who is "older": a 74-year-old person who backpacks every summer or a 58-year-old person who must carry an oxygen canister everywhere because of emphysema?

Three Stages of Old Age

Arthur Becker[1] suggests that there are three stages of old age. The young old are newly retired and very much in the prime of life. The middle old have slowed down and may have suffered major physical problems, but are still able to care for themselves. The frail elderly have suffered a combination of physical, financial, and emotional losses that leave them unable to care for themselves.

Caring for People Suffering Losses

Moving into old age is a series of losses. As people get older, they tend to lose physical abilities, grieve the losses of loved ones, lose their ability or opportunity to do meaningful work, and may even lose their ability to care for themselves. Finally, as they age, people may dread the ultimate loss that death brings even though they anticipate the joy of being with Christ forever. Therefore, the focus of this module is on caring for older persons when they suffer losses and as they live with the consequences of those losses. Stephen Leaders will not assign a Stephen Minister to a care receiver just because the care receiver is old. Rather, as with people of any age, older people will receive Stephen Ministry when they experience losses or other life crises.

Caring for older persons is, in many ways, the same as caring for younger persons. You join your care receiver in his or her pain and frustration so he or she doesn't experience them alone. You

help your care receiver understand and express feelings, you pray with and for your care receiver, and you find ways to encourage and enable your care receiver to care for him- or herself.

Module 22 Deals with Long-Term Care

Some may think that ministering to older persons means caring for people who are homebound or in a nursing home, who can no longer carry on extended conversations because of one or more physical or mental disabilities, and who are no longer competent to make their own decisions. Certainly there are older persons like that, but they are a small minority. The vast majority of older persons live in their own homes, are just as able to communicate as they ever were, and remain competent to manage their own affairs. What about caring for the small percentage of older persons who are greatly incapacitated? Module 22, "Ministering to Persons Needing Long-Term Care," is where you will learn more about caring for people who have physical or mental disabilities that make them unable to care for themselves, regardless of their age.

▶ Debunking Five Myths about Aging

Some myths about aging and about older persons lead to older persons' being stereotyped and treated prejudicially. These myths are patently false and need to be debunked.

---

1 Arthur H. Becker, *Ministry with Older Persons: A Guide for Clergy and Congregations* (Minneapolis: Augsburg Publishing House, 1986), pp. 36–37.

1. The Myth of Senility

Some think that most people, if they grow to be old enough, eventually will become senile, which they define as suffering confusion and major lapses in memory. Family members and caregivers may use this myth to account for behavior that they don't understand.

Only people who have a disease called senile dementia are truly senile, however, and that is only a small percentage of the older persons who suffer some confusion and memory loss. Much of what is called senility may be one or more of the following difficulties.

► Alzheimer's and related disorders
► Depression, grief, or anxiety
► Lack of social stimulation
► Overmedication
► Lack of a proper diet
► Cardiovascular problems
► Advanced alcoholism

When the problem is the result of some of the preceding situations, it may be controlled or reversed if the person receives the proper attention. Caregivers must be careful not to label as senile an older person whose problem might result from other treatable, reversible causes.

2. The Myth of "You Can't Teach an Old Dog New Tricks"

The myth of "you can't teach an old dog new tricks" assumes that there is a point in life when habits become so ingrained that people cannot learn, change, or grow. This myth also implies that all elderly persons are resistant to change and wish to keep things as they've always been.

Two pieces of evidence disprove this misconception. Many of the educational classes offered for the elderly fill up as soon as they are announced. Also, once enrolled in classes, older persons frequently outperform younger students in achieving academic excellence. Older people may learn at slightly slower rates, but their increased motivation often makes up for it. Their wisdom and life experiences give them greater ability to use what they learn.

Older persons are not any more resistant to change than they were earlier in their lives. Resistance to change has more to do with personality and past experiences than age.

3. The Myth of Chronological Age

The myth of chronological age pictures the aged as frail and infirm, though most of the elderly are not in this category. Many older persons are told that they are too old or that they are not capable of participating because of their age. The sad truth is that if you tell someone often enough that he or she is too old or not capable of something, that person will probably begin to believe you. As Malcolm Cowley says, "We start by growing old in other people's eyes, then slowly we come to share their judgment."[2]

Just because someone is x number of years old, however, does not mean that he or she is over the hill. A variety of

---

2 Malcolm Cowley, *The View from Eighty* (New York: Viking Press, 1980), p. 5.

factors can influence how "old" a person really is. These factors include physical health, the way the individual has lived, attitude and outlook, and the current social and emotional support available from family, friends, Stephen Ministers, and other caring resources. As one chaplain in a nursing home put it: "It's not how old you are; it's how you are old that counts."

4. The Myth That Older Persons Choose to Isolate Themselves

The myth that older persons choose to isolate themselves perpetuates the idea that older persons don't welcome the involvement of others in their lives. Some may accept this myth because it gives them an excuse not to become involved in the life of an older person and relieves them of guilt about not taking the time to visit.

The majority of older people are not socially isolated and lonely. Most older persons are healthy enough to maintain active social contacts and develop mutually satisfying relationships.

5. The Myth of Asexuality

The myth of asexuality asserts that as people age, they lose sexual desire or feelings and thus lose interest in sexual expression. "The fact is that sexual interest and capability, at varying levels of sexual expression, may continue into the 90s."[3] The lack of a suitable partner is a disturbing reality for many older persons, however.

▶ Losses and Gains Involved with Aging

While there are many losses that people must deal with as they age, there are also gains to acknowledge, celebrate, and take advantage of.

Physical Losses

As people age, they experience changes in their strength, senses, and appearance. Most changes are unwelcome. People whose sense of well-being has relied primarily on their looks and physical health may experience old age with its cumulative physical insults as a spirit-crushing downward physical spiral. All older persons are likely to grieve the loss of their physical abilities and appearance at times.

Loss of Job and Community Standing

A person's social role is a composite of work role, economic role, family role, and community role. As a person ages, all these roles will either diminish or come to an end.

Retirement may rob a person of goals such as financial self-sufficiency or the satisfaction of being productive. Unwanted idleness may leave the retired individual with no idea of what to do with time, talents, and energy. The retired person may feel useless, unwanted, no good, unworthy of respect, and sidetracked. These feelings can be very difficult to handle, especially when the person is still able to make significant contributions to a cause.

---

3 Becker, *Ministry with Older Persons,* p. 46.

Loss of Power

For most people, work is the primary avenue through which they express power and authority. The loss of a position in which a person supervised others or exercised his or her gifts and strengths may leave that person feeling helpless or useless. In reaction, the person may try to turn family members into supervisees under his or her authority.

This loss of power may be exacerbated by the loss of important roles in the church. The one-time board president, treasurer, or Bible study leader who is now given the message, "You're too old to do anything but sit in the pew," will experience added grief and loss.

Loss of Safety

Older persons often lack a sense of personal safety. The elderly can be much more afraid of violence or criminal attack. Unable to fend off attackers, or to escape, they may feel that they are easy prey for would-be attackers.

Older persons may fear falling and breaking a bone. They may be much more afraid to drive, especially at night. Bad weather may keep them at home because they don't trust their ability to cope with it.

Loss of Dignity

Some people think that growing older automatically means regressing into a second childhood. They tend to treat the elderly as small children, using a particularly patronizing tone of voice, speaking too loud, or using terms such as *honey* or *grandma* inappropriately.

People also can rob older persons of their dignity by not permitting them to participate in decisions that affect them.

Carobeth Laird wrote about how she was robbed of her dignity in a nursing home. After having published her first book when she was 80 and a second a year or so later, she was working on two more when she became physically incapacitated. She gave the ominous title *Limbo* to the book that described her experience in the home that she says was "neither the best nor the worst of nursing homes . . . it wasn't horrible, just dehumanizing." She fought a losing battle to maintain some independence. She was not permitted telephone calls, and her editor finally got through to her only by calling her "Professor Laird" and demanding that she be called to the phone. She was placed with patients who were severely incapacitated mentally, and she had to fight for her sanity by reading whatever she could get from the very limited nursing home library. "If I mentioned anything about my life or my books, the aides merely humored me with their condescending 'yes dear, no dear.' There was no respect for a person's dignity."[4]

Loss of One's Home

A home can be the essence of a person's identity—the core of all a person has done to establish a sense of self. Loss of the home usually occurs when an older person can no longer physically or financially manage to care for it. This may mean selling a beloved house, moving to an apartment, living with

---

4 Rita Rooney, "Carobeth Laird: An Old Woman Dreams— and Writes Books," *Parade Magazine,* July 30, 1978, 7.

children or in retirement housing, or even entering a long-term care facility. It almost always means decreased independence for the care receiver.

The move to a long-term care facility is especially painful since people generally perceive it as the final move they will make in their lives. Older people may project their anger about their circumstances and loss of independence onto family members. Even if they agree that it was for their own good, they may still interpret the move as a rejection.

Loss of Family and Friends through Death

Deaths of friends and family occur with increasing frequency as people grow older. Losing a close friend or relative means losing part of the past as well as the present. It is really the death of a part of oneself. The older person is made aware of the nearness and inevitability of death.

Even more painful is experiencing the death of one's own children. As people grow older, this too is more likely to occur. Such deaths go against the normal plan of things in which parents expect to die before their children. Caregivers should be especially aware of the very intense grief experienced by care receivers in these situations.

Losing One's Own Life

Older persons are regularly reminded that their days are numbered. The deaths of their friends and relatives and the gradual failing of their own bodies tell them that they are mortal.

Many older persons have come to accept death and are not afraid of it. Others, however, are terrified of death. Be very sensitive to how an older care receiver feels about his or her own death as you care for him or her, especially if the person is seriously ill, hospitalized, or dying. Also be aware of your own fears and try to be honest with yourself about them.

Impact of These Losses

All the losses just described are like small deaths. Aging may be filled with thousands of such bereavements. Because these losses usually overlap one another, the neat schedules of the grief process outlined by experts are not always relevant.

Suffering so many losses also can make someone question God's goodness and love. Distinctively Christian caregivers can talk about these questions with care receivers, letting them express whatever they are feeling as well as inviting them to deepen their relationship with God.

Gains Involved with Aging

People gain new freedom and wisdom as they age.

Freedom from Societal Definitions

Retirees may enjoy new freedom once their jobs no longer limit what they have time to do. They may now be able to try out new interests and avocations and realize the many hidden gifts and talents they possess. Others may find relief and joy in just being rather than perpetually doing.

More Time for Relationships

As people age, they may value and enjoy relationships more than ever before. They may also have more time for the relationships with family and friends.

Freedom from Fear of Death

Some aging people realize their own mortality more vividly than others. Others make peace with the fact that they will die. When they no longer fear or deny death, they enjoy new freedom and zest for living.

Spiritual Maturity

Some older persons grow to express a deep relationship with God and a profoundly spiritual perspective on life. Those who experience many physical and emotional losses of old age may find that their spiritual senses are sharpened. Read in Reference Box A the words Paul wrote about loss and gain.

REFERENCE BOX A

Loss and Gain

But whatever was to my profit I now consider loss for the sake of Christ. What is more, I consider everything a loss compared to the surpassing greatness of knowing Christ Jesus my Lord, for whose sake I have lost all things. I consider them rubbish, that I may gain Christ and be found in him, not having a righteousness of my own that comes from the law, but that which is through faith in Christ—the righteousness that comes from God and is by faith. I want to know Christ and the power of his resurrection and the fellowship of sharing in his sufferings, becoming like him in his death, and so, somehow, to

---

attain to the resurrection from the dead.

Philippians 3:7–11

Some older persons may emerge from their many losses transformed into people who fully realize Paul's bold dream of knowing Christ and the power of his resurrection.

▶ Getting Ready for the In-Class Sessions

The first module of Stephen Minister training, "The Person of the Caregiver," invited you to see that the most important gift you bring into the caring relationship is yourself. You will care best for older persons who wrestle with the losses of aging only when you face your own aging and address the losses you experience. You do not face these realities alone but in the presence of Jesus who is "the same yesterday and today and forever" (Hebrews 13:8). Read in Reference Box B what Henri Nouwen wrote about this.

REFERENCE BOX B

The Self as a Source of Healing

To care one must offer one's own vulnerable self to others as a source of healing. To care for the aging, therefore, means first of all to enter into close contact with your own aging self, to sense your own time, and to experience the movements of your own life cycle. From this aging self, healing can come forth and others can be invited to cast off the paralyzing fear for their future. As long as we think that caring means only being nice and friendly to old people, paying them a visit, bringing them a

---

flower or offering them a ride, we are apt to forget how much more important it is for us to be willing and able to be present to those we care for. And how can we be fully present to the elderly when we are hiding from our own aging? How can we listen to their pains when their stories open wounds in us that we are trying to cover up? How can we offer companionship when we want to keep our own aging self out of the room, and how can we gently touch the vulnerable spots in old people's lives when we have armored our own vulnerable self with fear and blindness? Only as we enter into solidarity with the aging and speak out of common experience, can we help others to discover the freedom of old age. By welcoming the elderly into our aging self we can be good hosts and healing can take place.[5]

No loss of aging can compare with the gain of knowing Christ and the power of his resurrection. Our faith in Jesus gives us the courage to face our own aging with honesty.

In preparation for the In-Class Sessions, think about yourself as an aging person. What do you hope for and fear in your old age? What kinds of care do you hope to receive when you experience losses related to aging?

---

5 Henri J. M. Nouwen and Walter J. Gaffney, *Aging: The Fulfillment of Life* (New York: Image Books, 1974) pp. 97–99.

Ministering to Those Experiencing Losses Related to Aging

Outline and Focus Notes

*"Listen to me, O house of Jacob,
all you who remain of the house of Israel,
you whom I have upheld since you were conceived,
and have carried since your birth.
Even to your old age and gray hairs
I am he, I am he who will sustain you.
I have made you and I will carry you;
I will sustain you and I will rescue you."*

Isaiah 46:3–4

I. The Gift of Old Age

II. Acting Your Age

FOCUS NOTE 1

Hopes and Fears When You Are Old

	Hopes	Fears
Physically		
Mentally		
Emotionally		

Socially		
Spirituality		

FOCUS NOTE 2

Personal Reflection Questions

1. As I imagine myself as an older person, what five aspects do I like best about myself?

2. As I imagine myself as an older person, what five aspects do I like least about myself?

3. What would be easiest about ministry to older persons?

4. What would be most difficult about ministry to older persons?

Discussion Questions

1a. If you made masks, show your mask to the others in your group, and explain what it says about your hopes, fears, and expectations of old age.

1b. If you wrote about hopes and fears, briefly tell whether you are mostly hopeful or mostly fearful about old age now and why.

2. Share your thoughts about what is easy and difficult about ministry to older persons.

3. Did this exercise help you to see more clearly any ageist attitudes, actions, or prejudices?

4. Did you learn anything from this exercise or the reading that might help you better prepare for and face your own old age?

III. Looking Ahead

IV. Opening

V. Caring for Older Persons

FOCUS NOTE 4

Panel of Older Persons

Use the space below to take notes on the questions asked of the panel and the responses panel members give.

Question:

Response:

Question:

Response:

Question:

Response:

Question:

Response:

Question:

Response:

A. Feelings

1. Responding to Reluctance to Share Feelings

FOCUS NOTE 5

Responding to Reluctance to Share Feelings

Care receiver: I was raised to keep personal issues private. There's no good that can come from complaining about your problems.

Don't say: While I respect your opinions and the way you were raised, I still think it's a good idea for you to share your feelings. I think if you try it you'll find that it helps a lot.

Do say: It sounds like you feel pretty strongly about keeping personal problems private *[or some other reflecting response that shows that you accept and respect the care receiver's opinion]*.

---

2. Responding When People Discount Feelings

FOCUS NOTE 6

Ways to Respond When Someone Discounts His or Her Feelings

Care receiver: But what I feel really isn't that important. I'm sure you don't want to listen to this.

Caregiver: Actually I do want to listen. Your feelings are important to me.

[or]

You think that your feelings aren't important.

[or]

You know, I wonder how you feel when you say that.

B. Listening

C. Distinctively Christian Caring

FOCUS NOTE 7

Losses Older Persons Might Experience
▶ Physical losses
▶ The loss of job and community standing
▶ The loss of power
▶ The loss of safety
▶ The loss of dignity
▶ The loss of one's home
▶ The loss of family and friends through death
▶ Losing one's own life

D. Telecare

E. Using Community Resources

F. Assertiveness

VI. Looking Ahead

VII. Opening

The Three Stages of Old Age

1. *Young Old:* Newly retired and very much in the prime of life

2. *Middle Old:* Have slowed down and may have suffered major physical problems, but are still able to care for themselves

3. *Frail Elderly:* Have suffered a combination of physical, financial, and emotional losses that leave them unable to care for themselves

VIII. Identifying Needs for Care

Situation 1

Mary is 82 and has lived alone for many years. Her passions are gardening, reading, and her church work. She has always been very involved with the women's group at church, and she taught Sunday school for 35 years.

Three months ago Mary had a bad fall and was hospitalized for several weeks. When she returned home, she and her children decided that it would be better for her to move into a retired persons' apartment complex where help would be available if something like that happened again. Unfortunately, the complex is 30 miles from her church, and she no longer drives.

Situation 2

The care receiver, Elizabeth, is 66 and partially blind. When her husband Tom died last year, financial problems made it necessary for her to sell her home. She moved into an apartment near her daughter, Susan.

Elizabeth enjoys her independence, but lately Susan has been worrying about Elizabeth's ability to care for herself. Elizabeth's eyesight has been getting even worse and her physician has suggested surgery to remove cataracts. Susan has suggested once or twice that Elizabeth move in with her and her husband and two children, but Elizabeth ignored the suggestions. She doesn't even want to think about living in someone else's home.

Situation 3

The care receiver, John, is 73. Last week he retired from a business he founded and made successful. While he plans to serve as a consultant, the majority of his time is now free. His wife, Becky, is a high school teacher who is looking forward to her own retirement in a year or two, but who is excited about the school year that will begin in a couple of weeks. Both John and Becky enjoy good health.

John agreed to meet with a Stephen Minister when Becky insisted he do so. They have met three times, but so far he hasn't had much to talk about with his Stephen Minister.

On the first day of his official retirement, John:
- watched Becky go off to work;
- forced himself not to call the office;

- tried to remember all the things he'd said he was going to do once he retired; and
- fumed over the list of "honey-do" projects that Becky handed him as she left for work.

IX. Caregiver's Compass Review

_____

_____

_____

_____

_____   _____

_____   _____

_____   _____

_____   _____

COMPASSIONATE · FULL OF FAITH · SKILLED · TRUSTWORTHY

_____

_____

_____

_____

X. Looking Ahead

FOCUS NOTE 12

Facing the Challenges of Aging Head On

On your own, brainstorm some specific tasks you can do to prepare for your own old age. Include the social, physical, emotional, financial, spiritual, and intellectual dimensions.

Make a covenant with yourself to do something specific to begin preparing for this time.

Prayer Partner Requests and Thanksgivings

My prayer partner is _____

Prayer requests and thanksgivings to share with my prayer partner

_____

_____

Prayer requests and thanksgivings shared by my prayer partner

_____

_____

Ministering to Persons Needing Long-Term Care

Preclass Reading

Contents

TM-22 PCR Ministering to Persons Needing Long-Term Care.doc C: 1/1/2000 R:

▶ Needs for Long-Term Care

Following are four stories that give glimpses of the dimensions of caring for long-term care receivers.

Pleasant Acres

Dwayne found out five years ago that he had amyotrophic lateral sclerosis, also known as Lou Gehrig's disease. A year later he had found out that his wife of 20 years was divorcing him. When he was 44 he had moved into a nursing home. He didn't know how many more years he would live, but he was positive he would not enjoy the rest of his life.

When his caregiver Ira would visit, Dwayne would say, "God, I hate this place. They call it Pleasant Acres but there's nothing pleasant about it. The smells in here are terrible and the crying and the moaning never quit."

Dwayne shook his head and got a faraway look in his eye. "Upwardly mobile . . . the fast track. I never thought I would end up here. Whatever I had the state has confiscated to pay for my 'care.' You know what's left? Behold, my kingdom: Pleasant Acres."

Deep Faith

Eunice had suffered from emphysema for ten years. She had to have her oxygen bottle with her at all times. At 78, she spent most of the day in her chair because every time she got up she felt painfully out of breath.

Vicki visited Eunice every Tuesday evening and called her at least once a week. Vicki loved talking with Eunice about books, especially mysteries.

Eunice and Vicki also talked about God. Eunice wanted them to say the 23rd Psalm, the Apostle's Creed, and the Lord's Prayer together every time Vicki visited, and then sing some old hymns. At first Vicki went along because it was what Eunice wanted. After a year or so of reciting with Eunice every week, however, Vicki found that she looked forward to that part of their visits. As she learned more about Eunice's faith, Vicki saw that God's Word had sunk in over the years and that Eunice had a deep reservoir of belief, hope, and peace. Vicki knew she wanted the kind of faith that Eunice had.

Healing

Matt's 17th birthday present had been a new motorcycle. By a week after his 17th birthday, the motorcycle was wrecked and Matt's physician had assured him that he would never walk again. Eighteen months later Matt was in the hospital with skin ulcers that were outward signs of his ulcerous inner anger. Matt's parents asked the pastor to visit, and she talked Matt into talking with a Stephen Minister.

Pete visited Matt for the first time when Matt was still in the hospital. Toward the end of the visit Matt said, "They tell me I'm in here because I don't take care of myself. Why should I take care of myself? What self is there to take care of?"

Pete visited Matt faithfully, even though Matt treated him rudely. Several times Matt asked, "Why do you keep coming back? You aren't doing any good and you can't enjoy being around me." Pete often asked himself that same question, and the answer he received was a sense of profound love for Matt. Pete didn't understand it, but he knew he couldn't abandon Matt.

Pete prayed fervently for Matt every day. He also asked the other members of his Supervision Group to pray for his care receiver and ask God to heal his deep hurt and anger.

A year after Pete started visiting, Matt learned that he needed more surgery and his anger doubled. In one visit Matt cursed God and ridiculed Pete for believing in a loving God. At the end of his outburst, Matt broke down and cried while Pete held him.

When Pete visited again after the surgery, Matt said, "After the way I unloaded on you, I thought I'd never see you again. Why *do* you come back?"

Pete thought for a moment and said, "There's a Bible verse that sums it up pretty well: 'We love because he first loved us'" (1 John 4:19).

"I Just Want Out"

At age 45 Marilyn had sent her one child, Debra, off to college. She had resumed her former career, while her husband, Barry, had recently been promoted and was making much more money than he had ever made before. Life seemed good.

Then Debra suffered a severe head injury that left her badly disabled. Unable to deal with Debra's injury, Barry divorced Marilyn and never visited his daughter. Debra went through vocational rehabilitation until she could get around with a walker and work in a

sheltered workshop. Marilyn was left to care for her alone.

One time Marilyn told her Stephen Minister, "I just wish I could go away for a time. I've become so irritable with Debra lately. I know it's because I'm worn out. My days seem endless. Work, home, no time out, no time off. If Debra could do more, that would help. But she can't. Some days I just want out."

Challenging and Rewarding Ministry

These stories show only a small sample of the situations that can cause people to need long-term care. Some people may think that long-term care receivers are only older persons, but tragic circumstances can happen to people at any age. In addition, sometimes people who care for chronically ill or disabled family members need a Stephen Minister's long-term care themselves.

As you read the descriptions of long-term care receivers, you may have wondered about caring for someone with these needs. Caring for long-term care receivers can be very challenging. It can require a lot of patience and commitment. It also can force the caregiver to consider the difficult spiritual issues of suffering, meaning, doubt, and faith.

Caring for long-term care receivers can also be extremely rewarding. Stephen Ministers can make a big difference for their long-term care receivers. Caregivers can emerge from the challenges of ministry with renewed faith and a deeper understanding of themselves and their own suffering. Caregivers for long-term care receivers follow the example of Jesus, who became one of us, suffered our pain, shared our joy, and has "borne our griefs, and carried our sorrows" (Isaiah 53:4 KJV).

How to Care for the Challenges of Long-Term Care Receivers

While long-term care receivers experience unique circumstances and individual needs, some challenges are common to many long-term care receivers.

Isolation and Loneliness

Long-term care receivers are often confined to their home or a long-term care facility. They may rarely have contact with people other than their caregivers. Former friends may stop visiting because they find the care receiver's situation too difficult to deal with. Care receivers who formerly enjoyed going to church may be unable to do so.

Long-term care receivers may therefore suffer painful loneliness. They may long for others' company and for the stimulation of getting out. They may feel hurt, angry, and deeply sad as a result.

Isolation and loneliness can create a vicious cycle. As the care receiver is isolated, he or she feels angry and depressed. Then, when someone visits, the care receiver has little to contribute other than painful feelings. This makes it much less likely that the visitor will return, which leads to greater isolation and more painful feelings.

In a different vicious cycle, the care receiver is so hungry for others' company that when someone visits, he or she comes across as extremely needy and tries to inspire guilt to manipulate the visitor into coming back again. Most visitors do not respond well to such manipulation and are not likely to visit very often in the future.

The care receiver's loneliness can be made worse by his or her relationships with the people he or she sees daily. Caregivers may be family members, visiting nurses, employees of a long-term care facility, or others. At times these daily caregivers can resent the long-term care receiver. They may resent how caring for the care receiver's needs limits their own lives. They may resent the care receiver's regular anger or continual sadness. Caregivers may feel just as trapped by the care receiver's disability as the care receiver is. When the only people a long-term care receiver regularly sees resent him or her, it tends to make him or her even angrier, sadder, and more resentful.

Eight Ways to Care for Isolation and Loneliness

When you understand the reasons for the painful loneliness that some long-term care receivers experience, you are more likely to find the courage and patience required to care for them. Here are some ideas for how to care for isolation and loneliness.

1. Be There

This is a simple yet most profound insight: Your caring presence—apart from anything you do—is an extremely powerful tool that God uses to bless the care receiver.

2. Make Regular, Planned Visits

Your long-term care receiver will look forward to your visits, even if he or she is too hurt and angry to tell you so. Your visit may be one of the highlights of his or her week. It is important to be a consistent visitor, therefore, and to keep your promises about when you will visit.

Even though your care receiver eagerly anticipates your visits, don't assume that you can just drop by. Planning your visits will make sure that you don't interrupt medical treatments or routine care. Planning shows respect for your care receivers and gives them something they can control. At the end of each visit, check to make sure that the next visit will be at a convenient time. If you must change the meeting time, mention that at the previous visit or call to arrange a different time.

3. Minister to the Care Receiver's Feelings

A great part of your ministry to a long-term care receiver will be to help him or her recognize, accept, and express his or her feelings. There may be special difficulties involved.

The care receiver may not see how talking about difficult feelings will help. Your ongoing empathy and unconditional positive regard may help him or her accept these difficult feelings over time.

The care receiver may be depressed and not communicate very much. Your challenge is to find ways to help your care receiver express feelings. Pay attention to nonverbal communication—facial expression, posture, eye contact, and dress. Then ask about these nonverbals as you would about spoken expressions of feelings. Reference Box A contains some examples.

REFERENCE BOX A

Reflecting Nonverbal Expressions of Feelings

"Your tears today seem to be saying that you are feeling very sad. Is that true?"

"You are looking off into the distance a lot today. I wonder if you are feeling sad or wishing you were somewhere else."

"When I mentioned your daughter, you frowned. Could you share what you are feeling about her today?"

"I see that you are wearing a bright and cheerful shirt, and I'm wondering if you might be feeling bright and cheerful today."

Sometimes you can use a psalm to give voice to a care receiver's feeling. Reference Box B provides examples.

REFERENCE BOX B

Using the Psalms

"As I listen to you, I am thinking of the psalm writer who said, 'Why, O LORD, do you stand far off? Why do you hide yourself in times of trouble? . . . Arise, LORD! Lift up your hand, O God. Do not forget the helpless' (Psalm 10:1, 12). Do you see a connection to your own situation?" If the person says yes, ask, "In what way?"

"Your words remind me of Psalm 4: 'Answer me when I call to you, O my righteous God. Give me relief from my distress; be merciful to me and hear my prayer' (Psalm 4:1). How close is that plea to your own?"

> "Your sense of the endlessness of your situation brings to mind the cry of the psalm writer, 'How long, O LORD?' (Psalm 13:1). In what way do those words pick up or reflect your feelings?"

4. Be Patient

Realize the difficult circumstances your care receiver may be living with, and assertively choose to bear with his or her anger or the monotony of caring for him or her. Seek the Lord's guidance for ways to get through the wall of bitterness or apathy that some long-term care receivers put up. For example, you might bring a single flower, a picture from a magazine, or a newspaper clipping each time you come.

Share your feelings of hurt, frustration, and helplessness with your Supervision Group in order to remain patient with your care receiver over time. Group members also can provide creative ideas for relating to your care receiver—something you can bring or do that can focus your time together.

5. Be Assertive

In attempts to end their painful loneliness, some care receivers may become manipulative. They may use guilt or pity to get their caregiver to stay longer or come back more often. You need to stay assertively within your boundaries as a Stephen Minister and say no to your care receiver when appropriate.

At other times you may give up your own rights for the sake of your care receiver. For example, a care receiver might be quite angry and express his or her anger at you inappropriately. You might decide to let your care receiver dump some undeserved anger on you because you believe it will do your care receiver good to express these feelings.

6. Help the Care Receiver Make Contact with Others

One antidote to isolation is more contact with others. A person who is homebound might appreciate being part of a weekly Bible study, prayer circle, or small group. Be aware of any help the person may need to participate. A long-term care receiver might enjoy a ministry of calling others on the telephone to make sure they are all right and to talk with them for a while. Some care receivers may be able to use the Internet to send and receive e-mail or participate in on-line chats. Care receivers can become pen pals with people needing encouragement. Examples include a foreign missionary, someone who is in prison, or a troubled teen.

As you help your care receiver make contact with others, resist the temptation to establish relationships for the person. Instead, discuss ideas and help him or her follow through.

7. Bring Worship to Your Care Receiver

Your congregation might have eucharistic ministers or others who bring Holy Communion to shut-in persons. If so, make sure your care receiver is on the list.

If your congregation does not have eucharistic ministers, bring a copy of the worship bulletin and talk about the service and the sermon.

8. Plan Stimulating Activities

Both the Stephen Minister and the care receiver need activities that keep the relationship fresh and help it to grow. As you get to know your care receiver, look for activities that you can do together. Reference Box C contains some ideas. The conversations that accompany these activities are where much of the relationship building takes place.

REFERENCE BOX C

Stimulating Activities

► Listen to an audiotape together and discuss it. Examples include:
  ▷ The Bible
  ▷ A Christian book
  ▷ Christian songs or hymns
  ▷ A Christian speaker's message
  ▷ A recent sermon or worship service
  ▷ A presentation about the situation faced by the long-term care receiver

► Sing together using a familiar hymnal, and talk about the significance of the hymns you sing or the memories they evoke.

► Watch a videotape and discuss it.
  ▷ A movie with a biblical theme like *The Ten Commandments*
  ▷ A videotape of a Christian speaker
  ▷ A videotape of a recent worship service
  ▷ A videotape of a special event in the care receiver's life or the life of a family member (e.g., wedding, baptism, graduation)

► Read together and discuss what you read.

► Create something together.
  ▷ A family history and stories for a book of memories or scrapbook that you can help assemble or write out
  ▷ A home altar for the care receiver that you also can use when you visit

---

  ▷ A letter of encouragement, with you serving as scribe or making an audiotape
  ▷ A symbol of faith to place on the wall

► Encourage using various art forms to express feelings or something of deep personal significance.

Adjusting to Change

Long-term care receivers frequently face difficult adjustments to changing circumstances, living arrangements, and abilities. Reference Box D lists some of these.

REFERENCE BOX D

Possible Changes Facing Long-Term Care Receivers

► Moving in with relatives or moving into a long-term care facility

► Living alone

► Illnesses or disabilities that will get worse and render them less and less able to care for themselves

► New caregivers (family, volunteers, or paid) who are undependable, impatient, unkind, dishonest, or ill-tempered, who handle them roughly or who do not understand them or their needs

► Lost hopes and dreams

► Lost relationships

► Reduced financial resources

► Loss of job

► Divorce

Adjusting to Multiple Challenges

Sometimes long-term care receivers have to face a number of challenges at the same time. For example, a man might find out he has multiple sclerosis, lose his job, learn that his wife is divorcing him, and have to move—all within several months. Other times a care receiver may begin adjusting to one loss when he or she is hit with another one. For example, a diabetic woman might be adjusting to a loss of eyesight when she discovers her right leg must be amputated below the knee. The more crises a person faces at once, the greater strain the person will experience.

Changes Bring Grief

Part of making adjustments is grieving the losses. Getting past denial to admitting the reality of a loss and allowing oneself to grieve can take quite a while when unrealistic expectations and dreams feed denial. Consider these situations: A person with a degenerative disease unreasonably believes in a miracle cure available only in a foreign country. A young adult who recently became a paraplegic asks his fiancée to postpone their wedding until he can walk down the aisle with her. In these situations and in many others, as long as a person refuses to admit to the reality of a loss, he or she cannot grieve or recover from it.

Need for Control

Care receivers facing multiple adjustments may try to control whatever they can. This can be very positive when care receivers concentrate on controlling themselves and their own responses to their circumstances. Trying to control other people may cause many difficul-ties. Care receivers can become so demanding, manipulative, or controlling that they alienate others, become even more isolated, and develop an even greater need to control. The end result is that care receivers feel even more hurt and vulnerable.

Three Ways to Care for Long-Term Care Receivers As They Make Adjustments

Long-term care receivers might need your care most when they are faced with adjusting to new challenges.

1. Grief Ministry

As care receivers experience losses, you can care for them in the stages of their grief. A person who learns that he or she will no longer be able to live alone is likely to experience the *shock* stage of grief. He or she may deny the loss. The best thing you can do in that stage is to be with the person. Trying to make him or her admit to the reality of the loss is not helpful.

Once the shock is over, the care receiver may enter into a long period of *recoil*. For example, a person who loses his or her sight due to diabetes may spend months or even years wrestling with depression, anger, and guilt. Your ministry is helping your care receiver deal with the feelings. In time a long-term care receiver may learn to live with new limitations and begin to *rebuild* his or her life. At that point, you and your care receiver might be able to talk about hopeful possibilities.

2. Dealing with Unrealistic Dreams and Expectations

Directly challenging unrealistic dreams and expectations is not likely to be helpful. Care receivers probably already know at some level that their expectations are not likely to be fulfilled. One way to deal with unrealistic dreams and expectations is to reflect back the hopes and fears that are wrapped up with them. You'll see these examples in Reference Box E.

REFERENCE BOX E

Reflecting Unrealistic Expectations

Care receiver: I just read in a tabloid that doctors in a foreign country are using pituitary glands from vampire bats to regrow severed spinal cords.

Stephen Minister: The way you said that indicates you're hoping this treatment might provide a cure for your condition.

[or]

Care receiver: My eyesight is getting bad, but it isn't that bad yet. I'm sure I'll be able to get my driver's license renewed.

Stephen Minister: I wonder if you're dreading the time when you can no longer drive.

[or]

Care receiver: I know that I've been getting weaker, but I have been praying about it. I'm sure God is going to heal me and turn this thing around.

Stephen Minister: You have a lot of hope that God is going to change your situation dramatically.

When you reflect the feelings that are behind unrealistic dreams and expectations, you nonjudgmentally offer care receivers a chance to talk about the real issues.

Once again the psalms offer an opportunity to facilitate discussion. See two examples in Reference Box F.

REFERENCE BOX F

Using the Psalms

"Sometimes the psalm writer struggled with the changes in life. When the changes became scary, the psalm writer would say to God, 'You are my hiding place' (Psalm 32:7). How might God be a hiding place for you right now?"

[or]

"Sometimes the psalm writer struggled with the changes in life and would cry out, 'My God, my God, why have you forsaken me? Why are you so far from saving me, so far from the words of my groaning?' (Psalm 22:1). I am wondering to what extent these words might express some of your feelings at this time?"

---

3. Responding to a Care Receiver's Need to Control

To a point, care receivers' need to control is understandable. You can help them control as much of their surroundings as is possible without trampling on others' rights. For example, a person caring for an elderly parent may have trouble keeping up with other household chores. You might help him or her assertively ask for more help from other family members. Another example would be helping a recently disabled care receiver ask others to speak directly to him or her about his or her needs or desires.

When a care receiver's attempts to control intrude on others' rights, respond assertively. For example, an elderly care receiver may try to manipulate people into spending time with her. Her Stephen Minister might say something like, "I do care for you and I will continue to. I have agreed to spend an hour a week with you and that's what I will do."

Maintain your boundaries with your care receiver, and do not give in to his or her attempts to get you to do what he or she is capable of doing. For example, if a care receiver who was perfectly capable of shopping were to ask his or her Stephen Minister to shop for him or her, the Stephen Minister should politely and firmly refuse.

Feelings of Uselessness

Long-term care receivers often wrestle with feelings of uselessness. Whatever made them feel useful in the past—for example, supporting their families, doing an important job well—is no longer possible. Their disability or illness has taken that away.

Attitudes of others can compound their feelings. People are usually considered successful and useful when they have a job, good income, a house, and other material signs of accomplishment. When a person can't even care for his or her own basic needs, people may consider that individual a drain on others.

Feelings of uselessness may get worse when people set unrealistic goals for themselves. For example, a shut-in person who no longer has the strength to walk more than a few feet at a time still expects to walk his or her dog. When the person cannot do so, he or she feels even more useless.

Four Ways to Care for Feelings of Uselessness

You can help your care receiver work through the feelings that come with his or her limitations and focus on what he or she can do.

1. Respond to Feelings

Do not make it your goal to get your care receiver to accept his or her limitations. Rather, support and minister to your care receiver as he or she faces his or her limitations.

A long-term care receiver's limitations are not likely to go away, so if anything changes it will be his or her feelings about the limitations. Encourage the care receiver to talk about his or her feelings and reflect them.

2. Focus on What the Care Receiver Can Do

Allow your long-term care receiver to do as much as possible for him- or herself. It requires substantial patience to watch someone take a very long time to do something you could do for him or her in a few seconds, but what is important is the care receiver's self-respect. You may also find it gratifying to do small tasks for your care receiver. Meet the care receiver's needs, not your own.

3. Doing for Others

Assist the care receiver to find ways to help others. Reference Box G contains some possibilities.

Ways Long-Term Care Receivers Might Help Others

1. Pray for others daily.

2. Serve on the congregation's prayer chain.

3. Minister over the telephone by:
   - calling others to check in with them;
   - calling people to remind them of meetings or service opportunities; or
   - making calls for charities that pick up used clothing and furniture from people's homes.

4. Speak to groups about what it's like to live with a disability.

5. Make useful items for less fortunate people.

6. Write caring cards to congregation members.

7. Write or dictate letters of encouragement to missionaries or people in prison.

Your long-term care receiver may need some encouragement to help others. The person may find it hard to imagine that he or she can do something that would help others or serve God. Biblical stories and passages like those in Reference Box H can provide help.

Biblical Encouragement for Those Feeling Useless

1. The prophet Jeremiah witnessed the ruin of Jerusalem and described his sense of total helplessness. Yet he shared his hope in the faithfulness of God (Lamentations 3:1–26).

2. The story of Anna (Luke 2:36–38) shows that worship, prayer, giving thanks, and sharing the Good News can be done by anyone.

3. Paul instructs Christians, regardless of their condition, to encourage others (1 Thessalonians 5:11) and to pray continually (1 Thessalonians 5:17).

4. Deciding How to Respond

Long-term care receivers can also decide how they are going to respond to their circumstances. Certainly your job as a caregiver is not to convince your care receiver that he or she has control over his or her responses. You can, however, treat responses as real choices and not as uncontrollable reactions.

Reference Box I shows a Stephen Minister helping a care receiver take responsibility for how he or she responds to his or her situation.

Helping a Care Receiver Take Responsibility

Dialogue 1

Care receiver: My doctor told me that I would have to come back for more tests next week and I just blew up at her.

Stephen Minister: You were angry.

Care receiver: I sure was. I'm sick of all these tests. Why can't they just leave me alone?

Stephen Minister: I wonder if you

really want them to leave you alone.

Care receiver *(after a pause):* No, I guess I don't. What I really want is for them to make all this go away.

Stephen Minister: And you're angry that they haven't done that.

Care receiver: Yeah, but I know it's really not their fault. They're doing the best they can.

Stephen Minister: Where else might you dump your anger?

Care receiver: Hmm . . . I suppose I could . . .

Dialogue 2

Care receiver: My daughter's piano recital is coming up soon. I wish I could go, but . . . This miserable wheelchair! *(The care receiver angrily pounds the armrest of the wheelchair.)*

Stephen Minister: You're pretty angry at that chair.

Care receiver: It ruins everything!

Stephen Minister: You'd like to go to the recital, but the wheelchair makes it impossible.

Care receiver: That's right! You can't imagine what a hassle it is to go somewhere with this thing.

Stephen Minister: I've not had to be in a wheelchair, so I can only imagine the hassle you face.

Care receiver: You have to depend upon so many people for help. It's embarrassing.

Stephen Minister: Asking for assistance. That can be tough.

Care receiver: It can be humiliating at times!

Stephen Minister: So if you went to the recital, you would have to be willing to risk humiliation.

Care receiver: Yeah . . .

Stephen Minister: If you stayed home you would avoid humiliation, but then you'd miss your daughter's piano recital.

Care receiver: Yeah . . . Some choice, huh?

Stephen Minister: A difficult choice indeed. How will you decide whether to attend or not to attend?

Other Challenges

Long-term care receivers may face other practical challenges where your care can assist them.

Maintaining Property

Long-term care receivers may no longer be able to do maintenance work on their property, and they may not be able to afford to pay others to do so. There are several ways that you might help a long-term care receiver do what he or she can.

Members of your congregation might help with painting or repairs. If your congregation has ChristCare Groups, one or more groups could help maintain the care receiver's property as their missional service project. Community resources may provide free or low cost home repair, or there may be government programs that can help. You could research the possibilities, and help your care receiver request assistance.

Obtaining Needed Medical Care

Long-term care receivers may see reporting a new problem to the doctor as just another step in the steady downhill journey. They may deny new problems, allowing them to get much worse. Care receivers may also resist following their physician's directions. Medications may cause unpleasant side effects. Daily exercises may be painful or burdensome. Some care receivers may not be able to afford the medical attention they need.

If care receivers deny that they need medical care and they are not in imminent danger, remain process-oriented and help them deal with their fears. Reference Box J provides an example.

REFERENCE BOX J

Responding to Denial

Stephen Minister: I've noticed that you haven't been able to move around as well in your wheelchair.

Care receiver: I'm doing fine.

Stephen Minister: You seem to be having trouble turning right.

Care receiver: I said I'm fine. Why do you keep harping on the subject?

Stephen Minister: I was wondering if you're experiencing new physical problems.

The care receiver looks away and refuses to answer.

The Stephen Minister remains quiet, waiting for the care receiver to continue the conversation.

Care receiver: I've been losing feeling in my right arm. Are you satisfied?

Stephen Minister: That sounds like it would be distressing.

Care receiver: Yeah, well, it is.

Stephen Minister: Have you talked with a doctor?

Care receiver: What's he going to do? He'll just tell me that pretty soon I'll be confined to a bed.

Stephen Minister: You're afraid this might mean big changes.

The care receiver looks away to hide the tears that are forming.

If care receivers need medical care and cannot afford it, investigate community resources. Clinics may offer free or low cost medical services. Get help from your Supervision Group or a Stephen Leader as you search for appropriate community resources.

Getting Sufficient Nutrition

If the care receiver is unable to do his or her own shopping, grocery stores in the area may deliver purchases. A nearby family member or congregation member might grocery shop for your care receiver.

Many communities provide home-delivered hot midday meals at little or no cost for people who cannot provide their own meals. You might help your care receiver investigate taking advantage of such a service.

If your care receiver is unable to afford nutritious food, you may be able to locate a charitable organization that provides food to those who cannot afford it.

If none of these solutions work and your care receiver is unable to get sufficiently nutritious food, he or she may need to move into a care facility that provides meals. You may need to help your care receiver come to that conclusion.

Retaining Personal Care Attendants

Long-term care receivers sometimes need personal care attendants or home health aides. Such assistance can be difficult to obtain and retain. Sometimes a care receiver:

► is eligible for a limited amount of personal attendant care under government programs but needs more care and cannot afford it;

► is eligible for a limited amount of such assistance but the current level of program funding falls short of providing the service to all who are eligible;

► does not meet certain requirements to receive public assistance; or

► can afford the services but can't find anyone willing to provide them.

Sometimes the people who provide personal care assistance:

► don't stay on the job very long;

► are not very intelligent or very caring; or

► steal from the care receiver or physically abuse him or her.

The care receiver may accept less than humane care out of fear that the attendant might quit.

How might you care? Listening empathetically will often help. In addition, you may speak on behalf of your care

receiver to government agencies, insurance carriers, or service providers. You might also help locate an agency that can teach the care receiver how to search for, interview, and screen potential attendants. You also could help search for nonprofit agencies that provide affordable home health services.

Minimizing Vulnerability to Crime

Long-term care receivers may be especially vulnerable to crime. You might help your care receiver check with the local police department to see if they provide or know of a service that inspects a home and recommends how to make it more secure. Community resources may install lighting, smoke alarms, or dead-bolt locks to make the home safer. Also make sure your care receiver has a phone available and knows how to report an emergency.

Your community may provide subsidized housing that is accessible and secure for people with disabilities. You could help your care receiver explore such housing options.

► Research Your Long-Term Care Receiver's Condition

Many injuries, illnesses, or other conditions can cause a person to be a long-term care receiver. To learn more about your care receiver's specific condition, look in the "Stephen Series Guide to Community Resources" in appendix A after the Preclass Reading for module 11, "Using Mental Health Professionals and Other Community Resources." Search the Internet; ask the care receiver, medical personnel, hospitals, and other organizations that provide informational seminars or sponsor support groups; monitor your local newspaper for helpful listings; or ask a librarian for assistance.

▶ Dealing with Challenges from Family Members

Family members may make it clear that your regular caring visits cause inconvenience or extra work. They may have to clean the house before you visit. Your visit may disrupt their daily routine of caring for your care receiver. Your need for confidentiality during your caring visits may mean that family members can't be in parts of the house where they would normally be. You may sense their frustration when you visit. They may interrupt your visit or make it uncomfortable for you.

Family members may feel guilty because they believe that your ministry to the care receiver means that they are not doing a good enough job. They may also have regular conflict with your care receiver and assume that he or she is telling you about it.

Family members may also feel overwhelmed by the challenges of living with a long-term care receiver. They may have no one who will listen and care for them, so they may dump their feelings on you.

Express Appreciation

Be sensitive to ways that your visits might cause extra work or inconvenience for the care receiver's family. Occasionally express your appreciation.

REFERENCE BOX K

Expressing Appreciation

"I know that you do a lot of things to prepare for my visits with your mother. I really enjoy my time with her. I appreciate your time and efforts in setting the stage for those visits. Thank you."

Respond Assertively to Interruptions

If your care receiver's family members interrupt your visits, respond with firm but gentle assertiveness. Remember what a challenge it is for them to care for your care receiver every day; politely ask them to give you the time and privacy you need.

REFERENCE BOX L

Responding Assertively to Interruptions

Stephen Minister: Would it be possible for us to talk for a moment before I go?

Family member: Sure, what do you need?

Stephen Minister: During the last three times I've visited with your father, you have come in to change the sheets on his bed.

Family member: Well, I do it at the same time every day, and your visits fall at that time.

Stephen Minister: I understand that you need to keep to a routine in order to care for your father and also meet all your other responsibilities. It is difficult for me to do my ministry with

> the interruptions, however; I wonder if I should arrange with your father to meet at a different time, or if you could change your routine on the days when I visit.
>
> **Family member:** If you could come a half-hour later, it would be a much more convenient time for me.
>
> **Stephen Minister:** I would be happy to come a half-hour later. Do you mind if I check with your father just to make sure he understands and agrees?

Maintain Confidentiality

Family members may ask you to reveal confidential information about your care receiver. They may have what they believe are good reasons for asking you to break confidentiality. Nonetheless, maintain confidentiality rigorously and encourage them to talk to the care receiver themselves.

Occasionally Care for Family Members

Sometimes it will be good to talk with family members for a while after you finish your visit with your care receiver. Ask them how they are doing and give them a chance to share some of their struggles. As long as family members only need you to check in with them occasionally, continue doing so.

Perhaps Suggest That Family Members Have Their Own Stephen Ministers

When family members need to share feelings regularly, you may recommend that they have their own Stephen Ministers. If a family member needs a Ste-phen Minister, check with your Stephen Leader, who will work toward an appropriate assignment.

▶ **Being a Stephen Minister to Primary Caregivers of Long-Term Care Receivers**

Primary caregivers may carry a very heavy load. They may provide much physical care, and they may be the only people that care receivers have to talk to most of the time. They may sacrifice their own free time, ambitions, and other relationships to care for the long-term care receiver for many years, carrying the responsibility alone. Such a primary caregiver may be affected almost as much as the long-term care receiver is, and he or she may also need a Stephen Minister.

Difficult Feelings

Primary caregivers may deal with difficult feelings as a result of their caregiving. They may feel angry over all they miss while caring for the long-term care receiver. Then they may feel guilty about feeling angry and tell themselves that they should be more giving. Long-term care receivers may be very difficult to live with, causing conflict between the primary caregiver and the care receiver.

Grief

Primary caregivers may grieve the losses that the long-term care receiver experiences and miss the person they knew before the illness or injury. They may also deeply grieve lost freedom and missed opportunities. They may see no hope for their life getting better.

Feeling Overwhelmed

Primary caregivers commonly feel overwhelmed meeting their own responsibilities and caring for the long-term care receiver. This can be more responsibility than they can bear, and they may need help figuring out what they can and cannot do. A caregiver can also help them deal with the feelings that come with their decisions. For example, if they decide to move the care receiver to a long-term care facility, they may need help dealing with guilt. If they give up their job to care for the care receiver, they may need help processing their anger.

Needing to Get Away

In the midst of this welter of feelings, the caregiver may long to get away.

REFERENCE BOX M

Taking Time Off

Perhaps the most important and valuable coping strategy is the arrangement of an adequate amount of "time off" to run errands and to engage in recreational and social activities. The research is quite clear that individuals who do not obtain a sufficient amount of time off feel a much greater sense of burden and have less success managing their emotional and physical health.[1]

---

1 Raye Lynne Dippel, "The Caregivers," in *Caring for the Alzheimer Patient: A Practical Guide*, ed. Raye Lynne Dippel and J. Thomas Hutton (Buffalo, NY: Prometheus Books, 1988), p. 20.

Caring for Primary Caregivers

Your basic Stephen Ministry skills and awareness of community resources are your best tools in caring for primary caregivers.

Listening and Sharing Feelings

Ministry to primary caregivers involves listening and helping them to get their feelings out into the open. Since primary caregivers may experience isolation due to the time they spend providing care, you may be the one who gives them a chance to unload.

Assertiveness

If the primary caregiver and the long-term care receiver have regular conflict, one or both of them may need to communicate more assertively. You may talk about assertiveness, or lend the primary caregiver your copy of *Speaking the Truth in Love* and discuss it.

Respite Care

Respite care means someone's taking over the primary caregiver's caregiving responsibilities for a while so he or she can focus on personal needs. You may offer to provide for the long-term care receiver's needs on occasion, enlist others in the congregation to spend time with the long-term care receiver, or help locate community adult day-care programs or respite care services.

Community Resources and Support Groups

You may also help primary caregivers investigate and use community resources and support groups that provide practical help and encouragement from experienced persons.

▶ Getting Ready for the In-Class Sessions

In this module's in-class continuing education you will consider the barriers to effective care for long-term care receivers, learn more about how to care for long-term care receivers, and think about the personal commitment and maturity necessary to care for long-term care receivers.

Appendix A

Caring for Long-Term Care Receivers in Nursing Homes

Nursing home residents are common recipients of long-term care. Many issues addressed in this module clearly pertain to ministry with persons in nursing homes. These issues are sometimes uniquely experienced in the nursing home, however. Stephen Ministers need to be aware of concerns.

▶ Challenges in Nursing Home Life

Some nursing home residents adjust very well to their new surroundings. People who have been living alone, for example, may welcome contact with others. They may be less anxious or fearful for their safety, or they may be relieved to no longer have the burden of maintaining a home. Many, however, find the transition to nursing home life difficult. They find much more to grieve and mourn than celebrate. Even persons who acclimate well to the nursing home can experience several key losses.

Loss of Autonomy

Long-term care receivers experience some loss of autonomy due to their disabilities. The institutional environment of a nursing home, however, can exacerbate this loss. Moving to a nursing home can signify handing the responsibility for one's life over to others. Family members may have made the decision for the care receiver, or there may have been no other available option.

The nursing home resident's loss of autonomy progresses as his or her stay continues. Nursing home residents have little control over their environment or schedule. They depend upon staff and family members to meet their life needs. The needs of the nursing home often override the personal preferences of individual residents.

Most nursing home residents also have little financial autonomy. Due to the high cost of nursing home care, many depend upon government resources and thus have little or no money to spend as they wish. Residents who do have adequate financial resources often ask family members to manage them. Even though it is the care receiver's money to spend, the person monitoring those finances may closely control them. The loss of such basic decision-making power can lead to feelings of helplessness and frustration.

Loss of Connection

Due to the lack of space, nursing home residents typically have few personal possessions. Treasured pieces of furniture are too large and valuables cannot be kept safely; thus, the person often has little to connect him or her with life prior to the nursing home. For residents with some mental limitations, this can lead to further disorientation and confusion.

Nursing home staff are the persons with whom residents spend the most time and they typically have not had prior contact with the resident. They may only see him or her as another sick person to care for. Both staff and residents miss out when daily life is focused on the care receiver's condition and not on the whole person, who is created in the image of God and who possesses unique interests, needs, and capabilities.

Loss of Companionship

The loss of familiar surroundings is compounded by the loss of meaningful companionship. Friends of elderly residents in nursing homes may have died or now live in other institutions. Some have no family in the area. Some may have moved from their home communities in order to find adequate care or be closer to relatives. Even those with family and friends nearby can experience long periods of solitude between visits.

Making new friends in the nursing home environment may be difficult. Residents typically have roommates, but this could be with someone who has completely different interests or an incompatible personality. A lucid person may be in a room with someone who is cognitively impaired, thus making a coherent conversation difficult, let alone a relationship.

Loss of Meaning in Life

Most nursing home residents know that this will be their last home. The future can seem predetermined and bleak. Care receivers undoubtedly have negative images of nursing home life from their culture and possibly from experiences with other relatives or friends. Residents may think they have little to offer to others. The thought that they have been put out to pasture can predominate, which can contribute to depression.

▶ Respect: The Key to Effective Nursing Home Ministry

With all the previously described losses, a care receiver may feel insignificant and not very valuable. The Stephen Minister must do everything possible to convey a sense of the person's worth and value. Treating your care receiver respectfully is the key. Address your care receiver by name, particularly at the beginning of your conversation. This creates a personal connection. Be especially diligent in maintaining eye contact and using reflective listening techniques to communicate your interest in what the care receiver says.

Although the physical environment may resemble a hospital, you are entering your care receiver's home. Treat his or her limited personal space as respectfully as possible. Wait until the person invites you to sit, turn on a light, or turn off the television. These simple acts can promote a feeling of control and ownership.

Respect can also be communicated by bringing small tokens like the weekly church bulletins, a devotional tract, or flowers. This shows the care receiver that you value him or her and also provides a remembrance of your visit.

Treat the other persons you encounter in the nursing home respectfully also. Greet any persons who address you as you enter or leave the building. Be especially aware of your care receiver's roommate. Say hello to him or her as you enter the room. You can also mention the roommate in prayers if this seems appropriate.

Be respectful also of nursing home staff. Call the nursing home first to determine their visitation policies. Are there set visiting hours? Do you need to sign in? Be sure to follow the proper procedures faithfully. Try to avoid visiting during mealtimes and other activities.

If a staff member is with your care receiver when you arrive, wait until he or she leaves before entering the room. If a doctor, nurse, or other caregiver comes while you are visiting, either step aside or leave the room while the other person attends to your care receiver. Staff members are often on a tight schedule, so your being flexible is important.

You also show respect when you keep opinions about your care receiver's caregivers or family to yourself. Do not criticize or defend any persons interacting with your care receiver. You may think that the care receiver's family members are not visiting often enough, but it will serve no purpose to share this belief with your care receiver. They may not visit often, but you have little if any knowledge of circumstances that may inhibit visitation. Your care receiver's memory may be faulty. A son or daughter could have visited an hour before you, but the care receiver may not remember. Focus on the care receiver's feelings and concerns and not your own.

▶ Ways to Meet Care Receivers' Needs in Nursing Homes

Most care receivers in nursing homes are glad to have a regular visitor. Your skills as a Stephen Minister can help make these visits particularly meaning-ful for your care receiver. Beyond being a good listener, however, you may become aware of ways that you can help improve your care receiver's quality of life.

If your care receiver has a lot of idle time, ask him or her about past interests and hobbies. Determine why he or she no longer pursues these activities. If the person is physically able, find out if any groups with compatible interests are currently offered by the nursing home. Discuss the possibility of his or her joining such an activity and listen carefully to concerns he or she may have. If your care receiver feels shy or insecure, offer to go with him or her to the activity once or twice if you can. This may help your care receiver establish a routine of doing something enjoyable.

If activities your care receiver enjoys are not available in the nursing home, talk to your pastor or Supervision Group about what resources might be available in the church or community for the care receiver. For example, if your care receiver is able to knit but does not have the money to buy yarn, see if a person or group at your congregation could provide the yarn for the person to knit scarves or mittens for the church fair or a local homeless shelter. Such activity will not only provide your care receiver with enjoyment, but can help him or her contribute to the community. Be sure to talk with other groups in your congregation about activities that some elderly persons might be able to do, such as sending cards to sick members or stuffing envelopes for church mailings.

Religious practices are also important to many elderly persons. Most nursing homes offer religious services. If your care receiver is not attending such services, discuss that possibility with him or her. Find out if other religious practices are or have been important to the person and see if there are resources that could help make these practices easier, such as a large print Bible or books on tape. Work with your care receiver to help ease the transition to any new forms of devotional material or worship.

If your care receiver is in relatively good health, explore the possibility of getting him or her out of the nursing home for special worship services or other activities. Check with the nursing home administration regarding the procedure for such an outing before discussing it with your care receiver.

▶ Advocating for Care Receivers in Nursing Homes

Even though your primary role is as an active listener, sometimes you may see problems and believe you must take action.

The best choice is usually to help the care receiver advocate for him- or herself. This can give the person a heightened sense of control. Work with the care receiver to explore ways to address his or her concerns, possibly roleplaying a conversation between your care receiver and the other person.

The second choice would be to inform the family of your care receiver's concerns so they can advocate for their loved one. Be sure to get your care receiver's permission before you share such information with his or her family.

If you suspect abuse or neglect of your care receiver, bring it up immediately with your Supervision Group or Stephen Leader in order to get the appropriate help.

Despite its many challenges, providing care for someone in a nursing home can be very rewarding. The attentive presence of a Stephen Minister can make a significant difference in a nursing home resident's life.

Ministering to Persons Needing Long-Term Care

Outline and Focus Notes

I was sick and you looked after me . . .

Matthew 25:36b

I. Looking for Jesus

FOCUS NOTE 1

The Last Judgment

"When the Son of Man comes in his glory, and all the angels with him, he will sit on his throne in heavenly glory. All the nations will be gathered before him, and he will separate the people one from another as a shepherd separates the sheep from the goats. He will put the sheep on his right and the goats on his left.

"Then the King will say to those on his right, 'Come, you who are blessed by my Father; take your inheritance, the kingdom prepared for you since the creation of the world. For I was hungry and you gave me something to eat, I was thirsty and you gave me something to drink, I was a stranger and you invited me in, I needed clothes and you clothed me, I was sick and you looked after me, I was in prison and you came to visit me.'

"Then the righteous will answer him, 'Lord, when did we see you hungry and feed you, or thirsty and give you something to drink? When did we see you a stranger and invite you in, or needing clothes and clothe you? When did we see you sick or in prison and go to visit you?'

"The King will reply, 'I tell you the truth, whatever you did for one of the least of these brothers of mine, you did for me.'"

Matthew 25:31–40

II. Barriers to Long-Term Caregiving

A. Barriers in the Care Receiver

1. Inability to Communicate

2. Depression

3. Anger

4. Manipulation and Boundary Issues

FOCUS NOTE 2

Four Types of Boundary Problems[1]

	Can't Say	Can't Hear
No	**The Compliant** Feels guilty or controlled by others, or both; can't set boundaries	**The Controller** Aggressively or manipulatively violates boundaries of others
Yes	**The Nonresponsive** Sets boundaries against providing love and care to others	**The Avoidant** Sets boundaries against receiving love and care from others

---

5. Faith Struggles

B. Barriers in the Stephen Minister

1. Motivation for Caregiving

---

1 Adapted from Henry Cloud and John Townsend, *Boundaries* (Grand Rapids, MI: Zondervan Publishing House, 1992), p. 59.

2. Lack of Results and Self-Esteem Issues

3. Boundary Issues

4. Faith Issues

C. Facing Barriers

FOCUS NOTE 3

Responding to Barriers

1. Working as a group, choose one of the barriers you just heard about, either a barrier for a care receiver or one for a Stephen Minister.

2. Brainstorm as many ways as you can think of to address that barrier.

3. Distill your brainstorming ideas and come up with a short answer to the question, "If I faced this barrier, in my care receiver or in myself, how could I respond to it?"

4. Write your group's answer in the space below and be prepared to share it with the rest of the class. Do all this in five minutes.

III. Looking Ahead

IV. Opening

V. Visiting with Long-Term Care Receivers

FOCUS NOTE 4

Sally Renberg's Tips for Visitors

1. Remember that you're dealing with individuals, so be careful you don't make your visits appear like "Official Calling Routines."

2. When you arrive, ask the person how he or she is; don't say, "You are looking well." This is because looks can be deceiving; especially if the person is an S.L.E. patient, has high blood pressure, or is taking certain medications.

3. Ask the person to let you know if you've stayed long enough. Don't count on getting an honest answer, however. Having company is too much fun even if exhausting. Instead, cut your visit off at any sign of fatigue. Ten minutes to one-half hour is a good range. As you visit again, you will learn to recognize signs that the person is getting weary and it's time to leave.

4. If you want the person to call you if he or she would like to talk, invite him or her to do so. Remember that the person may be reluctant to disturb you. Often it is when one is most upset that it is hardest to pick up the phone because one feels no one else could possibly be interested in one's problems.

5. Encourage the person to call by telling him or her when it is usually possible to catch you at home. If you think the person is depressed, call between visits. Even a brief sentence or two will lend encouragement. Soon you will be able to discern "moods," even on the telephone.

6. As a Stephen Minister, you probably won't be bringing gifts or flowers, but bring something of little monetary value, such as a funny cartoon or a couple of cookies (so you can sit down and enjoy them).

7. Here are some other gift suggestions: one flower from your yard; a wee bunch of sunny dandelions; two tea bags of a special herbal tea; a bright fall leaf; a tiny sprig of a bush almost ready to bloom; a copy of an amusing article; an unusual magazine; or photos of your children or grandchildren to share.

8. Be honest. Don't hesitate to ask questions about the illness or your care receiver's needs. Make it clear to your care receiver that you don't have to talk about the subject if he or she doesn't want to. Never lie.

9. If the individual has a chronic illness, ask if there is a book or arti-

---

cle on the subject he or she might share with you. Research the disease a bit before visiting. Many hospitals have brief telephone information tips about particular conditions.

10. If you believe the two of you have had a personality clash, make contact again immediately so that the person won't feel he or she turned you off.

11. Many of these ideas may seem trivial. Why would someone feel bad because you visited? Remember that those who are incapacitated have a lot of time to think about a lot of things.

A. Treat Care Receivers as Individuals

B. Ask the Person How He or She Is

C. Ask the Care Receiver to Tell You When You've Stayed Long Enough

D. Invite Your Care Receiver to Call You

FOCUS NOTE 5

Assertively Setting Limits on Telephone Calls

"We talked about how you are welcome to call me, and I'm glad that you are doing so when you need someone to talk to. For the past week, however, we've talked for over an hour every day. I'm afraid that I can't do that every day. I would like you to continue calling me, but I would like you to limit your calls to no more than two a week unless there's an emergency. I hope that's all right with you."

E. Bring Small Gifts

F. Find Out about Your Care Receiver's Illness or Injury

G. Respond Quickly to Clashes

H. Be Aware of the Care Receiver's Level of Sensitivity

VI. What You Bring to Long-Term Caregiving

Reflecting on Yourself as a Long-Term Caregiver

1. What about you—your experiences, your gifts and strengths, your faith, or your personality—will help you be an effective Stephen Minister with long-term care receivers?

2. What about you—your experiences, your weaknesses, your doubts, or your personality—might keep you from being an effective Stephen Minister with long-term care receivers?

3. How might you need to change in order to be an effective Stephen Minister with long-term care receivers? How do you think those changes could take place?

Characteristics

Characteristics That Make for Effective Caregiving	Characteristics That Make for Ineffective Caregiving

VII. Looking Ahead

VIII. Opening

IX. Support, Encouragement, and Accountability for Stephen Ministers Providing Long-Term Care

A. Skit 1: "Nothing ever happens. I'm bored."

FOCUS NOTE 8

Skit 1

Characters:
In-depth reporter **(IDR)**
Supervision Group Facilitator **(SGF)**
Stephen Minister **(SM)**

SGF: Pat, it's your turn to be in the spotlight and make an in-depth report about your caring relationship. Which in-depth tool did you choose?

IDR: I didn't really bother with writing out an in-depth report. There's really not a lot of point in it.

SGF: There's not a lot of point in writing out your in-depth report?

IDR: No, not really. *(Shrugs.)*

SM: Tell me more, Pat.

IDR: I could just use the report I wrote out a month ago or three months ago. Not a thing has changed with this care receiver since then.

SGF: I don't see how that could happen. Everybody changes.

IDR: You don't know my care receiver. *[He/she]* has talked about the same topic every single time I have visited. *[He/she]* says, "Oh, I wish my children would visit me more." I ask if *[he/she]* has invited them. Then *[he/she]* says, "Oh, no. I don't want to be a burden. They're so busy." So I ask, "Well, what do you want to do?" The reply is always the same. "Oh, I don't know. I do wish they'd come and visit more, though."

SM: Even if your care receiver never changes, what about you? Are you changing because of this caring relationship?

IDR: The only change I can see is that I become more bored every time I visit.

B. Skit 2: "I've tried everything I know to get my care receiver to change, and *[she/he]* just won't."

FOCUS NOTE 9

Skit 2

Characters:
In-depth reporter **(IDR)**
Supervision Group Facilitator **(SGF)**
Stephen Minister **(SM)**

IDR: So I guess the help I need most from all of you is to figure out what I can do to motivate my care receiver. I've tried everything I know to get my care receiver to change, and *[she/he]* just won't.

SM: What changes do you think your care receiver needs to make?

IDR: My care receiver has been through some very tough times in the last year, and I understand how *[she/he]* would be depressed and all, but *[she/he]* is still young with a whole life ahead. Sure, there are things *[she/he]* can't do anymore, but there are also many things *[she/he]* can still do. It's time to focus on the positive and look to the future.

SM: What does your care receiver say when you suggest that?

IDR: Not a lot. *[She/He]* hardly ever says very much anymore.

SGF: Is that a change?

IDP: Yeah, I suppose it is. *[She / He]* used to talk a whole lot more.

SGF: Can you remember if you started doing anything different at the time when your care receiver's amount of talking changed?

IDR: I imagine it was about the time when I started trying to get *[her / him]* to think about the future.

C. Skit 3: "I just don't know if I can stand *[her/his]* pain much longer."

FOCUS NOTE 10

Skit 3

Characters
In-depth reporter **(IDR)**
Supervision Group Facilitator **(SGF)**
Stephen Minister **(SM)**

SGF: Pat, you seem as depressed as you say your care receiver is.

IDR: Caring for my care receiver has been unbelievably difficult. *[She/He]* is in such terrible emotional pain, and as *[her/his]* Stephen Minister it's my responsibility to help carry that pain. I just don't know if I can stand *[her / his]* pain much longer.

SM: How has it affected you?

IDR: I seem to catch my care receiver's mood. Before the caring visit I'll be happy and carefree, but then when I visit my care receiver I come away with a stomachache and I feel helpless. Some nights I can't sleep because I can't stop thinking about *[her/him]* and wondering what I could do for *[her/him]*.

SM: Do you think your care receiver is benefiting from your ministry?

IDR: I suppose so. I'm afraid to ask. *[She/He]* certainly doesn't seem to be getting any better.

SGF: What do you think it would take for *[her/him]* to get better?

IDR: I just don't know. But I'm beginning to think that *[she/he]* needs someone other than me to help.

X. Caregiver's Compass Review

_____

_____

_____

_____

_____   _____

_____   _____

_____   _____

_____   _____

_____

_____

_____

_____

XI. Looking Ahead

Prayer Partner Requests and Thanksgivings

My prayer partner is _____

Prayer requests and thanksgivings to share with my prayer partner

_____

_____

Prayer requests and thanksgivings shared by my prayer partner

_____

_____

Ministering to Those Experiencing Divorce

Contents

▶ The Day After

Patrick sat in his apartment. Most of the boxes that contained his possessions were still packed and strewed around the twenty-foot-by-twenty-foot room that served as living room, dining room, office, and guest bedroom. He hated the mess and the lack of organization, but he couldn't summon the energy to get up and start putting things away. It was going to take a lot of organization to survive in an apartment this small, but he didn't see how he was even going to afford this one, with the child care and alimony payments and the lawyer bills.

"I wonder where Janie, Andy, and Sean will sleep when they come to see me," Patrick thought. "Not much of a place to bring kids to. That is, if Michelle actually lets the kids come here. She may just decide to stick the knife in and twist it again by finding some excuse to keep me from seeing my children."

Patrick had some work he needed to get to that evening. He had fallen far behind at the office with all the meetings with lawyers and having to find the apartment and move out. He really needed to get caught up. He was a failure as a husband and as a father now—he didn't know if he could stand being a failure at work too.

All he could think of doing, though, was going out barhopping as he had done with his friends in college over twenty years ago. He hadn't done that since he'd gotten married. It just hadn't fit his new responsibilities and position in life. Now, he didn't know what his position in life was. Going out drinking seemed just as natural—or unnatural—as the thought of getting ready to go to work in the morning.

He hadn't wanted the divorce. He believed that Michelle had been selfish to demand it. Now she had ended up with the house and custody of the kids, and Patrick had 14 packed boxes to show for the last 20 years of his life.

****

Ministering to those experiencing divorce, and to their families and friends, is a kind of caring that requires much acceptance and sensitivity. Divorce is an enormously painful experience—many say it is as difficult as when a loved one dies. Some people find it even more difficult because in divorce the other person is never really gone. To make matters worse, divorcing persons rarely receive the kind of care that is available to people who suffer other major losses such as the death of a spouse.

Divorce is often accompanied by judgment—from self, family, the church, and society. Divorcing persons may blame themselves and wonder what they did wrong. Children of divorce may believe the divorce is somehow their fault. Friends and family may become very angry and condemning. Divorcing persons may even feel judged by God.

This Preclass Reading will give you an idea of what the experience of divorce is like. You will better understand divorce from the point of view of divorcing persons, as well as their families and friends. Then you can use your distinctively Christian caring skills, all you have learned in other Stephen Ministry training sessions, and the love God has given you to care for people caught up in the tragedy of divorce. The Spirit will use your care to bring healing and new life.

▶ **The Pervasiveness of Divorce**

Divorce is an everyday reality in our society. Some estimates suggest that 40–50 percent of all marriages are expected to end in divorce. The ratio for divorce in second marriages appears to be even higher. There are few people in the United States who have not felt the sting of divorce—if not in their own marriages or those of their parents, then among friends, siblings, other relatives, or church members. To a greater or lesser extent, this is the case in many other cultures as well.

▶ An Opportunity for Christlike Care

Unfortunately, sometimes congregation members choose not to care for divorcing persons. They may believe that God's opposition to divorce means they should reject divorcing persons and their families and friends. They may fear that by accepting and loving those who have been touched by divorce, they will encourage others to divorce also. Churches sometimes simply don't feel up to dealing with the pain of divorce and the responsibility of caring for divorcing persons and their families and friends.

But Jesus said, "'It is not the healthy who need a doctor, but the sick. But go and learn what this means: "I desire mercy, not sacrifice." For I have not come to call the righteous, but sinners'" (Matthew 9:12–13). Divorce gives the church an opportunity to follow Jesus' example by bringing care to those who are in need. Those who are experiencing the pain of divorce—their own or someone else's—are some of the sick people Jesus said he came to save. As the body of Christ we are called to follow our Lord's example and give acceptance and care to those who need it the most.

▶ The Experience of Divorce for the Divorcing Couple

Divorce is more than a legal action. It is an emotional journey—one that often takes years. It can be helpful for caregivers to know some of the reasons why this journey is such a painful one.

What Makes Divorce So Painful?

An Open Wound

Many people describe divorce as a wound that never really heals. Even after the marriage ends, matters such as children, property, and money arrangements continue to need attention. For many people, it is impossible simply to cut all ties to the ex-spouse and get on with the work of grieving. Instead, the former couple must continue to deal with each other, reopening the wound again and again.

Take the case of a divorced couple with children. Not only are there custody and visitation arrangements to be worked out, but there are questions of schooling, discipline, religious training, holidays . . . the list goes on and on. Each issue may require anything from a short telephone call to a court battle to settle it. Each issue has the potential to become a battlefield between ex-spouses who want to pass on the hurt they themselves are feeling.

This makes it difficult to let go of the relationship and find healing. It is hard to get over difficult feelings like anger, hurt, and jealousy when they are regularly reinforced by new injuries, deliberate or otherwise. People may find it almost impossible to get on with their new lives while the old life is still demanding so much energy.

Failure

One of the most painful feelings that divorcing people experience is the feeling of having failed. Whenever they look at their children, they see how the failed marriage has caused pain. Friends and relatives say "I told you so," or, "Why did you ever marry *[him/her]* in the first place?" Even loan applications remind them of failure when they come to the heading *marital status* and are forced to mark *unmarried* or *divorced.*

Many people feel like failures because they were always taught that marriage is to be forever. They promised in a solemn church service to remain married for the rest of their lives, but were unable to keep that promise.

They may also feel like failures before God. They wince when they remember Jesus' words, "Therefore what God has joined together, let no one separate" (Matthew 19:6 NRSV). They often believe they have let God down and wonder if he still cares for them after they have failed to live up to his standards. These deep feelings of failure can lead to depression and loss of self-esteem.

Loss of Identity

Divorcing people face another struggle: the loss of identity. Many people build their self-image on their marriage and family. They feel complete as part of a couple, as part of a family. When that relationship is broken, they may start to wonder who they are and what their life means.

The loss of identity hurts in many little, unexpected ways. Many women face it whenever they sign their names. Should they retain their married name or go back to using their maiden name? The question becomes even more difficult when the ex-spouse has remarried and there is another Mrs. So-and-so to share a name with, or when children want their mother to have the same last name they have.

As they search for a new identity, divorcing persons may act in ways that are out of character. A quiet, stay-at-home person may start going out to bars and staying out very late. A responsible person may quit his or her job and make plans to become a beachcomber. While this behavior may seem bizarre, it is usually short-lived. It is one way the divorced person begins to carve out a new identity.

Loss of Structure

A related problem for some divorcing persons is loss of structure. Many of the responsibilities and expectations that gave their lives stability are gone. They no longer have to meet the expectations of a spouse (and sometimes children).

Divorced people may feel more free to leave the city or even the state. They may decide to switch careers or take up new interests. If they live alone, there is little pressure to abide by their former values. They may begin drinking more heavily or bring dates home to spend the night.

Rejection

One of the most terrible feelings of the divorce experience can be that of rejection. The essence of divorce is rejection. It is very difficult for individuals to think well of themselves when their spouses, who knew them better than anyone else in the world, have decided that they are not worth living with.

Family members may reject the divorcing person. Parents and siblings may blame him or her for failing to keep the marriage together. Children hurt by the divorce may withdraw from one or both of the divorced parents, causing them to feel even more rejected.

Friends may also stop socializing with the divorcing person. Sometimes friends do this because they simply don't know what to say to him or her. Other times friends who have known the person as part of a married couple may fear that this newly single person is a threat to their own marriages. No matter what the reason is, the divorcing person will probably feel rejected as a result.

A divorcing person can also experience painful rejection from people in church. This rejection may be subtle. People no longer talk much to him or her. People glance at the person and quickly look away. He or she is no longer invited to participate in activities. But rejection may also be more straightforward. Church members or leaders may quote Bible passages about the sin of divorce or even suggest that the divorcing person find a different church to join. Since the people of the church serve as God's representatives, the divorcing person can easily interpret their rejection as God's rejection. This can be very damaging to the divorcing person's relationship with God.

Feelings of rejection can lead to intense sadness and depression. Rejection can leave divorcing persons without the courage and support they need to face their pain and journey through it.

Stages in the Divorcing Process

As with any major loss, people who divorce go through several more or less predictable emotional stages. This module describes three broad stages—resistance, grief, and recovery—divorcing people may go through. These stages don't always happen in the order described below, nor does every person experience all of them. The stages described below are intended as a general road map to show what divorcing persons experience.

Stage One: Resistance

The initial reaction to a divorce is often to resist it or to resist the emotional impact of it. Some people will deny that the divorce is taking place or even continue to behave as if the marriage were still alive after it is dead. You might find divorcing people keeping the relationship alive, at least in their emotions, through extreme anger or guilt. Some people will resist the divorce by trying to bargain it away. Finally, however, in order to continue into the next stage of the divorce process, people must reach the point where they accept the reality of the divorce.

Denial

Denial is often what fuels the resistance stage of the divorcing process. People in denial cannot yet face the reality of the end of the marriage. Sometimes they deny the fact that the marriage is indeed over. At other times, they deny their feelings of hurt and loss.

Denial may start before anyone says the word *divorce*. When a married couple is in such pain that divorce crosses their minds, often their first reaction is to deny the reality of the pain. They tell themselves that the situation really isn't so bad and they can live with it. This can be true even in cases of spousal abuse where one partner is hurting the other very badly.

Denial can be very strong when one partner finally announces that the marriage is over. The other person may respond with disbelief: "You can't really mean that!" It takes a while for the news to sink in and sometimes it never really does. Sometimes people remain in denial for years after the marriage has ended, still expecting that they will eventually get back together with the ex-spouse.

A certain amount of denial is normal. Denial allows people the time to gather their internal resources in order to deal with the pain of a great loss. It is a kind of buffer that protects the person during the initial trauma. Yet when denial goes on too long, it becomes unhealthy. The only way to recover from a divorce is to grieve the losses that it brings. People in denial, however, can't grieve, because they can't admit that the loss has actually happened.

Another common way of expressing denial is to pretend that painful feelings don't exist. Often people will admit that the marriage is over but deny that they feel any sense of loss or sadness. They may hide these painful feelings from others and even from themselves, preferring to stay emotionally numb.

Again, some denial is normal. When people deny their feelings too long, however, they never have the chance to work through them in a healthy way. Instead, they may spend years stuck in terrible anger or irrational guilt. They may even quickly get married again to someone who is very similar to their ex-spouse, because it is easier to make the same mistake twice than to face the consequences of the first one.

Is everyone who shows very little sadness or hurt in denial? Not necessarily. Occasionally people are so relieved at the end of the marriage that they express very few painful feelings. In other cases, people have already done a great deal of the hard work of grieving before you meet them. Even so, don't assume that a care receiver who doesn't have many painful feelings is fully recovered. Instead, do a lot of careful listening to find out how your care receiver is feeling and reacting. Be patient and give him or her a lot of time to come to terms with painful feelings. If you suspect that your care receiver is stuck in denial, bring the issue up in your Supervision Group.

Anger and Guilt

In the resistance stage, many people experience extreme anger or guilt—feelings that seem out of proportion and often largely irrational. The feelings of anger or guilt may become so strong that they seem to consume the person.

During times of extreme anger, divorcing persons may lash out at their spouses. These attacks can be devastating because the spouses know each other so well that they know exactly what will hurt most. Some divorcing persons even use their children, friends, or family members in order to make their spouses hurt as much as they themselves are hurting. They may withhold needed support money even though this means their own children live in poverty. They may take or destroy items of great value to their spouses. Some even get so angry that they physically injure the other person.

Guilt can be another form of anger—one directed against the self. Those who experience guilt can also go to extremes. They may voluntarily give up the right to visit children or part with prized possessions in order to punish themselves. Some divorcing persons even consider or commit suicide as an expression of their extreme anger against themselves.

In most cases, these extreme feelings last only a short time. Feelings come back into proportion; feelings of anger and guilt subside to more reasonable, manageable levels. Divorcing persons continue to feel anger and guilt, but as time goes on these feelings are based more on actual wrongs rather than on an undefined, global feeling of hurt.

Unfortunately, there are a few individuals who remain stuck in terrible anger or guilt for years, leaving themselves crippled by these feelings. The divorce remains at the center of their lives for years and even decades. They can't let go.

This may be a form of denial: people are unwilling to let the relationship be completely over. Even though it hurts to feel anger or guilt, they hang on to these feelings rather than let go their last ties to the relationship.

Why do some individuals feel predominantly angry, while others experience mostly guilt? Sometimes it depends on personality. Some tend to blame others when things go wrong, while others blame themselves. Sometimes it has to do with who initiated the divorce proceedings, or with a particular event (such as an extramarital affair) that precipitated the divorce.

Don't expect feelings of guilt and anger to be based on logic. Guilt feelings often aren't logical and don't prove that the person was primarily responsible for the divorce. Feelings of anger don't always mean that the person was an innocent, injured party. Some individuals feel a great deal of guilt for leaving a spouse even in cases of child or spousal abuse. Others feel intense anger when their spouses finally leave them, even though they themselves did everything they could to sabotage the marriage.

Bargaining

Spouses may make one last try to salvage the marriage, promising to change certain behaviors. Others will finally agree to see a pastor or counselor. In some cases this works, and the divorce process stops. But in other cases, this last-ditch effort fails and one or both partners decide that the marriage is over.

Bargaining is one more way people put off facing the reality of the loss. People can get stuck bargaining, just as in anger or guilt. Some people continue to bargain for years, trying to resume the marriage even though the ex-spouse has made it clear he or she is not open to that. There have been cases in which one kept trying to salvage the marriage even after the other partner remarried!

Psychological Divorce

In a healthy recovery from divorce, there eventually comes a point when individuals give up most of their denial and admit that the marriage is really over. This milestone has been called *psychological divorce*. Once people admit to themselves that a major loss has occurred and cannot be remedied, they are ready to start the grieving process.

Stage Two: Grief

Grief is difficult, as you know from module 12, "Ministering to Those Experiencing Grief." Those in this stage of divorce continue to work through such painful emotions as anger, guilt, and depression. The insights you have gained from the grief module and from module 13, "Dealing with Depression: The Stephen Minister's Role," will help you care for divorcing people who are doing the hard work of grieving.

The Difficulty and Necessity of Grieving a Divorce

You have read that divorce can be as painful as the death of a loved one. Society has developed many supports for people who grieve the death of a loved one. Unfortunately, few if any of those supports are available to people grieving the loss of a marriage.

Immediately after a death there is often an outpouring of support. People may travel great distances to be with their relatives so that they won't have to be alone. Neighbors bring over meals, understanding that all of the emotional demands of grief make it hard to carry on with the normal responsibilities of life. The church supports grieving people in many ways, from pastoral visits to the funeral service.

After a divorce, however, there is rarely any support. Divorcing persons are left alone to deal with their pain as best they can. They may suffer rejection from those whose support they need most— their family members, friends, and the church. There is no funeral service, no public ceremony where loved ones can gather to admit the terrible reality of the loss. Instead people often refuse to talk about the subject, even if the divorcing person brings it up.

How do divorcing people cope with their grief? Often they try to suppress their pain, to pretend it isn't there. They may find it too difficult to face alone. They may also suppress their pain because friends and family tell them that sadness is wrong. They may hear advice such as "You should be relieved to be finished with that marriage. Why are you crying? Get on with your life."

Yet suppressing pain is not a healthy way for people to deal with divorce. The feelings will come out, one way or another. If people cannot face their feelings, they may develop physical problems, get into new and unhealthy relationships, remain stuck in guilt, or continue to take out their extreme anger on others.

Divorcing people need to do the hard work of grieving. They need to recognize, accept, and express the feelings they are having, so that they can eventually work through them.

Taking a Life Apart to Put It Back Together

As a divorcing person grieves, he or she learns to live without a relationship that has been very important, perhaps at the center of his or her life. This is a time of taking the old life apart and getting used to the fact that some of the parts don't work anymore.

Taking apart the old life really hurts. The divorcing person may experience intense feelings of sadness, anger, hurt, loss, frustration, guilt, regret, depression, and despair. This can go on for months and even years. Many times the divorcing person feels as if the pain will never end.

Stage Three: Recovery

Finally, however, many divorcing persons reach the point where the feelings aren't as intense anymore. Most (although not all) of the grieving is over. They find themselves thinking more about the future and less about the past. They find the energy to do new things. They establish new relationships. It's time to construct a new life.

This stage is called *recovery*. While this is generally a happier and less painful stage, it has its own difficulties. It takes courage to try out new ways of living. Finding a new set of friends can be difficult. It can also be difficult to start dating again. Divorce tends to deflate a person's self-confidence, and it takes a lot of time and patience to build it back up.

Recovery is rarely complete. Most people must continue to deal with reminders of the old life—children, money arrangements, and possible problems with the ex-spouse. These parts of the old life can cause problems in the new one—for example, conflict between a new spouse and children from the old marriage.

Nevertheless, this is a time of hope. Those who have done the hard work of grieving can come out of the divorce with new self-confidence and coping skills. They may have a new understanding of self that can only come from having been through such a challenging experience. These gifts can even make it possible for them to establish a much more satisfying and successful relationship the next time around.

▶ The Experience of Divorce for Children

While Stephen Ministers do not care for minors, they do care for parents who have responsibility for their children. This section will help you understand what the experience of divorce can be like for children. Equipped with this knowledge, you can then help a divorcing care receiver understand and interpret his or her children's experience of divorce and decide how the care receiver can care for his or her children.

Many times children are the forgotten participants in a divorce. Because they are young and have difficulty expressing their feelings directly, many people assume that they have no major need for care. They assume that children will bounce back quickly.

Unfortunately, this is not the case. Children experience many of the same needs that adults do, but have far fewer resources for meeting them. One study found that only ten percent of children had anyone to talk to about divorce. Very often parents have a lot of trouble meeting their children's needs for care because they have all they can handle dealing with their own divorce crisis. Your care for a divorcing parent can help him or her become emotionally able to care for his or her children.

How do children experience divorce? First, you will take a broad look at this. Then the chart that follows this section, on pages 603–605, gives greater detail on specific ways that children of different ages may express their feelings.

Divorce As Loss

For children, as for adults, the divorce process is a time of loss. Chief among these losses are loss of security and loss of relationships.

Children derive feelings of security from a predictable, safe family life. This changes during divorce. One parent is largely absent. This means that all the activities and family rituals that centered around him or her are changed also. Someone else—either the other parent or a babysitter—may be making toast, picking the children up from school, or tucking them into bed. Little League or swimming lessons may fall by the wayside, now that the involved parent is no longer available. Money problems may force the custodial parent to work different or longer hours than before, also affecting the family routine. If the children must move because of the divorce, they also lose the old home, neighborhood friends, and school. To children it may seem that the world has turned upside down.

Emotional security is jeopardized as children experience the fallout of their parents' painful experience. Children may hear their parents getting loud and angry with each other, seemingly out of control. They may see a parent crying, whom they've never seen cry before. If parents express their worries for the future, children may doubt the family's ability to survive.

The other major loss children face is that of relationships. In most cases, one parent has custody of the children and the other has visiting rights. This means that the children's relationship with the visiting parent may change greatly. Now their time together is limited, planned in advance, and special. Many times it is given over to special events such as a trip to the beach or to the science museum. The parent is no longer centrally involved in the child's daily life—fixing dinner, asking to see school papers, or handing out discipline. Children recognize the change in the relationship, and while they may welcome it, they may also grieve at the same time.

In some cases the child's contact with the visiting parent becomes less frequent and finally stops altogether. In such a case, the child has lost a parent, and grieving is an obvious response.

The partial or complete loss of the visiting parent also means the loss of a role model. If the visiting parent is the same gender as the child, the child may grow up not knowing what it means to be a man or a woman. Without a parent to model him- or herself after, the child may turn to peers for examples. Boys without fathers may become overly aggressive or macho, or in some cases they may become too passive. Girls without mothers may become sexually active at an early age, or they may do their best to ignore that part of themselves.

When the visiting parent is the opposite gender from the child, there can also be difficulties. Both girls and boys may grow up with impaired knowledge of how to relate to people of the opposite gender. The nervousness they feel can lead to problems in later life.

Children may also lose other relationships through divorce. If parents divide custody of the children, brothers and sisters may lose their relationship with one another. Children may lose contact with their relatives on one side of the family. For example, if children live with their mother, they may rarely see their paternal grandparents, aunts, or uncles. This can cause grief, especially if there has been a close relationship.

The losses of divorce for children can be summed up as a loss of childhood. Children whose parents divorce often experience much more anxiety, fear, and grief than other children do. They may take on adult roles and responsibilities, such as shopping, cooking, cleaning, and caring for younger siblings. In addition, they must face these additional pressures without the complete support of their parents, who are preoccupied with their own problems. Children of divorce often are forced to grow up much more quickly than other children do.

How Children Respond to Divorce

How do children deal with the losses of divorce? The same way adults do: Children may experience denial, bargaining, anger, depression, and finally recovery and acceptance.

Denial

Children may deny the reality of the divorce in obvious or subtle ways. It is normal for children to resist the news of divorce when they first hear it. This is true even when the family situation has been intolerable for a long time and the child is old enough to know what's coming. Many children, particularly younger ones, continue to deny the re-

ality of the divorce for weeks or even months. They may tell friends, teachers, and even the parents themselves that there is no divorce happening; they may make up tall tales to explain the absence of one parent.

Denial persists even after children appear to have accepted the fact of the divorce. Most children, even adolescents, cherish the dream that their parents will reconcile. They may continue to fantasize about this for years. If the divorce is sudden or children have seen little parental conflict, this dream may become even stronger. This form of denial is often at the root of children's resistance to a parent dating again or remarrying.

Bargaining

As the fact of the divorce sinks in, children often move into bargaining. The younger a child is, the more likely he or she is to explain the divorce egocentrically. "[Daddy/Mommy] left because I wasn't good enough." This kind of thinking can be present right up to the brink of adolescence, and can appear there as well.

Following this kind of logic, children may reason that if they can only be good enough, the absent parent will return and everything will be the way it used to be. Children may throw themselves into school activities or attempt to be unnaturally good at home in order to appease the absent parent. Elementary-school-age children may make bargains with God or use magical thinking in an effort to undo the divorce.

Anger

Anger is another way children respond to divorce. It's important to remember that many times children don't realize that they are angry. The younger children are, the less likely they are to express their anger directly. Instead, anger may take the form of physical problems such as stomachaches and headaches.

Children may turn their anger against playmates and siblings. They may also become uncooperative at home, refusing to do what parents tell them. As the child matures—especially in adolescence—he or she may begin to express this anger verbally toward the parent.

Depression

Another feeling children work through as they struggle with a divorce in their family is depression. Crying a lot is an obvious sign of depression in children, but there are many other signs. Young children may regress or fail to make progress developmentally. For example, they may forget how to use the toilet or demand a bottle again. Children of any age may seem listless and withdraw from friendships and activities they formerly enjoyed. They may seem unable to concentrate. Their schoolwork may suffer. Conversely, children may become overinvolved in school or a hobby as a way of escaping their feelings of sadness. Adolescents may sleep or eat too much, or get involved in drugs or sex as a way of avoiding their feelings or expressing their anger.

Do what you can to help parents stay alert to the possibility of deep depression and suicide. Even young children may act in self-destructive ways. If they notice anything that gives them concern, encourage them to get professional help immediately.

Acceptance and Recovery

As children do the difficult work of grieving, they may eventually come to the final stage of recovery. This is the point where children have substantially accepted the fact of the divorce and largely adjusted to the new situation. In recovery, children begin to put the divorce behind them and move forward in their lives. The strains of the divorce have either ended or children have found strategies for coping with them.

Remember that this stage may take years to reach, no matter how well a child seems to be adjusting. Older elementary school children are especially good at appearing to be well-adjusted when they have only managed to put their distress on hold or express it in ways—such as physical problems—that parents do not catch on to. Encourage your care receiver to look for hidden problems, even when a child seems to have adjusted to the divorce well in a short time.

A Closer Look at Children's Reaction to Divorce

Reference Box A, on pages 603–605, gives more detail on how children at each age level may react to divorce. You might show it to your care receiver, or share ideas. Keep in mind that the ages given are only approximate. Children in one age group may respond like those in age groups on either side of their own. Be sure to look at the age groups on both sides of the ones that your care receiver's children are in.

	Infancy (0–2 years)	Preschool (3–5 years)	Early Elementary (6–8 years)
Denial		Forgetting and asking when Daddy or Mommy will come home	Verbal denial; telling friends, teachers, and even the parents that no divorce is taking place
Bargaining		Promising good behavior if the absent parent returns home	Being or promising to be unnaturally good in order to bring the other parent home; making bargains with God
Anger		Tantrums, uncooperative behavior	Uncooperative behavior at home or school; picking on siblings or playmates
Depression	Listlessness and withdrawal	Listlessness and withdrawal; crying; lack of interest in food or activities; regression or failure to progress normally in development	Withdrawal; crying; lack of interest in treats or activities; inability to concentrate; schoolwork falling off; self-destructive behavior or comments; stomachaches or headaches
Insecurity	Regression from previously attained developmental milestones; failure to progress normally	Regression or failure to progress; excessive separation anxiety	Worries about losing custodial parent; may worry about money or housing problems if parent has mentioned them
Fears	Resonates to parental emotions, even without understanding them; may develop new or stronger separation anxiety	Fears abandonment, kidnapping, losing a parent; invents egocentric explanation for the divorce; develops expectations for the future based on this theory	Worries about who will take care of the absent parent; egocentric thinking still common
Acceptance		Problems largely resolved; able to accept a parent's new partner	Problems largely resolved; able to accept a parent's new partner

	Later Elementary (9–13 years)	**Adolescent** (14–18 years)
Denial	Clings to hope that parents will reconcile, and may resist anything (a move, parental dating, remarriage) that threatens this hope; may try to hide the divorce from friends and teachers	Hopes parents will reconcile; resists parental dating or remarriage
Bargaining	May try to be extra good in order to bring absent parent back home; may make bargains with God or use magical thinking	May use negative behavior as a way of bargaining with parents: "I'll stop this and do what you want if you reconcile"; may offer a parent advice on how to save the marriage, and use bargaining to ensure that the advice is taken
Anger	Continues to express anger through being uncooperative at home, picking on siblings and playmates, and physical complaints such as headaches and stomachaches; becomes somewhat more aware of his or her own angry feelings and is more able to express them verbally; however, may not express those feelings for fear of rejection and losing the parent	Better able to recognize his or her own anger and to express it verbally; however, acting out is still common; normal rebellion of these years is accentuated
Depression	Listlessness, withdrawal, crying, and evident sadness; self-destructive or suicidal behavior possible	May withdraw from the family or from activities and friendships; may escape from sadness by sleeping too much, becoming overinvolved in school or an activity, or abusing drugs, alcohol, food, or sex; self-destructive or suicidal behavior possible
Insecurity	More aware of any money or housing problems, and may worry about them; if worried about a parent's distress, often tries to help parent by becoming a housekeeper, confidant, or behavior monitor and caretaker for younger siblings	May feel out of control without old stability of family; has more freedom and responsibility than he or she knows how to handle; may worry that parents are no longer there as a lifeline for him or her while exploring lifestyle choices
Fears	May fear for the safety or well-being of a parent, particularly if he or she sees parents become extremely angry with each other; may also develop unrealistic fears for a parent based on comments made by the other parent about his or her health, finances, or moral standards; may develop unrealistic fears for own safety when with the other parent	May fear parental suicide; may doubt his or her ability to begin and maintain a permanent male/female relationship; if too closely attached to one parent, may be afraid to leave home and the parent who depends on him or her

	Later Elementary (9–13 years)	Adolescent (14–18 years)
Acceptance	Life settles into a fairly predictable routine; behavior or schoolwork problems disappear; able to accept parental dating or remarriage without overreacting; fantasy of parental reconciliation substantially given up	Schoolwork and behavior problems subside, although some problems are common during adolescence; comes to terms with parental dating and remarriage; fantasy of parental reconciliation is substantially given up; relationship with both parents becomes stable and predictable

▶ The Experience of Divorce for Other Family Members and Friends

Divorce can lead to loss and grief even for those who are not the spouses or children involved. It can cause deep distress even if the divorcing couple live thousands of miles away. Anyone who has been close to the couple will probably be touched in some way by the divorce. What might these individuals experience as the couple proceeds with the divorce?

Parents/Grandparents

The parents of divorcing persons can be deeply affected. The closer their relationship with the divorcing couple and children, the more upset they are likely to be. To some extent their family is being disrupted.

Often they grieve for the pain their child is experiencing. They may wish they could fix the situation so their child wouldn't hurt so much, and become frustrated or depressed because this isn't possible. They may also grieve for the loss of their son- or daughter-in-law. Occasionally people say, "I actually like my *[son-in-law/daughter-in-law]* better than I like my own child. I will miss *[him/her]*."

Along with sadness may come anger and guilt. In addition, some parents consider divorce immoral and selfish and severely judge their child's decision. Parents who have a stable marriage may feel angry that the divorcing couple hasn't worked harder to keep the marriage together. Parents who themselves have been divorced may feel guilt for setting a bad example.

Parents of a divorcing couple may also feel angry or concerned about the effect the divorce is having on their grandchildren. Grandparents may have little or no say in what happens to their grandchildren, and this can leave them feeling helpless. They may not even be able to keep up a relationship with their grandchildren if the custodial parent moves or refuses to allow the children to visit.

Other Relatives and Friends

Sisters, brothers, aunts, uncles, cousins, close friends—all may experience pain in the wake of a divorce. They feel deeply for the divorcing couple and wish they could do something to make the pain go away. They may wonder why the divorce happened. Sometimes they begin to worry about how stable their own marriages are.

While some friends and relatives become very judgmental, in most cases friends and relatives want to show loving support. Unfortunately, they often just don't know how.

Some friends and relatives never mention the divorce at all. If the divorcing person mentions the divorce or the spouse, they change the subject and talk about something else. Other friends may simply stop seeing the divorcing person altogether.

Why do people do this? They may feel unable to cope with the intense feelings of the divorcing person. They may fear that listening means they are taking sides in the divorce—something they might not want to do. They may think they have to offer advice or make the divorcing person feel better—and they don't know how to do that.

Friends and relatives need to work through their own feelings of hurt, fear, and loss. Then they will be able to continue their relationship with the divorcing family without being scared away by the feelings the divorce creates.

▶ Ministering to Those Experiencing Divorce

Divorce ministry is grief ministry. As you care for a divorcing person, you will walk together with your care receiver through the long and often painful journey of grief.

There will be many times when it may be difficult for you to relate to your care receiver. You may feel frustrated because he or she seems to be stuck in denial, holding on to a relationship that will never work out. At other times, you may listen to a great deal of anger or depression. Your care receiver's situation may cause you to think about issues in your own life or marriage that you'd rather not face.

As you care for divorcing persons, you need to remember one key word: *trustworthy*. Divorcing persons experience a great deal of rejection. They need to know that you will be there for them even when they feel most unlovable. As you continue to accept and care for them, they will come to trust you. Often God will use your faithful care to bring healing.

Whether your care receiver is a divorcing person or a friend or relative of a divorcing person, there are several ways of caring that are the same for all.

Build and Maintain a Trusting Relationship

At the center of any caring ministry you do as a Stephen Minister is the trusting relationship you build with your care receiver. As you care for your care receiver, you learn to trust each other more and more until your care receiver can talk to you about subjects that he or she may not be able to share with anyone else. This helps your care receiver find the courage to face up to the difficult memories, feelings, and choices of divorce.

Be extremely careful as a caregiver to avoid any actions or words that communicate judgment or rejection. People affected by divorce are often hypersensitive to criticism. If you care for someone affected by divorce, be sure that you give him or her the gift of unconditional positive regard, which, of course, you can only do with God's aid. (Note that unconditional positive regard for your care receiver does not include being critical of his or her spouse or ex-spouse. Even though the care receiver may be very critical, you must care for his or her feelings without joining in the criticism.)

Encourage the Expression of Feelings

As you build a relationship with your care receiver, work together to get feelings out into the open. Use all the skills you've learned in module 2, "Feelings: Yours, Mine, and Ours," and module 3, "The Art of Listening." In addition, you can do the following.

Ask about Specific Feelings

At times as you listen to and observe your care receiver, you may suspect that he or she is experiencing feelings that he or she is not talking about. For example, your care receiver may express a great deal of anger toward an ex-spouse, but it seems to you that there is a lot of unexpressed hurt there also. In such a case, you might choose to ask about the unexpressed feeling as Reference Box B suggests.

REFERENCE BOX B

Reflecting Feelings

Care receiver: I'm so angry with my ex-spouse for what he said about me at that party.

Stephen Minister: You're very angry. I'm wondering if there is also some feeling of hurt when he criticizes you to others.

Remember Together

As your care receiver does the hard work of grieving, occasionally you will want to encourage him or her to remember both the most joyful and most painful events in the marriage. You can do this by asking questions such as:

▸ What are some of your best memories of your marriage?

▸ What were some of the most difficult times?

▸ How did you meet?

▸ When did you first realize that the marriage wasn't going to work out?

Why encourage your care receiver to remember these events? They bring up many different feelings for your care receiver. Sorting through feelings is one way people grieve. By encouraging your care receiver to recall these events and sort through his or her feelings about them, you are helping him or her to grieve.

Obviously, such questions should only be used with gentleness and sensitivity. You will want to wait until you and your care receiver have a deeply trusting relationship before you ask him or her such intimate questions. You will also need to use your judgment about what to ask. Some topics may be too painful for your care receiver to talk about yet. When used carefully, however, such questions can be a powerful way of caring.

Listen for Incongruities and Explore Them

Be sure to listen not only to the words your care receiver says, but also to his or her tone of voice and body language. Sometimes you may notice that what the person is saying does not match his or her gestures or voice tone. For example, the care receiver may say, "The divorce has been a great relief. I'm just so happy to be out of that marriage." Yet you notice that he or she is saying this with a tight jaw and isn't making eye contact with you. Perhaps he or she is fiddling with a ring or pencil. There seems to be more going on than just happiness and relief.

Gently explore such incongruities. At times you might want to point out the behavior that seems incongruous to you and ask about it. At other times, you might not bring up the behavior at all, especially if you think it might upset your care receiver. Instead you would simply ask about other feelings: "You say you feel very relieved, and I'm sure that's true. Sometimes people can feel angry or upset at the same time, though. Have you ever felt that way?"

Respond Compassionately

Keep in mind that you are not called upon to fix difficult feelings. You are there to listen and care. Allow your care receiver to express feelings of hurt, anger, guilt, and worry without discounting them or offering solutions. Remain process-oriented and rely on God to bring repentance and healing.

Caring during Stages of Divorcing

Be aware of where your care receiver is in the divorcing process, and focus your care on the different needs during resistance, grief, and recovery.

Gently Respond to Denial

How can you care for divorcing care receivers who are in denial? It usually isn't helpful to confront them. Instead, help them to discover for themselves that they aren't seeing the situation from a realistic perspective.

You can do this by repeatedly bringing up, in a gentle and nonconfrontational way, topics the care receiver is denying. For example, you might say, "It seems to me that you hope someday the two of you will get back together." Allow your care receiver to talk about the subject. Encourage him or her to explore the subject more thoroughly by asking gentle questions, such as, "When do you think this might happen?" or making gentle requests such as, "Tell me more about how you see this happening." Often, as people think through the details of what they are denying, they come to realize the truth of the situation.

If a care receiver is stuck in denial of some sort for several months you will want to discuss it with your Supervision Group and perhaps with a Stephen Leader or your pastor. It could be that the care receiver needs a referral to a mental health professional.

Grief and Special Dates

One very thoughtful way for you to care as your care receiver grieves is to be aware of special dates that can cause pain. The first Christmas after a separation can be very difficult; as can days like Valentine's Day and Mother's or Father's Day. The divorced couple's wedding anniversary is an obvious date to watch for. Your care receiver may also find other dates especially difficult, such as the anniversary of the first time they met or the anniversary of the separation. Near any of these dates, it's a good idea to encourage your care receiver to talk about the feelings the date brings up for him or her.

Make a special point of being there for your care receiver on the day the divorce becomes final. This day officially puts an end to the marriage, and all kinds of feelings are apt to come out in response—even feelings that the care receiver didn't know he or she had. Be there to listen and care.

Be Aware of Concerns for Others

You may notice that your care receiver is very concerned about the effect the divorce is having on others, especially children. Often a divorcing person feels concern or even guilt about this and needs to talk it through. Give him or her that opportunity.

Journey through the Rebuilding Process

As your care receiver moves through the hard work of grieving and begins to rebuild his or her life, continue to be there for him or her. Your care can make this journey much easier.

Be a Safe Listener

Following a divorce, individuals try out new ideas and new ways of living. During this time, divorced persons need someone safe that they can talk to about their ideas, fears, successes, and failures. They need a listener who can help them sort through their options in a balanced way without judging them.

As caregivers continue to listen with acceptance and care, care receivers gain courage to make changes in their lives. They know they can try something out and even risk failure, because their caregivers will still be there for them. Stephen Ministers will continue to accept them as they try out new identities and new ways to live.

Encourage Them to Try Out New Ways of Being

It can be frightening to be newly divorced and facing many choices. Reentering the job market, going back to school, finding a new place to live, beginning to date again—all these can be intimidating.

When your care receiver seems ready, gently encourage him or her to try out some of these new ways of being. This doesn't mean you should push him or her into anything—for example, dating. He or she may not be ready yet. But when your care receiver expresses an interest in one of these life changes, encourage him or her to talk about it. Reflect the interest you hear. Ask about the feelings this new way of being arouses in your care receiver. Discuss the many big and little changes it would bring to your care receiver's life.

Continue to Work through Remaining Grief

Keep in mind that people will continue to work through grief over the divorce even after they have substantially recovered. Continue to work through remaining feelings of anger, sadness, hurt, and guilt.

Caring for Other Family and Friends

Encourage care receivers to talk about their loss. Care receivers may try to play down their feelings of loss at the divorce of a friend or relative, believing that they have no right to feel pain since the divorce isn't happening to them personally. Let them know that it's okay to have these feelings and to express them.

If care receivers express concern over not knowing what to say to the divorcing person, discuss this issue together. Draw on your own training to help care receivers discover ways of reaching out with care to their divorcing friends and relatives.

▶ Getting Ready for the In-Class Sessions

In the In-Class Sessions for this continuing education module you will look at what the Bible has to say about divorce and hear how people who have experienced divorce describe it. In preparation for the In-Class Sessions, think about your experiences with divorce and consider how you would feel if you were assigned to care for a person experiencing divorce.

Ministering to Those Experiencing Divorce

Here is a trustworthy saying that deserves full acceptance: Christ Jesus came into the world to save sinners—of whom I am the worst. But for that very reason I was shown mercy so that in me, the worst of sinners, Christ Jesus might display his unlimited patience as an example for those who would believe on him and receive eternal life.

1 Timothy 1:15–16

I. Rejected and Accepted

II. Christian Care for Divorcing Persons

A. How God Regards Divorce

FOCUS NOTE 1

The Biblical Word about Marriage

What does God think about marriage?

The LORD God said, "It is not good for the man to be alone. I will make a helper suitable for him."

Now the LORD God had formed out of the ground all the beasts of the field and all the birds of the air. He brought them to the man to see what he would name them; and whatever the man called each living creature, that was its name. So the man gave names to all the livestock, the birds of the air and all the beasts of the field.

But for Adam no suitable helper was found. So the LORD God caused the man to fall into a deep sleep; and while he was sleeping, he took one

---

of the man's ribs and closed up the place with flesh. Then the LORD God made a woman from the rib he had taken out of the man, and he brought her to the man.

The man said,

> "This is now bone of my bones
>   and flesh of my flesh;
> she shall be called 'woman,'
>   for she was taken out of man."

For this reason a man will leave his father and mother and be united to his wife, and they will become one flesh.

Genesis 2:18–24

[Jesus said], "But from the beginning of creation, 'God made them male and female.' 'For this reason a man shall leave his father and mother and be joined to his wife, and the two shall become one flesh.' So they are no longer two, but one flesh. Therefore what God has joined together, let no one separate."

Mark 10:6–9 NRSV

FOCUS NOTE 2

The Biblical Word about Divorce

What does God think of divorce?

Some Pharisees came to him to test him. They asked, "Is it lawful for a man to divorce his wife for any and every reason?"

"Haven't you read," he replied, "that at the beginning the Creator 'made them male and female,' and said, 'For this reason a man will leave his father and mother and be united to his wife, and the two will become one flesh'? So they are no longer two, but one. Therefore what God has joined together, let man not separate."

"Why then," they asked, "did Moses command that a man give his wife a certificate of divorce and send her away?"

Jesus replied, "Moses permitted you to divorce your wives because your hearts were hard. But it was not this way from the beginning. I tell you that anyone who divorces his wife, except for marital unfaithfulness, and marries another woman commits adultery."

Matthew 19:3–9

Another thing you do: You flood the LORD'S altar with tears. You weep and wail because he no longer pays attention to your offerings or accepts them with pleasure from your hands. You ask, "Why?" It is because the LORD is acting as the witness between you and the wife of your youth, because you have broken faith with her, though she is your partner, the wife of your marriage covenant.

Has not the LORD made them one? In flesh and spirit they are his. And why one? Because he was seeking godly offspring. So guard yourself in your spirit, and do not break faith with the wife of your youth.

"I hate divorce," says the LORD God of Israel, "and I hate a man's covering himself with violence as well as with his garment," says the LORD Almighty.

So guard yourself in your spirit, and do not break faith.

Malachi 2:13–16

FOCUS NOTE 3

The Biblical Word about When Divorce May Be Permissible

What does the Bible say about when divorce is allowable?

"It has been said, 'Anyone who divorces his wife must give her a certificate of divorce.' But I tell you that anyone who divorces his wife, except for marital unfaithfulness, causes her to become an adulteress, and anyone who marries the divorced woman commits adultery."

Matthew 5:31–32

To the rest I say this (I, not the Lord): If any brother has a wife who is not a believer and she is willing to live with him, he must not divorce her. And if a woman has a husband who is not a believer and he is willing to live with her, she must not divorce him. For the unbelieving husband has been sanctified through his wife, and the unbelieving wife has been sanctified through her believing husband. Otherwise your children would be unclean, but as it is, they are holy.

But if the unbeliever leaves, let him do so. A believing man or woman is not bound in such circumstances; God has called us to live in peace.

1 Corinthians 7:12–15

FOCUS NOTE 4

What God Thinks of People Who Divorce

What does God think of people who divorce?

If we claim to be without sin, we deceive ourselves and the truth is not in us. If we confess our sins, he is faithful and just and will forgive us our sins and purify us from all unrighteousness.

1 John 1:8–9

"For God so loved the world that he gave his one and only Son, that whoever believes in him shall not perish but have eternal life. For God did not send his Son into the world to condemn the world, but to save the world through him."

John 3:16–17

While Jesus was having dinner at Matthew's house, many tax collectors and "sinners" came and ate with him and his disciples. When the Pharisees saw this, they asked his disciples, "Why does your teacher eat with tax collectors and 'sinners'?"

On hearing this, Jesus said, "It is not the healthy who need a doctor, but the sick. But go and learn what this means: 'I desire mercy, not sacrifice.' For I have not come to call the righteous, but sinners."

Matthew 9:10–13

So if anyone is in Christ, there is a new creation: everything old has passed away; see, everything has become new! All this is from God, who reconciled us to himself through Christ, and has given us the ministry of reconciliation; that is, in Christ God was reconciling the world to himself, not counting their trespasses against them, and entrusting the message of reconciliation to us. So we are ambassadors for Christ, since God is making his appeal through us; we entreat you on behalf of Christ, be reconciled to God. For our sake he made him to be sin who knew no sin, so that in him we might become the righteousness of God.

2 Corinthians 5:17–21 NRSV

B. Caring for Divorcing Persons

1. Marriage Is a Serious Commitment

2. Divorce Requires Forgiveness in Several Ways

3. The Caregiver's Attitude Matters a Lot

III. Looking Ahead

IV. Opening

V. Panel of People Affected by Divorce

FOCUS NOTE 5

Panel of Those Experiencing Divorce

Use the space below to take notes on the questions asked of the panel and the responses panel members give.

Question:

Response:

Question:

Response:

Question:

Response:

Question:

Response:

Question:

Response:

VI. Looking Ahead

VII. Opening

VIII. Avoiding Pitfalls in Divorce Care

FOCUS NOTE 6

Skit 1: Giving the Marriage Another Try

Care receiver 1: I was just thinking yesterday that Chris and I might get back together. It's been a month now and I think it's time to give the marriage another try.

Stephen Minister 1: You're thinking you might get back together now.

CR2: Yes. I think Chris just needed some time alone to work things out. *[He/She]* talked about wanting a trial separation. Maybe we've been separated long enough.

SM2: Didn't you tell me that Chris is about to file divorce papers?

CR3: Yeah. That's why I've decided to talk to *[him/her]* about this now, before *[he/she]* takes a step that we'll both regret.

SM3: You believe there's still a chance that you will get back together.

CR4: Of course. Our marriage isn't over. This is just a bump in the road.

SM4: Has Chris done anything to make you think the marriage isn't over?

CR5: No, but *[he/she]* doesn't have to. I know. I'm a part of this marriage too, and I know.

SM5: I think what's going on is that you are stuck in denial. I can assure you that Chris is never going to come back to you. Your marriage is over, and the sooner you admit that and come to terms with it, the sooner you'll be able to get over Chris and move on with the rest of your life.

Skit 2: Payback Time

Stephen Minister 1: I've noticed that your children are home today. I thought you told me that they were spending this week with Pat.

Care receiver 1: Oh, I decided to keep them home this week.

SM2: Hasn't Pat been making plans for this week? I thought you said that *[he / she]* had taken the week off from work and was taking the kids camping.

CR2: Yeah, well, *[he'll / she'll]* get over it.

SM3: I think I remember this kind of thing happening before. What does Pat think about it?

CR3: I don't care one bit what *[he / she]* thinks. *[He's / She's]* only getting what's coming to *[him / her]*.

SM4: Doesn't your divorce settlement give Pat the right to spend time with the kids?

CR4: It doesn't matter. *[He / She]* doesn't have enough money to hire an attorney, so there's nothing *[he / she]* can do about it.

SM5: How do you think this is affecting your children?

CR5: They'll get over it. The sooner they realize what a jerk *[he / she]* is, the better.

SM6: You seem to be extremely angry at Pat.

CR6: It's nothing *[he / she]* doesn't deserve. *[He / She]* should have thought about this before sleeping around and killing our marriage and ruining our family.

SM7: How do you think it affects you to hold on to such anger at Pat?

CR7: I think it helps me feel human. Pat treated me so badly that the only way I can maintain any self-respect is to get back at *[him / her]* any way I can.

SM8: Have you ever thought about forgiving Pat?

CR8: Fat chance of that.

SM9: Well, I have to tell you that your lack of forgiveness isn't doing anyone any good. It may be hard to forgive, but for your children's sake and for your own sake, that's what you have to do. The longer you hang on to your bitterness, the more it is going to hurt you and your children. If you don't let go of it, it will eat you alive. Besides, Jesus said we should forgive our enemies and love those who treat us badly.

CR9 *(sarcastically):* Ummm. Maybe Jesus should try going through divorce before he hands out such advice.

SM10: Jesus went through quite a bit for your sake. Do you want me to look up the passage for you?

CR10: Yeah. Sure. Whatever.

FOCUS NOTE 8

Skit 3: Getting Started Again

Stephen Minister 1: Isn't this the three-year anniversary of your breakup with Casey?

Care receiver 1 *(does some mental calculations):* Actually Monday was.

SM2: Tell me how it makes you feel to remember that.

CR2: You know, I was thinking back to a year ago, how emotional I was about this anniversary. It seems as if I've really changed.

SM3: What are your feelings now?

CR3: I don't know. I suppose it's mostly resignation. I still feel sad, but I know there's nothing I can do about it.

SM4: You sound as if you've reached a point where you can accept the past.

CR4: Yeah, I suppose I have. As a matter of fact, I have been thinking a lot about the future.

SM5: Tell me more.

CR5: For the longest time, I didn't see how the future could be hopeful at all. Recently, however, I've actually been feeling optimistic. It's great.

SM6: It sounds wonderful. Have you been feeling hopeful about anything in particular?

CR6: Actually, yes. I met someone at the church picnic, and I think *[he/she]* seemed interested in me.

SM7: Wow. How did that feel?

CR7: At first I thought I must have been imagining things, but the more I thought about it, I felt flattered and excited.

SM8: Do you know *[his/her]* name?

CR8: Well . . . yes.

SM9: Great. Is *[he/she]* a member of the church?

CR9: Yes . . .

SM10: This is so exciting. Where's your church directory? We can look up the phone number and you can give *[him/her]* a call and ask *[him/her]* out on a date. It must feel good to get back into the stream of things.

CR10: Well, I'm not sure. The whole idea of dating scares me.

SM11: Oh, you just have a case of the jitters. Once you make the call you'll feel great. Let's get your directory.

CR11: I don't think so. I just don't feel ready.

SM12: Well, you're going to have to get started sometime.

IX. Caregiver's Compass Review

_____

_____

_____

_____

_____   _____

_____   _____

_____   _____

COMPASSIONATE · FULL OF FAITH · SKILLED · TRUSTWORTHY

_____

_____

_____

_____

X. Looking Ahead

Prayer Partner Requests and Thanksgivings

My prayer partner is _____

Prayer requests and thanksgivings to share with my prayer partner

_____

_____

Prayer requests and thanksgivings shared by my prayer partner

_____

_____

Crises of Pregnancy and Childbirth

Contents

► Challenges and Concerns of a Normal Pregnancy

Peggy eased herself into the chair with a sigh. Leaning down, she extracted one swollen foot from her shoe, then the other, lifting one foot at a time up onto the hassock. She hadn't seen her anklebones in weeks. No one had told her that her feet would look so fat, so puffy. Her legs just seemed to flow straight into her shoes these days.

Being seven-and-a-half-months pregnant certainly wasn't all it was cracked up to be. A week ago, she caught a glimpse of herself in a mirror—sideways. Unbelievable! Did she really look like that? She never dreamed that she would see the weight that the nurse recorded last week. It's one thing to talk about gaining twenty-five to thirty pounds during a normal pregnancy—it's another to see twenty of those pounds already racked up! Would she ever be able to wear that pale blue satin dress again?

Ouch! She grabbed her side as the baby's feet pushed vigorously at her rib cage from inside and under. She managed to get the tiny leg to move over a bit farther. It hurt when a foot found her ribs and squeezed them that way! Sometimes, though, she just couldn't get the baby to move. Nobody had told her about that, either.

This baby moved a lot. Was it a boy or a girl? She sort of wanted a girl to cuddle and dress up and enjoy. Doug said he didn't care whether the baby was a boy or girl as long as the baby was healthy—but Peggy wondered whether he secretly wished for a boy. She hoped he wouldn't be disappointed with a girl.

She wondered whether Doug was happy. He had been wonderful during those first few months when she had felt so blue, tired, and nauseated. He encouraged her to stay home for the first six months after the baby's birth and then return to work part-time. He said it was important for the baby to have its mother when it was so little, and that they'd be able to manage on just his salary. But was she just being selfish?

That was another worry, though—whether they could make ends meet. They hadn't saved a great deal and losing Peggy's income would definitely make a difference in their lifestyle!

Having the baby would change their lives a lot. She and Doug had been used to spontaneously going out for dinner or a movie. Now, since they would need to pay a babysitter to go out for a few hours, they probably couldn't afford to go to dinner or a movie.

Peggy felt tears prickle her eyes. There were going to be a lot of changes—and a lot of questions. Would they be good parents? Would they do everything right?

It was all so frightening and confusing. When she told Doug's sister that she was planning to breast-feed the baby, Rhonda said, "Why in the world would you want to tie yourself down that way? I'd never do it! Besides, what if you don't have enough milk? You'll just have to supplement with formula anyway—why even bother?" She'd heard a lot of criticism over her decisions to breast-feed and to work only part-time after six months. Everyone wanted to run her life. Yesterday a stranger patted her stomach and commented, "You look as if you're about ready to pop any day!" As if he knew!

Could she make it through labor? Almost every woman in her office told at least one horror story about labor and delivery—her own or somebody else's. Was it really like being ripped in half? Would their baby be all right? If she ate something or did something that she shouldn't have, would the baby be deformed or even die? She'd heard all sorts of stories—perfectly healthy babies who died because they were born with the cord around their necks and they strangled!

Peggy took several deep breaths and tried to push down the panic. Sometimes she just hated being pregnant and wished it were over and that everything was back to normal. But would there ever be a normal again?

****

Even when pregnancy progresses normally and the baby is born healthy and beloved, pregnancy and childbirth can be a time of crisis for a family. The birth of the first child signals a couple's transformation into parents, and the awesome responsibility of this can be overwhelming. For a family that already has one or more children, a new baby causes major changes in the established order of the family's life.

Pregnancy is not always a time of joy and elation; it is a time of worry as well. Heidi Murkoff has written about this time of worry, as quoted in Reference Box A.

REFERENCE BOX A

Worry during Pregnancy

Worry, according to one study, is one of the most common complaints of pregnancy, affecting more expectant women than morning sickness and food cravings combined. Ninety-four out of every hundred women worry about whether their babies will be normal, and 93% worry about whether they and their babies will come through delivery safely. More women worry about their figures (91%) than their health (81%) during pregnancy. And most worry that they worry too much.[1]

This worry is often unnecessary. The vast majority of successful pregnancies end in the birth of a healthy, normal baby. Modern prenatal care has made pregnancy and childbirth safer than ever before. Most babies will be just fine. But not always, as Susan Borg and Judith Lasker point out in Reference Box B.

REFERENCE BOX B

Birth Tragedy Statistics

And yet birth tragedies are not as rare as we like to think. In one year, in the United States alone, according to the National Center for Health Statistics, close to one million families are affected. Of the 3.67 million infants born alive, over 25,000 (one in 144) die during the

1 Arlene Eisenberg, Heidi E. Murkoff, and Sandee E. Hathaway, *What to Expect When You're Expecting*, 2nd ed. (New York: Workman Publishing, 1996), p. xxiii.

first twenty-eight days of life and are counted as neonatal deaths. An additional 30,000 babies (about one in every 123 deliveries) are stillborn, having died between the twentieth week of pregnancy and the time of birth. These rates have been declining steadily, yet they are still higher in the United States than in many other countries. And no matter how rare a tragedy, when it happens to you, it is 100 percent.[2]

Miscarriages occur in about 15 to 20 percent of all recognized pregnancies.[3] Cases of ectopic pregnancy, in which the fertilized egg implants in an area other than the uterus—usually in the fallopian tube—have almost quadrupled in number since 1970, possibly due to an increased number of pelvic infections and the use of IUDs.[4]

Other problems can surface at birth. Certain illnesses like rubella, which the mother may contract during pregnancy, can cause deformities in the baby. Medicines and environmental toxins can also affect the baby. Babies of mothers addicted to drugs like heroin or cocaine or to alcohol are born similarly addicted. Cigarette smoking during pregnancy has been linked to miscarriages, to premature labor and delivery, and to babies who are born with lower birth weights: "And being born too small is the major cause of infant illness and perinatal death (those that occur just before, during, or after birth)."[5] Certainly pregnancy is a time for a mother to take care of herself to help her baby be born strong and healthy.

Parents whose babies die will need special care to help them to grieve the loss of their child. Similarly, parents of babies with mental or physical deficiencies will need support to help them cope with the challenges of their baby and to grieve the loss of their ideal child. Parents-to-be who struggle through the dangers and stresses of a high-risk pregnancy may welcome a listening ear and the caring support of a Stephen Minister.

But even parents whose pregnancy, labor, and delivery progress uneventfully and who find themselves parents of a perfectly normal baby may find pregnancy and childbirth to be a crisis. Stephen Ministers can help resolve the crisis so the parents find greater wholeness rather than deeper brokenness.

Depression

A woman undergoes a major shift in hormones during pregnancy that may cause mood swings. Such mood swings may easily be mistaken for depression and are usually temporary: "You may experience periods of moodiness, but these shifts in emotions usually disappear by the fourth month; once hormone production levels off and comes into balance, your emotional well-being will also come into balance."[6] Usually eating

---

2 Susan Borg and Judith Lasker, *When Pregnancy Fails: Families Coping with Miscarriage, Ectopic Pregnancy, Stillbirth, and Infant Death*, rev. ed. (New York: Bantam Books, 1989), p. 8.

3 Borg and Lasker, *When Pregnancy Fails,* p. 9.

4 Borg and Lasker, *When Pregnancy Fails,* pp. 8, 42.

5 Eisenberg, Murkoff, and Hathaway, *What to Expect When You're Expecting*, p. 54.

6 Bruce Hayman, *A Miracle in the Making* (Chicago: Budlong Press, 1998), p. 17.

well, getting enough rest and exercise, and talking the feelings out can relieve the worst of the emotional stress.

About 10 percent of women do suffer mild to moderate depression during pregnancy. Symptoms of depression to watch for include:

▸ feeling down, empty, and flat;

▸ sleep disturbances;

▸ changed eating habits (not eating at all or eating endlessly);

▸ prolonged or unusual fatigue;

▸ extended loss of interest in work, play, and other activities or pleasures; and

▸ exaggerated mood swings.

If the symptoms last longer than two weeks, the mother may need professional help to deal with her depression.[7]

Physical Changes and Concerns

Traditionally, a woman is supposed to glow and bloom when she is pregnant. Some pregnant women do feel healthier, happier, and more beautiful than at any other time in their lives. Other women, however, may experience great concern over the loss of their prepregnant body image. A woman who had a petite, trim figure before pregnancy may well be aghast at the view in a mirror by her eighth or ninth month of pregnancy. Varicose veins, stretch marks, constipation, back pain, shortness of breath, swollen fingers and ankles, a pronounced waddle when she walks—all may unite to make the woman feel uncomfortable and unattractive.

---

7 Eisenberg, Murkoff, and Hathaway, *What to Expect When You're Expecting*, p. 104.

Emotional Demands of Pregnancy

A first-time mother in particular may find the demands of caring for both herself and her unborn baby a bit overwhelming. A pregnant woman is under pressure to give up smoking, drinking, and careless eating habits; for perhaps the first time in her life she is called upon to care for another person even more carefully than she might care for herself. Pregnancy may signal adulthood in a more tangible way than any other rite of passage so far. The demands are unrelenting throughout pregnancy and are likely to increase once the child is born. Such demands may occasionally give rise to some resentment and nostalgia for her previous, more carefree lifestyle.

Loss of Privacy

At no other time in her life is a woman so likely to feel that her private life is on public display. Her coworkers may ask whether the baby was planned or an accident, or run an office pool to guess the baby's weight and actual delivery date. Anyone who has had a baby or known someone who has had a baby may want to regale the new mother with horror stories of cousin Betty's 32-hour labor or sister Sue's 42-stitch episiotomy. Total strangers may pat the new mother's stomach and offer advice. Although well-intended, the invasive questions and comments may make the mother want to hide until after she's had the baby. Worse, the advice, criticism, or war stories may undermine the confidence of the parents-to-be in the choices they have made on such issues as where to deliver the baby, whether or not to breast-feed, whether or not the mother will return to work after she has the baby and—if so—how soon.

As much as possible, the mother- and father-to-be need to be confident in the decisions they have made. Only they know the particular circumstances that make up their situation; only they will be able to decide what is best for their family.

Concern for the Health of the Baby

Most pregnant couples worry over the health of their baby, even in spite of the overwhelming odds that their baby will be perfect. Sometimes these concerns have a real basis: if the couple knows that a genetic defect runs in their families, or if the mother has come down with German measles, for example.

Financial Concerns

For most parents, a baby introduces some degree of financial stress. If the mother was working prior to having the baby, the loss of her income may be a concern. Childcare may introduce a significant expense. Some may face such difficult financial challenges that they will need to be referred to a financial counselor.

Concern about Changes in the Couple's Relationship

A baby brings changes in a couple's relationship. After the child is born, lack of sleep and constant demands on the mother and father may leave the couple with no time or energy to nurture their own relationship. They may wonder if they have to give up their special closeness to become parents.

To Work or Not to Work

Every woman who works outside the home before and during her pregnancy faces the decision of whether or not she will return to work after she has the baby and, if so, how soon after delivery. This may be one of the most stressful decisions a couple faces, and one that depends on the particular circumstances of that family. Some of the considerations are as follows.

What sort of maternity leave does the company provide? Will the company ensure that the woman will still have her position (or a similar one) if she is home with the baby for four weeks, six weeks, or even six months? With so many women working outside the home today, many companies provide flexible options for maternity leave that allow the mother to stay home for a time and still return to her position. She may even be able to combine sick leave with unpaid leave to extend her stay long enough to provide a good start for her baby. Fathers also may be able to take family leave to help mother and baby adjust or to extend the time before arranging for childcare.

In the United States employees who are covered by the provisions of the Family and Medical Leave Act of 1993 may be able to take up to 12 weeks of unpaid leave to care for their baby or spouse without losing their original (or an equivalent) position, health coverage, or other benefits. Additional information can be obtained by contacting the local branch of the U.S. Department of Labor—Employment Standards Administration, Wage and Hour Division.

If the mother decides to stay home permanently after the baby is born, will the family be able to manage financially on the father's salary alone? This is certainly a concern for new parents. Some may find that by careful budgeting, the mother or father can stay home with the baby.

Some families make their financial decision based not only on income, but also on costs. The cost of childcare for an infant can be very high. When the cost of a working wardrobe is factored into the equation, staying home with the baby may well prove financially advantageous. Staying home is also easiest for breast-feeding mothers.

If the mother or father decides to stay home after the baby is born, will all her or his intelligence and career skills atrophy? Will all her or his concerns revolve around Sesame Street *and finding the best preschool?* A parent who stays home with a child may long for the company of adults or for the stimulation of work. The parent may worry about losing ground in a career and wonder if she or he will ever catch up. The work of caring for a very young child can be emotionally demanding but not very stimulating. The parent may sometimes long for more rewarding work.

Some parents do become thoroughly absorbed by the baby. They think or talk about little else. Most parents are happiest, however, when they have some interests other than the child and are able to get away from the baby now and then.

If both parents decide to pursue their careers after the baby is born, will they be able to find appropriate childcare? Will the baby be safe? Will the baby feel abandoned? Will the mother or father lose out on all the important events in the baby's life?* These concerns are well-founded, and parents who know that they cannot stay home to raise their children are wise to begin early to find childcare. Many families cannot afford to have a parent stay home full-time, and those children are still well-adjusted, loving, and nurtured. The parents need to find a caregiver who shares their values and who values their child.

What other options might be available for parents besides returning to work full-time? With such a high percentage of women who work outside the home, many employers have become more open to various options. A mother or father may be able to return to work part-time, continue in her or his normal job at home rather than in the office, or continue her or his work on a freelance basis. Exploring the creative solutions for simultaneous working and parenting are well worth the effort.

No matter what decision a couple makes about parents working after the baby is born, they are likely to face criticism. They need to remember that this decision is a personal one, based on their own needs and circumstances. Unless the parents-to-be are asking someone to take an active role in caring for their child, neither parent's choice is anyone else's business.

To Breast-Feed or Not to Breast-Feed

Whether or not to breast-feed her baby is a very personal decision for the mother, based on her knowledge of the benefits of breast-feeding and her own feelings about it. The mother-to-be needs to become familiar with all aspects of breast-feeding before she decides how to feed her infant.

Most medical professionals strongly endorse breast-feeding as ideal for both the baby and the mother. Breast-feeding is inexpensive, safe, and often convenient. The baby benefits because breast milk is the best possible food for the infant, and no formula can duplicate the nutrients found in it; the baby even receives the mother's immunities in the colostrum during the first few days of life. Few babies are allergic to their mothers' milk. The act of nursing the baby helps the mother's body heal more readily from childbirth and may make premenopausal breast cancer less likely.[8]

Some women, however, may not want to breast-feed their babies. A mother may decide that she can provide for the baby's needs more readily and predictably by bottle-feeding. Bottle-feeding allows the father to help with the feedings and helps him bond with the baby. Millions of infants who have been bottle-fed have grown up healthy and loved.[9]

Even when a mother wants to breast-feed, doing so can be difficult. During the first few days of breast-feeding, mothers can worry about whether their baby is getting enough nutrition. Such worry can hurt the mothers' self-

confidence. This is a time when some mothers need someone to listen to them and reassure them.

If a woman decides that she is not comfortable with breast-feeding, her decision needs to be respected. Some people are so enthusiastic about the benefits of breast-feeding that those who choose not to breast-feed can feel judged by the enthusiastic supporters. Mothers who choose to feed their babies with bottles may need to talk about their feelings about that decision and to receive support and encouragement from friends, family, or their Stephen Ministers.

► Major-Crisis Pregnancies

Regrettably, not all pregnancies are normal or welcome. For some, pregnancy can be a major crisis.

Unwanted Pregnancy

The positive pregnancy test is not always a source of joy. The news may be unwelcome for many reasons.

Pregnancy for a Woman Who Does Not Want Children or Does Not Want Any More Children

Some couples do not want to have children. Some families may have already had the number of children they planned to have. In these cases, the discovery that the woman is pregnant may precipitate a crisis for her and possibly for her family. At the very least, the pregnancy will force the woman to re-evaluate her goals and her plans for the future to accommodate the new baby. The new child may have a profound impact on career plans, financial stability, and perhaps even family dynamics.

---

8 Adapted from Hayman, *A Miracle in the Making,* p. 122, and Eisenberg, Murkoff, and Hathaway, *What to Expect When You're Expecting,* pp. 251–252.

9 Adapted from Eisenberg, Murkoff, and Hathaway, *What to Expect When You're Expecting,* p. 253, and Hayman, *A Miracle in the Making,* p. 124.

Women who face such a crisis need to be able to talk through their fears, anger, and frustration. They need someone to listen as they think about their future and develop new plans and hopes.

Such an unwanted pregnancy may affect the entire family's happiness and plans. The mother may feel somewhat responsible for disrupting the family. She may also feel angry with the father for his part in the pregnancy. She may feel hurt or frustrated by family members' reactions to the pregnancy and may believe they are blaming her.

Teenage Pregnancy and Single Motherhood

When an unmarried teenage girl becomes pregnant, the crisis can take on the proportions of tragedy. As one father put it, "From the moment I heard my fourteen-year-old daughter say, 'Daddy, I'm pregnant!' I knew God would be stretching me beyond anything I'd ever experienced."[10]

A teenage girl who finds herself pregnant faces many issues—not the least of which may be breaking the news to her parents. If the parents continue to give their love and support, many of the other issues can be resolved. If not, she may need help with such basic issues as food and shelter. A major issue will be what to do once the baby is born. Will the mother want to keep the baby herself? Will she marry the father? Will her parents take on the task of raising their grandchild along with their daughter? Will the mother make an adoption plan?

A young mother usually will not be able to provide adequately for herself and her new baby, so financial considerations will be a major issue. Completing her education will also be an issue; even if the girl remains at home, someone will need to care for the child while she is in school. Often, if the father of the baby is as young as the mother, marriage is not a solution.

Helping the teenager make good choices about the pregnancy is crucial. She will need help finding prenatal care and ensuring that the baby will have the best possible future. She will need help deciding whether to parent her baby or make an adoption plan. Nonjudgmental care and support will allow the girl to find the best possible resolution of her crisis. Both public and private counseling programs are available to help pregnant teens through pregnancy, labor, and delivery.

Older single mothers may face similar difficulties as described in Reference Box C.

REFERENCE BOX C

Difficulties of Older Single Mothers

The many poor single women, no longer teenagers but still without the means to assure good nutrition and medical care, are also prone to serious complications. If they are on welfare, perhaps supporting other children, their reception by the medical and social services is sometimes less than sympathetic during pregnancy and delivery.[11]

---

10 Author: A Dad Named Bill, *Daddy, I'm Pregnant* (Portland, OR: Multnomah Press, 1987), p. 9.

11 Borg and Lasker, *When Pregnancy Fails*, p. 102.

They often lack the support of family and must face the challenges of pregnancy alone. They may need a caring and nonjudgmental listener to help them as they try to make the best choices for the baby and themselves.

High-Risk Pregnancies

For the woman who faces a high-risk pregnancy, "Pregnancy is a time of fear, anxiety, constant medical care, frequent hospitalization, and a feeling that 'no one else knows what it's like.'"[12]

Who faces a high-risk pregnancy? "Women under 18 and over 35 need additional care and observation . . . to reduce the risks to themselves and their babies."[13] Women with conditions such as diabetes, asthma, chronic hypertension, multiple sclerosis, eating disorders, a physical disability, epilepsy, coronary artery disease, sickle-cell anemia, or lupus will also need to take special precautions.[14] Pregnancy in couples who may have a genetic tendency to inherited diseases or defects such as diabetes, Down's syndrome, hemophilia, Tay-Sachs disease, clubfoot, cleft palate, or sickle-cell anemia may also be classified as high-risk.[15]

Multiple pregnancies (when a woman is pregnant with more than one fetus) are usually classified as high-risk pregnancies as well. Multiple pregnancies increase the risk for both mother and babies, intensifying the general discomforts of the mother and increasing the likelihood that the babies will be born at least two to five weeks before the due date.[16]

Even a woman whose pregnancy has been textbook-perfect may develop conditions during pregnancy that will make her pregnancy high-risk. Gestational diabetes, preeclampsia (pregnancy-induced hypertension, also called toxemia), eclampsia (convulsions during late pregnancy), difficulties due to the placement of the placenta, or preterm labor, for instance, may develop quite suddenly and put the baby and the mother in serious danger. With careful monitoring some conditions can be controlled, but others may demand serious restrictions in diet or activity, or even hospitalization.

The couple who faces a high-risk pregnancy will be under a great deal of stress from the time the pregnancy has been diagnosed as high-risk. They will probably be feeling fear, resentment, guilt, inadequacy, constant pressure to do everything perfectly, marital stress, and pressure to plan ahead financially for an expensive childbirth. The couple will need to be particularly aware of each other's needs as they go through this difficult time.[17]

▶ The Emptiness of the Lost Baby

Sometimes babies do not make it safely to birth. Some couples lose their babies

---

12 Eisenberg, Murkoff, and Hathaway, *What to Expect When You're Expecting*, p. 339.

13 Hayman, *A Miracle in the Making*, p. 41.

14 Eisenberg, Murkoff, and Hathaway, *What to Expect When You're Expecting*, pp. 325-341.

15 Hayman, *A Miracle in the Making*, p. 37.

16 Hayman, *A Miracle in the Making*, pp. 41-42.

17 Eisenberg, Murkoff, and Hathaway, *What to Expect When You're Expecting*, pp. 339-341.

in either the first or second trimester through miscarriage. Sometimes the egg implants in an area that cannot sustain the fetus, and the resulting ectopic pregnancy endangers the life of the mother as well as the baby. Sometimes the baby dies just before or during birth. Some babies live only a few minutes, a few hours, a few days—allowing far too few memories for the parents who will grieve for them for a long time to come. Some couples are unable to conceive, and spend years yearning for the baby that would fill their hearts and their empty nursery with joy. Some parents, unable to offer their baby a secure and stable life, make an adoption plan for their baby so that a loving couple can provide the care they wish they themselves could.

When the pregnancy ends tragically, the parents may need help to grieve the loss of their baby and of their dream.

The Lost Baby: Miscarriage, Ectopic Pregnancy, Stillbirth, Infant Death

When babies die or pregnancy ends unsuccessfully, a major challenge tends to be the misunderstanding that surrounds these situations. Many people who have not experienced such loss fail to understand the couple's grief. Often parents experience feelings of grief and guilt. Even though friends and family may not consider it a major loss, the couple will often need the kind of care that a Stephen Minister provides.

Miscarriage

Miscarriage—the loss of the pregnancy before the 20th week—occurs in as many as 15 to 20 percent of all known pregnancies. But people rarely understand the emotional and physical trauma involved in this loss. Parents who lose a baby, even in the fairly early stages of pregnancy, experience a real loss. It is the death of their child. The fact that they never got to know that child can be a source of deep grief as well.

The fact that the baby was not full-term seems to negate the significance of the loss for some of the family and friends, who tend to dismiss the loss as a minor setback—or even one to be welcomed. The well-meant platitudes utterly trivialize the couple's experience of loss:

▸ "The baby must have been deformed or sick. Miscarriage is nature's way of getting rid of its mistakes."

▸ "You're probably lucky you lost the baby."

▸ "You can always have another baby."

No matter how many children the couple may go on to have in later years or how many children they already have had, the miscarriage is the loss of this unique child, and most parents never forget those babies.

Grief over a miscarried baby is like grief over any other death or loss, except that it's more private and less sanctioned. People don't expect parents to grieve the loss of these children, and are more embarrassed than sympathetic toward these parents. For many, the grief is borne in silence.

Most couples feel guilt when their baby miscarries, wondering what they have done to cause it. And despite all the warnings to avoid one thing or another, most women have done nothing to cause the miscarriage. Still, when a miscarriage occurs and no concrete explanation is available for it, the couple may tend to blame themselves and try to figure out how they might have prevented it.

Most couples are also unprepared for the physical aspects of the miscarriage. As Susan Borg and Judith Lasker explain, "Few couples expect a miscarriage to occur at all. When it does, they are surprised by the event and frightened and overwhelmed by its intensity."[18] The individual symptoms vary in degree, but most women are shocked and dismayed at the heaviness of the bleeding, the intensity of the pain of the contractions, and the passage of the clots that signal the loss of the pregnancy.

The grief of parents who have lost a child through miscarriage resembles the feelings of those in any bereavement. They feel emptiness and sorrow for the loss of the baby who had become very real to them both. First-time parents may fear that if they have miscarried once, they may never bear a healthy child. Parents who have lost a baby through miscarriage need emotional support and caring to help them as they work through the weeks and months ahead—not embarrassed silence or platitudes.

Ectopic Pregnancy
A couple who experiences an ectopic pregnancy also needs time to grieve. In ectopic pregnancy, the embryo implants outside the uterus—usually in the fallopian tube. It is a life-threatening condi-

tion for the mother, because as the embryo grows, it pushes against the walls of the tube, and unless the condition is detected early enough, the tube will burst, causing internal hemorrhaging and possibly death.[19]

Ectopic pregnancy is difficult to diagnose, especially since the woman may not even be aware that she is pregnant. Since ectopic pregnancies can become emergencies without much warning, most couples have little or no time to adjust. Sometimes friends' and family's relief that the woman has survived obscures for them the loss of the child. The couple may feel sorrow, guilt, and fear over the loss of their child, but they may not find much understanding for their loss.

Most couples who miscarry can go on to have healthy children. Couples who have had an ectopic pregnancy, however, may face difficulties in future pregnancies as well: "The studies which have been done found that between one-third and one-half of women who have had an ectopic pregnancy eventually have a baby. The possibility becomes smaller with each subsequent ectopic pregnancy."[20]

Stillbirth and Infant Death
Babies who are born dead are a source of special grief to parents. The pregnancy and the long labor usually result in a joyful consequence; to have it end in tragedy is unexpected and devastating. Sometimes the baby dies days, even weeks, before labor starts, and the

---

18 Borg and Lasker, *When Pregnancy Fails*, p. 30.

19 Borg and Lasker, *When Pregnancy Fails*, pp. 42, 46.

20 Borg and Lasker, *When Pregnancy Fails*, p. 47.

mother must carry her grief as well as the child until natural labor begins. Other times there is no warning that the baby is having problems.

Parents long to know what caused their baby to die, and all too often there simply is no satisfactory information for them. According to Borg and Lasker, "In up to half of all fetal deaths, the cause of death is never determined."[21] Some possible reasons include problems with the umbilical cord, which supplies oxygen and nutrition to the baby, or with the placement of the placenta.[22]

Even when the cause of death can be identified, however, it rarely alleviates the concern over future children or relieves the aching emptiness and deep grief the parents feel.

Some babies are born alive but very ill. Sometimes the doctors can tell that the child will live only a few hours, days, weeks, or months; other times they simply won't know. Such parents are in limbo—unable to rejoice in their new baby because they have no assurance that the baby will ever come home; unable to grieve effectively because the baby is not yet gone; unable to feel any release from the stress of uncertainty.

Parents may need special support after the loss of a child. They have cherished hopes and dreams for this baby. They may need help to accept and grieve the loss of their baby.

Infertility

For some couples, the crisis of childbirth is their inability even to conceive a child. Some 15 percent of all couples are infertile, which means that they have not been able to conceive after one year of regular sexual intercourse without the use of any kind of birth control.[23] Specialists may be able to recommend tests and techniques for these couples to try, and sometimes fertility drugs will allow couples who have been unable to conceive a child to become pregnant. But for some couples, month after month and year after year will pass, and pregnancy will simply not occur. Fertility clinics will be very expensive and probably not covered by insurance.

For these couples, the sight of babies and pregnant women may bring on a sense of longing and of loss. They may grieve the child that they will never have. All too often, their friends and family may not understand their grief and may tell them to snap out of it and get on with their lives. But for the infertile couple, the lives they have to get on with are not the lives they had planned for themselves, and their loss is real.

Adoption

Sometimes the mother cannot provide appropriate care for her child, and she decides to make an adoption plan. Allowing a loving couple to parent her child is a heart-wrenching decision. The mother who makes an adoption plan

---

21 Borg and Lasker, *When Pregnancy Fails*, p. 66.

22 Borg and Lasker, *When Pregnancy Fails*, pp. 66-67.

23 The American College of Obstetricians and Gynecologists, *ACOG Guide to Preconception Care*, reprinted from ACOG Guide to *Planning for Pregnancy, Birth, and Beyond* (Washington, D.C.: American College of Obstetricians and Gynecologists, 1990), p. 26.

faces the emptiness of the baby's loss and the longing for the child. She may grieve over her decision even while she knows it is the best one to make. She may feel guilt. And there may be no one with whom she can share her feelings. This grieving mother needs someone to listen to her feelings nonjudgmentally and empathetically and to help her accept her decision.

► The Anguish of a Sick or Premature Baby

Some babies are born sick or with disabilities. Others are born too early to function entirely on their own. The joyous event that the birth should have been becomes a time of even greater anxiety as parents watch their baby struggle for survival, or realize that even if their baby survives, he or she will never be the perfect infant they dreamed about.

Premature babies struggle to breathe with immature lungs. They must gain enough weight that they are not so fragile—which is difficult if the baby is so tiny that he or she cannot nurse strongly. Many of these tiny babies, however, have an excellent chance at a normal life.

Babies who are ill or afflicted with severe disabilities may not have as good an outlook. The babies may face surgery to repair developmental problems or congenital deficiencies. Or the disabilities may cause the child to die within a few days, weeks, months, or years.

Parents of these children may need much support and help coping with continued visits to the hospital. If the mother is trying to breast-feed the baby, she may need to make daily trips to the hospital. Parents may need help with childcare for their other children, especially if the baby's stay is long.

The parents may also need help with the expenses of their baby's extended hospital stay. Knowing what resources are available may relieve some of the stress.

Parents of a sick or severely disabled baby may also need help coming to terms with their grief over the loss of their ideal child. While they may love their baby, a child with severe problems will demand time, attention, and resources that go far beyond the needs of a normal child. The parents' lives will never again be the same. At times, the parents may wonder why this happened and feel resentment. They may feel ambivalence about becoming too attached to this child, especially if the child is not likely to survive to adulthood. They may feel that they somehow have failed by not producing a perfectly healthy baby. They may need someone to listen to their feelings nonjudgmentally and to allow them to deal with the issues in their own way and at their own pace.

► Postpartum Sadness

Postpartum letdown is not a universal experience, and how and when it appears varies also. Sometimes the depression is partly due to rapid hormonal changes just after childbirth, and a woman's sensitivity to those hormonal shifts help explain why about half of women experience some degree of postpartum depression, most commonly about the third day after delivery. They may feel weepy, sad, irritable, or moody, and this feeling can last anywhere from 48 hours to six or eight weeks. But this depression can occur any time during the first year and affects second-time mothers more often than first-time mothers.[24]

Factors other than hormonal shifts may also contribute to postpartum blues.

Exhaustion

Giving birth is extremely hard, tiring work. Trying to rest up in the hospital can be difficult with the normal interruptions of hospital routine, and the aches and pains that follow even a normal delivery can make sleep elusive. And just when the woman needs her rest the most, she must begin adjusting to the needs of a tiny infant who depends on her for everything, all the time. Many new mothers would give a king's ransom for a single night's uninterrupted sleep.

Most physicians advise new mothers to rest whenever the baby sleeps. But instead of resting, some mothers use the quiet time to catch up on chores, and end up so tired that they almost cannot cope with the baby or their own needs. The situation is compounded if the mother has older children who also need her care and time and energy. It may all seem overwhelming.

The new father has also gone through the anxiety and sleeplessness of the labor and delivery, and often has to return to work the next day. Once his wife and baby have come home from the hospital, he is probably also short on sleep. Newborns do not sleep through the night, and many fathers share getting up in those early hours, even if their wives are breast-feeding the baby. And through all this, the father is expected to function at work as though nothing has changed.

Exhaustion is one of the likeliest reasons that a new parent might become depressed. New parents can avoid fatigue by accepting help, by "being less compulsive about doing things that can wait," by using the baby's naps and even feeding times for rest periods, and by "nursing or bottle-feeding in bed or in a comfortable chair with your feet up."[25] To care for someone as dependent as a newborn takes great stamina and patience, and new parents need to make sure they get adequate rest.

Physical Discomfort and Dissatisfaction with Postpartum Appearance

Although a woman who is expecting a baby may bloom with health and well-being for the entire nine months, most women who have just had a baby look rather the worse for wear. The extreme pressure exerted by the mother in pushing the baby through the birth canal can leave her with black or bloodshot eyes and tiny red dots or actual black-and-blue bruises all over her face or upper chest.

A new mother is usually coping with a host of physical discomforts after the

---

24 Eisenberg, Murkoff, and Hathaway, *What to Expect When You're Expecting*, p. 398.

25 Eisenberg, Murkoff, and Hathaway, *What to Expect When You're Expecting*, p. 399.

delivery as well. Often there are stitches—either from a cesarean delivery or from the episiotomy or any tearing—which may hurt or itch. Even if the delivery went smoothly, the mother may experience pain in the perineal area because of the stretching and bruising the delivery caused. The mother may find it difficult to sit or walk for some time. If the delivery was difficult, she may be generally sore from the pushing. Most women have some degree of constipation after delivery. And about the third or fourth day, the mother's milk comes in, often leaving the breasts swollen, hard as a rock, and painfully tender until the mother and baby are able to establish a workable routine for nursing. Nursing mothers often experience some nipple soreness as their breasts become irritated by the frequent nursing; the nipples may even crack or bleed until they finally become toughened by the baby's nursing. The first week or two postpartum can be a time of considerable discomfort for the mother.

Most doctors suggest some therapies to ease postpartum discomfort, most of which do not involve drugs that would pass into the mother's milk if she is nursing. Healing certainly takes time, but getting enough sleep and eating properly can help the postpartum woman overcome many of the discomforts she faces.

A few women might be able to fit into their prepregnancy clothes at just a week postpartum, but the vast majority of women—especially women who have previously had children—probably won't be wearing anything form-fitting for at least a month. Nine months of pregnancy is enough—to look somewhat

pregnant afterward is very disappointing to the new mother. A person who feels unattractive or who is experiencing constant discomfort may feel trapped and frustrated.

Encourage the woman who has just had a baby to be patient with herself. A Stephen Minister can help to put her frustrations and anxieties into perspective simply by listening and reflecting them to her.

Concern over the Relationship with the Baby

Many new parents experience some disappointment after the baby is born. They expect their first meeting with the new baby to be a joyous occasion—that at the drum roll they will immediately feel like the perfect mother and father with a gush of love for this tiny creature that is theirs. Often, this is not the case. The baby is screaming, red, wrinkled, and not at all cuddly. "One study found that it took an average of over two weeks (and often as long as nine weeks) for mothers to begin having positive feelings toward their newborns."[26]

Not to feel this gush of motherly or fatherly love may be disconcerting to new parents. But this is a normal reaction. Parents need to get to know their infant in order for this bonding to take place. As long as the closeness and comfort with the baby increase as the days and weeks go by, matters are progressing as they should. Only if the parent finds him- or herself developing an anger or antagonism toward the baby should he

26 Eisenberg, Murkoff, and Hathaway, *What to Expect When You're Expecting*, p. 383.

or she begin to feel concern and enlist the help of the pediatrician.[27]

Anticlimax

For some parents, the ending of the pregnancy results in anticlimax—a flatness, wondering whether this is all there is to it. The attention and the excitement that had focused on the mother-to-be has shifted to the new baby, and the attitude of many toward the new mother may shift to near disapproval. Through their comments or body language people may convey questions like, "Why are you still looking pregnant now that you've delivered?" All the classes, the prenatal visits, the showers, the excitement are over, and the parents are left with an overwhelming sense of responsibility and even worry. The parents may feel a sort of after-the-holidays letdown. It can seem as if all that lies ahead is a lot of work. It can be pretty discouraging.

Usually this feeling of flatness will change with time. The parents' former lives have changed irrevocably; finding the new paths to becoming a family can take time and can feel very strange. The parents need to become comfortable with their new self-images. As they become more comfortable with the little stranger who has changed their lives, the strangeness and flatness is usually replaced by confidence and the knowledge that they, more than anyone else, know best what their baby needs. This growth takes time and patience, and a Stephen Minister who can walk with a new parent through his or her trials will make the passage to confidence much smoother.

Postpartum Depression

Some 10 to 20 percent of women experience postpartum depression, which does not diminish but intensifies as the weeks pass after delivery. If the care receiver has had her baby two to four weeks earlier and the symptoms of her depression are not improving but are actually getting worse, the Stephen Minister will probably want to suggest that the care receiver seek professional evaluation. The warning signs of postpartum depression[28] are listed in Reference Box D.

REFERENCE BOX D

Warning Signs of Postpartum Depression

▶ Crying spells

▶ Nervousness

▶ Frequent irritability

▶ Low energy

▶ Appetite loss

▶ Sleep disturbance

▶ Trouble caring for oneself

▶ Not wanting to be with the baby

▶ Fears about one's own or about the baby's health

If the care receiver is indeed suffering from depression, the Stephen Minister will need to ask the professional caregiver whether she should continue to

---

27 Adapted from Eisenberg, Murkoff, and Hathaway, *What to Expect When You're Expecting*, p. 383.

28 Adapted from "Coping with Postpartum Adjustment" by Diane G. Sanford, Ph.D., (St. Louis, privately published), n.d.

meet with the care receiver and then follow the decision of the professional. The ultimate goal for the Stephen Minister is the best possible treatment for the care receiver.

The Stephen Minister needs to recognize the signs of depression in the father as well as the mother. Childbirth is a crisis for men and women alike, and the father may also be in need of support and care to resolve the crisis in the direction of greater wholeness.

▶ Pregnancy and Childbirth as a Crisis—the Father's Perspective

Fathers-to-be are all too often the forgotten members in this new family equation. The attention tends to be focused on the mother-to-be, and the expectant father may feel left out. Yet fathers have a vital role in the entire pregnancy and childbirth and provide support and encouragement to their wives. They also face many changes and challenges during and after pregnancy and childbirth.

Some fathers experience some of the physical effects of the pregnancy along with their wives. This is called the couvade syndrome and is described in Reference Box E.

REFERENCE BOX E

Description of Couvade Syndrome

Couvade is the common but poorly understood phenomenon whereby the expectant father experiences somatic symptoms during the pregnancy for which there is no recognized physiological basis. Symptoms commonly include indigestion, increased or decreased appetite, weight gain, diarrhea or constipation, headache, and toothache. Onset is usually during the third gestational month with a secondary rise in the late third trimester. Symptoms generally resolve with childbirth.[29]

The father should be encouraged to be involved in the pregnancy. If possible, he should go with his wife when she sees the obstetrician, particularly when the doctor will first be listening to the heartbeat or performing a sonogram. The father can also become as informed as possible about the process of pregnancy and childbirth—knowledge will help him know what to expect and how best to deal with problems and concerns. Decorating the baby's room and shopping for the items the baby will need can keep the father involved.

Establishing contact with the baby will also make the baby more real to the father. Babies can hear and feel through the womb, and a father can talk or sing or read to his baby and can feel the baby's kicks. Such contact can make the father feel more connected to this baby—and to the mother as well.

The father may feel some frustration over his wife's moodiness. He may feel the weight of the responsibility of giving his wife support to maintain all the good habits that will ensure the best pregnancy possible. He may worry about

---

29 From an abstract of H. Klein, "Couvade Syndrome: Male Counterpart to Pregnancy," *Int J Psychiatry Med*, 21: 1, 1991, 57-69, which appeared in "Couvade: Sympathetic Pregnancy" in the Childbirth.Org Home Page [on-line, cited 4 December 1998; 11:11 A.M. CST]. Available from the World Wide Web: <http://pregnancy.miningco.com /library/weekly/aa033197.htm>.

falling apart during his wife's labor. Concerns about sexual intercourse during the pregnancy and after the birth may arise. If the pregnancy is high-risk and the wife is confined to bed, the demands on the father will be particularly heavy, as he will have to assume the household chores and taking care of his wife's needs as well as his regular work. The father-to-be needs to be able to talk out his feelings of frustration, loneliness, and anxiety and figure out how best to deal with them.

A father-to-be needs the same support and nurturing as the mother-to-be. His needs just may not be as obvious.

▶ Getting Ready for the In-Class Sessions

In the In-Class Sessions you will use what you have read in this Preclass Reading to assess the needs of hypothetical care receivers and decide how to care for them. You may want to review this Preclass Reading right before each class so it is fresh in your mind.

Crises of Pregnancy and Childbirth

Outline and Focus Notes

*"A voice is heard in Ramah,
mourning and great weeping,
Rachel weeping for her children
and refusing to be comforted,
because her children are no more."*

Jeremiah 31:15

I. Comfort in the Midst of Crisis

II. Ministering to a Parent-to-Be in a Normal Pregnancy

A. Types of Care Not to Provide

B. Appropriate Care for a Stephen Minister to Provide

III. Caring for Crises in a Normal Pregnancy

FOCUS NOTE 1

How Stephen Ministers Care

▶ Listening, which includes reflecting content, feelings, and spiritual concerns and asking open-ended questions

▶ Empathizing and helping care receivers recognize, accept, and express their feelings

▶ Sharing distinctively Christian caring resources (biblical stories and verses, prayer, forgiveness, blessings, and "a cup of cold water") in ways that are appropriate and sensitive to a care receiver's needs

▶ Remaining process-oriented and leaving the results to God

▶ Relating assertively

▶ Maintaining boundaries

- ▶ Maintaining confidentiality
- ▶ Recommending professional care when the care receiver's needs exceed the care the Stephen Minister can provide

---

FOCUS NOTE 2

Needs and Concerns during a Normal Pregnancy

- ▶ Depression
- ▶ Physical changes and concerns
- ▶ Emotional demands of pregnancy
- ▶ Loss of privacy
- ▶ Concern for the health of the baby
- ▶ Financial concerns
- ▶ Concern about changes in the couple's relationship
- ▶ Difficult decisions about whether or not to go back to work
- ▶ Difficult decisions about whether or not to breast-feed

FOCUS NOTE 3

Situation 1: Celeste

"I just don't know how I'm going to cope with another six months of this," said Celeste, clearly exasperated. "In spite of being sick every single morning for the last six weeks, I've gained four pounds already, from eating almost nothing but crackers! I'll need to be in maternity clothes in no time—and I don't have any.

"And it isn't as if I have time to be sick, either. I've never been so busy at work. I'm beginning to wonder if they want me to do the whole year's work in the next six months before I have the baby. I don't feel as if I have any time for myself.

"Terry isn't all that much help, either. You should see my house! Up until now I've always done the cleaning and have managed to keep it looking nice. But when I get home now, all I want to do is stretch out on the sofa and take a nap, and there goes my evening. But does Terry ever lift a finger to help? Oh, he'll load the dishwasher and stuff—he'll even pop some frozen dinners in the oven. But dust? Or clean the kitchen floor? I don't think he even notices. Oh, I know he's been busy at work too; he's brought work home the last few nights. But I can't do everything by myself."

Discussion Questions

1. Which of the needs and concerns of a normal pregnancy does the care receiver seem to be experiencing?

2. In what process-oriented ways could a Stephen Minister offer care and support?

Situation 2: Michael

"I am really worried," Michael said. "I don't know how we're going to manage when Laurie has the baby. We're planning to have her stay home with the baby for at least a year. But her salary amounts to about a third of our total income. That's going to be hard to lose! I honestly don't know how we're going to make ends meet. We've decided she isn't going to go back to work in six weeks, but I still wonder whether that is the right decision.

"I know that we have a good doctor and that she will do everything that can be done for Laurie, but I still worry about Laurie and the baby. If the baby isn't healthy I don't know how I'll handle it. Also, when I was a child I had an aunt who died in childbirth. I don't think that will happen to Laurie, but I feel so out of control in this situation. Once she starts having the baby, there's nothing I can do to help except be there. I can't imagine trying to raise a child alone.

"This has been so crazy. Laurie started with morning sickness, and I started throwing up too. She laughed and thought it was 'sweet,' but I was embarrassed by it. She seems so preoccupied with this baby. I wonder if our relationship will ever be the same."

Situation 3: Melissa

"I am just so miserable," sobbed Melissa. "I'm seven-and-a-half-months pregnant; I've gained 20 pounds. I'm ugly. Look at my legs—I don't even have ankles anymore!

"I hate being pregnant. I look like a walrus and I waddle like a duck. I can't eat garlic or onions or green peppers because I'll taste them for two days. I love garlic and onions and peppers, and I hate all the milk I'm supposed to drink.

"Everyone seems to think that my pregnancy is their business. They ask when the baby is due, and when I tell them they make a face like I shouldn't be this big this early. What business is it of theirs? I've started feeling really hostile whenever anyone mentions anything about my pregnancy.

"Everyone says I should breast-feed the baby, but I really don't want to. I don't want to be tied down like that, and I don't want to be the only one who has to get up at 2:00 in the morning to feed the baby. When I told my friend, Sheila, what I've been thinking, she was shocked. She made me feel really guilty, but I'm not going to change my mind.

"I'm tired of my back hurting. I'm tired of being too tired to do anything fun. I'm tired of not being able to sleep. I know I shouldn't eat so much, but sometimes that's the only thing that makes me feel better. The further this pregnancy goes, the more isolated I feel. Sometimes I can hardly force myself to get up in the morning.

"There are days when I'm sure I'll be the only pregnant woman who stays pregnant forever. But other days I dread the childbirth. I've heard it's awful—that your whole body feels ripped in half. I hate pain. I just know I'm going to be an absolute baby about it, and all the nurses will make fun of me and my doctor will be mad at me for making such a fuss."

IV. Looking Ahead

V. Opening

VI. Caring for a Parent-to-Be in a High-Risk Pregnancy

FOCUS NOTE 7

Dorothy

"I just don't know how I'm going to get through the next three months!" Dorothy exclaimed. "I've been flat on my back—almost, anyway—for a whole week now, and I think I am going to go out of my mind. What am I supposed to do with myself? I hate soap operas and daytime talk shows, I don't have any good books right now, and you can only watch so many movies. Besides, it just makes me realize how lonely it is here.

"I miss being at work. Sometimes one of my friends will call to say hi, but most of my friends work, so they're gone all day, which is when I really feel lost. It's better when Joe is home—he tells me what's going on at his work and all. But I feel so out of everything—it's just as if my whole life is on hold!

"Poor Joe comes home from a long day at work, and then he has to start dinner and bring it to me. He's been so good about making sure I have everything I need for the day before he leaves for work in the morning. I did all the cooking until last week, when the doctor said I had to stay put. Joe tries hard, but he got involved in watching the news the day before yesterday and burned both the chops. We had to throw them away and have hot dogs.

"I feel so bad about all the extra work he's facing. I know he's got a lot going at work right now—it's time for their fiscal year closing, and he's bringing work home almost every night. But it kills me to see the laundry mounting up and the dust gathering on everything. I wish I could get up and take care of it all.

"But I know I can't. The doctor said that the pregnancy is precarious enough that I have to stay absolutely off my feet, except to go to the bathroom, for at least a month and maybe for the whole three. The baby seems to be doing fine at this point—I know I just need to be patient. I don't want to risk losing this baby! But I just don't know if I can stay lying down when I feel fine and I know I have so much to do!"

Charles

"I am at the end of my rope!" Charles said, his voice tight with frustration. "I just don't know how I'm going to make it through the rest of the nine months! Trudy has been on total bedrest now for about a month, and I'm run ragged. I come home from work at night so tired I can hardly stand up, and right away I have to start cooking dinner. And it can't just be TV dinners or anything simple because the doctor says those prepackaged meals are too high in sodium for Trudy. So I end up actually having to cook.

"And if I want clean shirts for the week, I'd better make sure I've washed them on Saturday. I forgot about the clothes in the dryer last week and ended up having to iron an entire load of shirts. I'm just not used to this stuff.

"It's not fair. Does she really have to stay totally on her back for the rest of the pregnancy? Sometimes it makes me crazy, trying to do my work and all the work around the house too. Not that I'm doing that much cleaning or that the house looks great or anything—I just don't notice whether or not I've put the dishes away or picked up the living room before I go to bed.

"What I really have trouble with is not ever being able to get away from it. Even on Friday night—Trudy and I always used to eat dinner out and go to a movie on Fridays. But now I feel really guilty about leaving her alone to go out and do something with my friends, because she's already been home alone all day and is just dying for someone to talk to. But by the end of the day, all I want to do is crawl into a hole and drag it in after me. It's all I can do to listen. I'd love to get out once in a while.

"And when people do come over, everybody is always fussing over Trudy. Everything is Trudy, Trudy, Trudy—how hard she has it and how awful it is to have to stay in bed all day every day. What about me? I've never worked so hard in my life, and I get no credit whatsoever for it. I'm stuck at home too! At times I really resent the whole situation."

Five Important Facts about High-Risk Pregnancies

1.

2.

3.

4.

5.

Additional ideas:

FOCUS NOTE 10

Five Needs Those Experiencing High-Risk Pregnancies May Have

1.

2.

3.

4.

5.

Additional ideas:

Five Ways to Care for People Experiencing a High-Risk Pregnancy

1.

2.

3.

4.

5.

Additional ideas:

VII. Ministering to Those Who Are Infertile

FOCUS NOTE 12

Susan

"I can't believe I broke down right in the mall," Susan sobbed. "Right there in the middle of all those people, with all their little boys and girls. But there they were, all waiting in this long line to see Santa Claus. The little girls were all dressed in pretty party dresses, red and green and pink, velvet and chiffon—just as sweet as anything you've ever seen! And the little boys in their Christmas best! This one little fellow had the cutest little red and white polka-dot bow tie—I just wanted to grab him and hug him!

"And then it was all too much. Just two weeks ago the doctor gave us the bad news that we can't have children. And it just hit me like a ton of bricks. I'll never be waiting in a line to see Santa as my mother had for me. I'll never take pictures of my little ones tearing into presents on Christmas morning or singing in a Christmas pageant at school with their little faces looking like angels'. And I couldn't help it—I just started crying and crying. And I couldn't stop! I drove all the way home with tears streaming down my cheeks. I've never felt so totally alone, so absolutely devastated. I don't think it had hit me until then what it would mean not ever to have children of my own.

"We've exhausted all the possibilities for having our own children. Ron suggested that we might consider adopting a baby. I don't know—I can't even think about that yet. I just can't even comprehend not having a baby of my own. Why us? There are so many teenagers out there who get pregnant without even trying! Why can't we?"

VIII. Looking Ahead

IX. Opening

X. Ministering to a Parent Who Has Lost a Child

A. A True Experience of Great Loss and Grief

FOCUS NOTE 13

The Grief That Comes from Losing a Child

Any pregnancy is a time of major emotional and physical changes. Psychologists consider pregnancy—especially the first—an important life crisis, a turning point in the individual's development as significant as puberty. Ordinarily this crisis is resolved by the birth of a healthy child. When this does not happen, the crisis deepens. Parents may feel they have suffered a major setback in their lives. They wonder if they will have to live their lives without children or without as many as they wanted.

These parents suffer a loss of self-esteem. The plans and dreams they shared during the pregnancy have been destroyed. They experience the pain of failure, the failure to fulfill one of the most fundamental of human acts: to give birth to a healthy child.

They experience these feelings alone, isolated from others. Most of their family and friends do not understand what sort of emotional support is needed. "At least you never knew this child," they will say, hoping to ease the pain. Or "It could have been worse." Or "You'll have another one." In their own way they might be trying to offer hope for the future, but to the bereaved parents it often seems that these people do not comprehend the enormity of what has happened.

What others do not understand is that the parents are grieving for the loss of a very real person. As pediatricians Marshall Klaus and John Kennell have shown, "bonding" between parent and child begins early in pregnancy. Long before the actual birth, parents are readying themselves for the arrival of their son or daughter. An image develops of how the infant will look and act. Parents may talk to the baby and even call him or her by name. The mourning after an unsuccessful pregnancy may be different from the mourning for the loss of an older child, but it is still grief for someone who already exists in the parents' minds.

Many professionals who come in contact with the mourning couple—medical people, clergy, funeral directors—often fail to provide appropriate support and counseling. This is true in many situations of

---

death and when a miscarriage, an ectopic pregnancy, a stillbirth, . . . or an early infant death occurs, it is especially important for professionals to assist parents in beginning to grieve. They can do this by helping to create concrete memories for the parents to hold on to. Yet in too many hospitals, still, all reminders of the baby are removed quickly, and parents are not encouraged to consider a funeral or other formal mourning practices.[1]

B. Discovering Needs for Care

FOCUS NOTE 14

Joyce

When Ellen answered the phone, it was her care receiver Joyce. "Ellen, can you come right over? I woke up this morning spotting, and I'm scared to death."

Ellen hurried right over to Joyce's home, where she found Joyce lying on the couch. Joyce was almost three months pregnant with her first child.

"Thank you so much for coming," Joyce said. "I talked to the doctor this morning, and he told me to stay off my feet and just to relax. But when I asked him if everything was going to be all right, he didn't say—all he would say was that he couldn't be sure, but that I should call him if the bleeding got any worse or if I feel cramping."

"Has it gotten any worse?" Ellen asked.

Joyce hesitated. "I suppose it has. I've had cramping for the last three or four hours—but not quite as bad as menstrual cramps, and the bleeding has gotten a little heavier. I'm sure everything's going to be all right. Don't you think so? I've been praying since I got up this morning, and I told God that if this baby is all right, I'm going to be the greatest mother this world has ever seen. I'm sure that the bleeding isn't serious."

1 Susan Borg and Judith Lasker, *When Pregnancy Fails: Families Coping with Miscarriage, Ectopic Pregnancy, Stillbirth, and Infant Death*, rev. ed. (New York: Bantam Books, 1989), pp. 7-8.

Ted

It was just a week before the estimated due date when Ted's wife, Alison, noticed that she hadn't felt the baby kicking for several hours. When Alison called her obstetrician, she told them to come to the office immediately. Her face was grave as she listened through the stethoscope for the baby's heartbeat. She shook her head. "I can't find a heartbeat." Their baby was dead.

The doctor advised Ted and Alison to wait until labor began on its own. Four very difficult days passed, with Alison crying for several hours each day. Ted carried on. It was Ted who took down the baby bed in the little nursery, who folded the tiny outfits and sleepers and booties and put them into boxes for storage, who put away the mobile and the brightly colored pictures, who took the bassinet they had borrowed back to the Wilsons. He answered the telephone and fielded the questions from well-meaning friends, passing on the news as needed. He worked tirelessly after he returned from work each day to make things go smoothly. Friends commented that he was a tower of strength for Alison.

When labor began, he helped Alison breathe through the early contractions and brought her to the hospital when the doctor said he should. The birth progressed fairly uneventfully, and Ted helped Alison, who was heavily sedated against the pain, complete the labor and delivery. After the baby was born, the nurse washed the little bundle and wrapped him in a blanket. "It was a boy," she said softly, and brought him to Alison.

Alison held the still form and looked at him through her tears. "Why, Ted, he's beautiful," she said.

Ted patted her shoulder. He looked for a short time at the baby and then looked away. He moved over to the doctor and asked, "Will Alison be all right?"

Joan

Marge arrived at Joan's house for their fourth caring visit. Joan had miscarried a few weeks earlier; she had been about two months into the pregnancy. Marge had been assigned to help Joan through this difficult time.

When Joan opened the door, her eyes were red and swollen and full of tears. "Come on in," Joan said, stepping aside.

The house looked cluttered. A bunch of half-empty cups and glasses stood on the TV tray in front of the sofa, along with a saucer holding a dried-out peanut butter sandwich with a few bites taken out of it. Several magazines lay on the floor next to the sofa, and the newspaper lay scattered on the table. A few bags of trash and some boxes lay near the front door. Marge recognized some of them from the week before.

Joan sat wearily on the sofa and ran her hand through her rumpled hair. Her sweat suit was wrinkled, as though she had been sleeping in it. "I don't know what's the matter with me," she told Marge. "I just can't seem to get motivated.

"All the time I keep thinking about the baby—wondering whether it was a boy or a girl, whether it was healthy. I keep wondering what I could have done to save the baby.

"It was so awful! When I started spotting, I just figured it was normal stuff. Nobody ever has anything go wrong with their pregnancies—why should I? And when the bleeding started so badly and the pain got so terrible, I just couldn't believe it. Why was this happening? What had I done to deserve this? And why did my baby have to die?

"Then, after it was all over and I was lying in the hospital bed that night, I realized what had happened." Joan leaned forward, her eyes full of tears. "I never told anybody this, but I have to tell someone. The evening before I lost the baby, Mark and I had this terrible argument. He shouted at me, and I cried and cried—for over an hour." She covered her face with her hands. "I know that's when the baby died, and that it's all my fault. I shouldn't have gotten so upset. You have to stay upbeat when you're pregnant, and I didn't. That's why I lost the baby."

Five Needs

Complete the needs for your group's assigned care receiver. Later take notes for the other two care receivers.

Five Needs That Care Receiver Joyce (in Focus Note 14) Might Have

1.

2.

3.

4.

5.

Five Needs That Care Receiver Ted (in Focus Note 15) Might Have

1.

2.

3.

4.

5.

Five Needs That Care Receiver Joan (in Focus Note 16) Might Have

1.

2.

3.

4.

5.

Five Ways to Care

Complete five ways to care for your group's assigned care receiver. Later take notes for the other two care receivers.

Five Ways to Care for Care Receiver Joyce (in Focus Note 14)

1.

2.

3.

4.

5.

Five Ways to Care for Care Receiver Ted (in Focus Note 15)

1.

2.

3.

4.

5.

Five Ways to Care for Care Receiver Joan (in Focus Note 16)

1.

2.

3.

4.

5.

XI. Caregiver's Compass Review

_____

_____

_____

_____

_____   COMPASSIONATE · FULL OF FAITH · SKILLED · TRUSTWORTHY   _____

_____   _____

_____   _____

_____   _____

_____

_____

_____

_____

XII. Looking Ahead

> ### Prayer Partner Requests and Thanksgivings
>
> My prayer partner is _____
>
> Prayer requests and thanksgivings to share with my prayer partner
>
> _____
>
> _____
>
> Prayer requests and thanksgivings shared by my prayer partner
>
> _____
>
> _____

Providing Spiritual Care

Preclass Reading

Contents

▶ Stories of People Who Need Spiritual Care

Art sat at home and watched the Sunday morning news programs. He looked at the clock and noted that the worship service was just starting. He thought, "It'll be a cold day in hell when they see me there again."

When Irene, his wife of 43 years, was diagnosed with cancer, Art had been so worried; there were so many important issues to think about. He hadn't thought about calling the church. Within two months Irene died and no one from the church ever visited. When he called the church to arrange for the funeral, the pastor was surprised to learn that Irene had been ill. No one contacted Art after the funeral. He had been left alone to grieve the loss of the love of his life.

Since then, Art had missed church eight Sundays in a row, and no one called to see if he was okay. It was obvious that he could have died too and no one at the church would have given it a second thought.

Art clicked the remote from one television program to another. The church hadn't missed him when he hadn't showed up, so he sure wasn't going back now.

****

Gretchen sat in her nightgown and stared out the glass doors to the backyard. She sighed as she remembered the swing set that used to sit in the middle of the yard and the children who used to play on it. She was so busy during those years, running kids everywhere, doing her duty with the Parent Teacher Organization, and making sure homework got done. At times Gretchen had dreamed about when the kids would be grown and gone and she could have a life again. Now that time had arrived, and the dream had become a nightmare.

Gretchen saw her reflection in the window and wondered how she had ever reached this predicament. She used to be outgoing and happy all the time. Now she wanted to stay home and hide from the world. She tried praying about her life, asking God for some answers or some help, but when she prayed she felt empty and alone. She didn't believe God heard her prayers anymore. At times she wasn't sure that there was a God.

****

Sylvia stood by Lamar's hospital bed and gripped the cool metal rail. She was afraid she would collapse if she didn't hold herself up. The doctor had just left after delivering the news: The good news was that Lamar would live; the bad news was that he would never move his arms or legs again.

Sylvia's grip on the rail tightened as she thought how stupid Lamar had been, and how out-of-character that was for him. The model teen, the straight-A student, had been drinking at a party and then tried to drive three friends home. Now one friend was dead, and the casualty list might number two before the day was over.

One of Sylvia's tears splashed on the bed rail as she wrestled with so many conflicting feelings. She felt so much sorrow for Lamar and the life he now faced. She felt resentment as it dawned on her how Lamar's changed life would change her life also. She felt her stomach knot as she worried about the other parents suing her and her husband, Cedric. She felt guilty for not being a better parent, for not somehow preventing this from happening.

When she thought about preventing the accident, she wondered where God had been when this happened. She always thought God was watching over her family and protecting them. That was what she always prayed for.

Most of all she felt a profound sense of loss about another way she had lost her son: her deeply entrenched anger at Lamar grew stronger by the minute and she knew she would never be able to forgive him for all this.

► You Are Already a Spiritual Care Provider

You may wonder why you are encountering a module on "Providing Spiritual Care" now. Does someone think that the care you have learned and provided has not been spiritual? By no means. From the beginning of your training you have brought Christ's care to your care receiver. You are already a spiritual care provider.

Your training and experience are very important for providing spiritual care. You've learned to remain process-oriented and respect the care receivers' boundaries. Those are essential skills for spiritual caregivers because it would be the height of presumption to take over the management of another person's relationship with God.

The purpose of this module is to deepen your understanding of providing spiritual care to others. The Preclass Reading and In-Class Sessions will help you to recognize situations where people—including you—need special care for spiritual pain, understand better the reasons for those spiritual needs, and know even more how to give and receive spiritual care. You may also grow in faith as you understand better your needs for spiritual care and the resources you can turn to for help.

► What Is Spiritual Care?

Spiritual care has a simple definition. *Spiritual care is helping people hear and believe that God loves them.*

The definition is simple, but the care is profound. Providing it requires God's help and also some vital skills. When Stephen Ministers give spiritual care, they realize that all their caregiving abilities—their compassion, faith, skills, and trustworthiness—are necessary, but are not enough. In order for care receivers to obtain the healing and wholeness that they need and desire, they need to hear and believe God's promises and receive his gracious love. Anything short of the blessings God gives will never be enough care; it will never provide all that the care receiver needs.

God's Activity

The most important activity in spiritual care is God's activity. The Holy Spirit is the one who gives faith and makes it possible for people to believe. Therefore, the most important activity for a spiritual care provider is to stay connected to God and entrust the care receiver to God's care.

The Caregiver's Role

There is also a role for the caregiver, which includes:

1. recognizing spiritual needs;

2. discerning which conduits of grace are blocked (what is keeping people from hearing and believing); and

3. allying themselves with God to help others find ways to hear and believe more fully.

This Preclass Reading will help you learn to fulfill your role even more confidently and effectively.

▶ Recognizing Spiritual Needs

Sometimes, people are more aware than usual of their need for God. Spiritual needs become critical; they bubble to the surface and create a lot of unhappiness and pain. When this happens, people usually experience other kinds of needs also, but it is important to recognize and respond to the spiritual needs, the ones that no amount of human caregiving will solve, needs that only God can address. You might even call these *God-sized needs* because they are so fundamental and so difficult that they take a crucified and resurrected Savior to solve them.

The stories of Art, Gretchen, and Sylvia at the beginning of this Preclass Reading illustrate such spiritual needs.

▶ Art needs someone to care for his deep hurt and anger by listening and reflecting feelings, but that will not be enough. Art's pain has led him to push away not only God's people but also God. Eventually Art needs to deal with the pain of his grief, and only the hope of the resurrection will be enough to help and heal him.

▶ Gretchen is very sad and seems somewhat depressed. She may need professional care. She also needs a renewed sense of meaning and purpose in her life and the assurance that God is there for her, does hear her prayers, and still loves her.

▶ Sylvia faces a constellation of needs: emotional, financial, relational, and physical. She will need many kinds of care from medical personnel, people who will help her learn to care for Lamar in her home, friends and family, a Stephen Minister, and maybe an attorney and a mental health professional. It won't be long, however, before Sylvia will have to face her need to forgive Lamar, and only her gracious, forgiving God will be able to help her come to terms with that need.

It is possible to misunderstand needs for spiritual care by thinking that any time a person has a spiritual need, he or she is in severe spiritual peril; that having a spiritual need means a person's relationship with God is in danger of ending. *That is not true.*

Everyone has spiritual needs. Jesus said, "I have come that they may have life, and have it to the full" (John 10:10b). Since people fall short of enjoying the full life that Jesus promised, they need spiritual care to hear and believe that God loves them.

A first step in caring for those with spiritual needs is to recognize the spiritual nature of their pain or unhappiness. One way to detect that people have spiritual needs is to know the characteristics of a healthy life of faith in God and then to notice when such characteristics are missing or distorted for them.

Seven Signs of God's Grace in a Person's Life

When people hear and believe that God loves them they are affected by the free flow of God's grace and love. Following are seven signs of God's activity in people's lives.[1] They identify seven ways people are changed when they hear and

---

1 These signs are adapted from *The Minister as Diagnostician: Personal Problems in Pastoral Perspective* by Paul W. Pruyser (Philadelphia: Westminster, 1976), pp. 60-79.

believe that God loves them. These signs overlap somewhat; no one shows these signs perfectly, and everyone will show some of them more than others. Nevertheless, they are present to some extent in lives of faith. When they are noticeably absent or distorted, that is a sign that people are having trouble hearing and believing that God loves them.

1. Awareness of God's Presence

As people hear and believe the promise of God's love, they usually have some sense of God's presence and care for them. Whether they experience God in public worship, private meditation, a small group, or while pondering the majesty of his creation, they have a sense that God is real, that he truly loves them, that he hears their prayers, and that they can count on him to care for them.

2. Faith

Faith is a way of living[2] that demonstrates trust in God. People who hear and believe that God loves them tend to live in ways that show that belief. They have confidence because they know that God is caring for them. They are able to take risks and embrace change because they know that God is in control of the outcome.

Jesus talked about such faith when he said, "'So do not worry, saying, "What shall we eat?" or "What shall we drink?" or "What shall we wear?" For the pa-

---

2 Sometimes people use the word *faith* to mean what they believe about God. According to that definition, the act of faith is one of giving intellectual assent to a body of beliefs or doctrines. The meaning of faith here is different. Here it means what people do based on their beliefs.

gans run after all these things, and your heavenly Father knows that you need them. But seek first his kingdom and his righteousness, and all these things will be given to you as well'" (Matthew 6:31–33). People with faith in God tend to live as Jesus taught, because they know God will take care of them, no matter what.

3. Hope

To hope is to believe in the possibility of a favorable future; it is the opposite of worry, fear, and despair. Hopeful people live positive and fruitful lives. Hope implies a certain discontent with the way things are and propels people to work for a more desirable, God-pleasing future. People who hear and believe the good news about Jesus' resurrection will hope in God, even when all human reasons for hope are gone.

4. Love

When people hear and believe that God loves them, their response is to love God and others. Jesus said, "By this everyone will know that you are my disciples, if you have love for one another" (John 13:35 NRSV). Jesus identified love as the most important command (Mark 12:28–31), and Paul called it the first fruit of the Spirit (Galatians 5:22). Paul wrote, "the greatest of these is love" (1 Corinthians 13:13b), and, "The entire law is summed up in a single command: 'Love your neighbor as yourself'" (Galatians 5:14).

As the Holy Spirit enables people to hear and believe that God loves them, the Spirit also helps believers grow to love God more deeply and to serve the needs of others ahead of self. Love is the energy of the Spirit that empowers God's people to extend themselves for the spiritual growth of others as well as of themselves.

5. Gratitude and Openness to Grace

People who hear and believe that God loves them are grateful people. They remain open to receiving God's love without thinking they have earned it. When they ask God to forgive them, they believe that he does, and they don't cling to their guilt. They know that God loves them because of who Jesus is and what he did and in spite of who they are and what they have done.

As a result they live gratefully. They regularly recognize the daily gifts and favors God gives them—everything from the beauty of a sunrise to help in a dangerous driving situation—and they know that those are not just happenstances but expressions of God's never-ending love. The more they recognize God's minute-by-minute love the more grateful they are.

6. Repentance and Humility

When people hear and believe that God loves them, they become free to admit their faults and to turn away from their sins. To repent is to turn back from behaviors that are disobedient to God, that hurt others, damage relationships, or are self-destructive. God's love frees people from slavery to such behaviors so that they reject sin and turn toward God's abundant life.

Repentance is an enemy of false pride. In *My Utmost for His Highest*,[3] Oswald

---

3 Oswald Chambers, *My Utmost for His Highest* (Uhrichsville, OH: Barbour and Company, 1935, 1963).

Chambers speaks again and again about surrendering to God the right to oneself. That's what Jesus did when he "did not consider equality with God something to be grasped" (Philippians 2:6b), and that's what Christians do when they humbly give up their rights in order to serve God and care for others. Repentance means turning away from one's own rights and surrendering to God's will. That is true humility.

7. Community

Those who hear and believe the promise of God's gracious love understand that God has adopted them and that they are now part of a very big family. They are in community with all God's other children and with all humankind. While they maintain their individuality, they don't let it selfishly rule their behavior and relationships. They seek out others with whom to share their gifts, their lives, and their dreams.

These people feel connected rather than isolated from other people. They rejoice in being with others, and they recognize Jesus' presence in others. They are comfortable with people who are different from them, knowing that their connection with others as God's beloved creatures is stronger than any differences. They reach out to other people and care for them.

Detecting Spiritual Needs

No one is perfect or self-sufficient. Everyone needs spiritual care. Such an admission doesn't mean a person is spiritually defective or doesn't have enough faith. It means that the individual is normal, that each of us needs a

Savior, and can rejoice in the Savior God has given us.

Why Detect Spiritual Needs?

Spiritual needs are powerful; they can make people especially vulnerable. Since such needs are so powerful, and since no one this side of heaven is completely free from sin, it is important to state what are *not* reasons for detecting spiritual needs. Caregivers do not detect spiritual needs in order to:

▶ take over another person's spiritual life or relationship with God;

▶ try to control another person;

▶ condemn another person or impose guilt;

▶ prove themselves superior to those whom they have proven to be so needy; or

▶ get rid of their own guilt by proving that someone else is worse.

Simply put, caregivers detect needs for spiritual care so that they can plan how best to care for their care receivers. Once they understand their care receivers' spiritual needs, they find ways to communicate God's grace that speak directly to their care receivers' hurts and needs. You may wonder why it is so important to make such a point of the motivation for detecting spiritual care needs. To understand the necessity of this repeated emphasis, you need only imagine the damage that would be done if someone misused such information.

Look Inside

To detect spiritual needs in others, you first must be aware of your own God-sized needs. How are the seven signs of God's grace evident in your life? If you are aware of your own need for God's love, you are more likely to assess others' needs accurately.

There are ways to establish a discipline of looking inside and taking your own spiritual temperature. You might regularly write about your life with God and others in a journal. Your entries will make you more aware of your spiritual growth as well as interruptions to your own hearing and believing. You may be part of a small group where members talk about how they are doing spiritually. You may even be involved in a mentoring, discipling, or spiritual direction relationship with another Christian who has your permission to ask hard questions about your life with God.

Detecting Others' Needs for Spiritual Care

How, then, do you detect spiritual needs in others? One way is to observe to what extent the seven signs are present in a person's life.

Sometimes it is easy to figure out that people aren't experiencing a lot of God's love. If people are bitter and antisocial, if they typically relate in cruel or hurtful ways, if they only embrace as much life as they can rigidly control, then they probably aren't hearing and believing that God loves them. Their selfishness and fear show their separation from God. In such cases you can safely conclude that the person has deep and painful spiritual needs.

With other people, however, the needs are less obvious. A person may attend church regularly and even practice a discipline of daily devotions, including reading the Bible and praying. You might notice, however, that he or she is anxious and fearful or is very judgmental: severely criticizing others, or holding tightly to everything that is his or hers. Even though this Christian is regularly in the path of God's word, it seems that something is blocking God's love from getting through. Another example is a person who seems happy and content and talks about God regularly. Whenever there is a disagreement, however, it is always someone else's fault. This person never acknowledges his or her own need to change and grow. Something is blocking the free flow of God's grace to him or her.

Still other people have spiritual care needs that are difficult to detect. They demonstrate the seven signs of God's grace to a great extent, but still experience spiritual needs. The only way to detect these needs is to know what they were like a month or a year before and see the difference in how they are feeling and living now. For example, a person may have previously taken every opportunity to enjoy Christian community. But then he or she suffered a deep hurt from a fellow Christian and became less trusting and more cautious around others. If you talk to the person, he or she seems friendly and interested in you, so you might not conclude he or she had a problem with community. If you compare the person now with how he or she was a year ago, however, you might see the effects of the hurt on his or her ability to trust others.

Wholistic Needs

Another way to detect spiritual needs is to look for other types of needs. Everyone has interconnected, wholistic needs, not only spiritual needs but also physical, emotional, social, and intellectual ones. Such needs do not exist in isolation. Since people's needs are all interconnected, it is certain that when a person has physical or emotional pain, for example, there is also spiritual pain. Reference Box A contains what a hospital chaplain wrote about the connection between spiritual and other needs.

REFERENCE BOX A

The Connection between Spiritual and Other Needs

Our spiritual lives in general and our spiritual needs and resources at any particular moment are strongly influenced by what is happening in the rest of our life. The power of these dimensions to influence our spiritual well-being is one reason for attending to them in the process of spiritual assessment.

But there is another reason as well. Our spirits are not separate from our bodies, our emotions, and our thoughts. Each of us is one whole person. Our ways of thinking about ourselves often limit us to considering only one dimension at a time, but that does not mean those dimensions are separate or discrete. Our wholeness, the way in which the spiritual aspects of who we are are expressed in all aspects of our lives, requires that spiritual assessment be whole person assessment. When I begin spiritual assessment, therefore, I first review the information I have about all aspects of the person's life.[4]

4 George Fitchett, *Assessing Spiritual Needs: A Guide For Caregivers* (Minneapolis: Augsburg Fortress, 1993), pp. 42-43.

There may even be times when spiritual needs bring about other needs. Someone who is unable to forgive may suffer painful feelings of anger or guilt. Those feelings can lead to physical ailments, such as ulcers. Furthermore, such a person may become so bitter that he or she withdraws from relationships and ends up friendless.

When you see people suffering pain, deprivation, great unhappiness, loneliness, or frailty, pay close attention. They may also be struggling to hear and believe that God loves them. The lack of connection with God's love may also be the cause of some of the other maladies.

▶ Discerning Which Conduits of Grace Are Open and Which Are Blocked

God earnestly wants people to hear and believe that he loves them, and his gracious love is always flowing to people through conduits of grace. Yet people can block the free flow of God's grace. You will better understand a care receiver's spiritual care needs by noticing which conduits seem open and which appear blocked.

What Are Conduits of Grace?

The dictionary defines *conduit* as a "channel through which something . . . is conveyed . . . a means of transmitting or distributing."[5] So conduits of grace are ways in which God transmits or distributes his gracious love and helps people hear and believe that he

---

5 *Merriam-Webster's Collegiate Dictionary,* 10th ed. s. v. "conduit."

loves them. Following are nine conduits of grace.

1. The Bible

Paul wrote, "Consequently, faith comes from hearing the message, and the message is heard through the word of Christ" (Romans 10:17). In Ephesians you read, "And you also were included in Christ when you heard the word of truth, the gospel of your salvation" (Ephesians 1:13a). Jesus quoted Moses when he said, "'One does not live by bread alone, but by every word that comes from the mouth of God'" (Matthew 4:4 NRSV). Clearly God's Word is a powerful conduit through which his saving, faith-creating grace flows into people's lives.

God's Word gets inside people through both ears and eyes. When people read the Bible regularly, they obey Paul's admonition to "Let the word of Christ dwell in you richly . . . " (Colossians 3:16a). God works through his Word to tell them about his love and help them believe it.

Some people hear God's Word read in church services, in small groups, in family devotions, on audiotape while driving to and from work, or on a Christian radio or television station. The Bible was written to be read aloud; Paul wrote to the Thessalonians, "Greet all the brothers and sisters with a holy kiss. I solemnly command you by the Lord that this letter be read to all of them" (1 Thessalonians 5:26–27 NRSV).

2. Worship

Worship is an intimate way to express our relationship with God. Our worship is so important to our right relationship with God that he commanded us to worship only him. In worship we hear God's Word, we pray, and we may receive his gifts of love through the sacraments. Whenever we open our hearts to worship our gracious God, his grace flows into us, as Richard Foster writes in the quotation in Reference Box B.

REFERENCE BOX B

In Worship, Jesus Leads

Genuine worship has only one Leader, Jesus Christ. When I speak of Jesus as the Leader of worship, I mean, first of all, that he is alive and present among his people. His voice can be heard in their hearts and his presence known. . . . Christ is alive and present in all his power. He saves us not only from the consequences of sin but from the domination of sin. Whatever he teaches us, he will give us the power to obey.[6]

When we worship, we stand squarely in the strong current of the river of God's grace.

3. Prayer

Prayer is another conduit of God's grace. When we pray, we pay attention to God, talk to him, and listen to him, and our God, who is so eager to give us his gracious love, meets us in prayer and communicates his love to us. God bids us approach his throne of grace, as the author of Hebrews wrote, as quoted in Reference Box C.

REFERENCE BOX C

God Bids Us Approach

Therefore, since we have a great high priest who has gone through the heavens, Jesus the Son of God, let us hold firmly to the faith we profess. For we do not have a high priest who is unable to sympathize with our weaknesses, but we have one who has been tempted in every way, just as we are—yet was without sin. Let us then approach the throne of grace with confidence, so that we may receive mercy and find grace to help us in our time of need.

Hebrews 4:14–16

In prayer we approach the throne of grace and receive God's mercy and help.

4. Confession and Forgiveness

Richard Foster wrote, "To understand his (God's) grace is to understand our guilt."[7] The New Testament Greek word for *confession* literally means "to say the same thing, to agree." When we confess, we say what God says, we agree with him that we are sinners in need of mercy and grace. We also hear what God says, that he accepts and forgives us because of Jesus.

What a gracious truth it is that "If we confess our sins, he is faithful and just and will forgive us our sins and purify us from all unrighteousness" (1 John 1:9). Forgiveness is pure grace. It is only and always available because of Jesus' death and resurrection.

---

6 Richard Foster, *Celebration of Discipline: The Path to Spiritual Growth*, rev. ed. (San Francisco: Harper and Row, 1978, 1988), p. 165.

7 Foster, *Celebration of Discipline*, p. 160.

5. Sacraments

In some Christian traditions, believers regard sacraments as conduits of God's grace. They believe that God graciously gives eternal life when they receive baptism and that Jesus meets them and graciously forgives them through Holy Communion. They may also believe God meets them in special ways through other sacraments.

6. Meeting Jesus in "The Least of These"

Jesus told a story that reveals another conduit of God's grace. It's in Reference Box D.

REFERENCE BOX D

You Did It to Me

"When the Son of Man comes in his glory, and all the angels with him, then he will sit on the throne of his glory. All the nations will be gathered before him, and he will separate people one from another as a shepherd separates the sheep from the goats, and he will put the sheep at his right hand and the goats at the left. Then the king will say to those at his right hand, 'Come, you that are blessed by my Father, inherit the kingdom prepared for you from the foundation of the world; for I was hungry and you gave me food, I was thirsty and you gave me something to drink, I was a stranger and you welcomed me, I was naked and you gave me clothing, I was sick and you took care of me, I was in prison and you visited me.' Then the righteous will answer him, 'Lord, when was it that we saw you hungry and gave you food, or thirsty and gave you something to drink? And when was it that we saw you a stranger and welcomed you, or naked and gave you clothing? And when was it that we saw you sick or in prison and visited you?' And the king will answer them, 'Truly I tell you, just as you did it to one of the least of these who are members of my family, you did it to me.'"

Matthew 25:31–40 NRSV

In Jesus' story the righteous are surprised that they had met the king. They were simply caring for people in need, as Christians do. Jesus graciously turned their care into occasions to meet and care for God himself, and he graciously invited them to receive the kingdom he had prepared for them. It is still true today: When Christians care for the least of these who are members of Jesus' family, they care for him, and he turns their care into an opportunity to give them his grace.

7. Practicing Other Spiritual Disciplines

You read about spiritual disciplines in the first module of your Stephen Minister training, "The Person of the Caregiver." Spiritual disciplines can be conduits of God's grace. Richard Foster explained how. His words are in Reference Box E.

REFERENCE BOX E

How Spiritual Disciplines Are Conduits of God's Grace

The apostle Paul says, "he who sows to his own flesh will from the flesh reap corruption; but he who sows to the Spirit will from the Spirit reap eternal life" (Gal. 6:8). Paul's analogy is instructive. A farmer is helpless to grow grain; all he can do is provide the right conditions for the growing of grain. He

---

cultivates the ground, he plants the seed, he waters the plants, and then the natural forces of the earth take over and up comes the grain. This is the way it is with the Spiritual Disciplines—they are a way of sowing to the Spirit. The Disciplines are God's way of getting us into the ground; they put us where he can work within us and transform us. By themselves the Spiritual Disciplines can do nothing; they can only get us to the place where something can be done. They are God's means of grace. The inner righteousness we seek is not something that is poured on our heads. God has ordained the Disciplines of the spiritual life as the means by which we place ourselves where he can bless us.[8]

You may want to read again the description of spiritual disciplines on pages 10–16 in volume 1 of your *Stephen Ministry Training Manual*.

8. Getting Together with Other Christians

Jesus said, "For where two or three come together in my name, there am I with them" (Matthew 18:20). Jesus is graciously present when Christian people gather in his name.

God uses gatherings of his people as conduits of grace. One example is getting together with other Christians for weekly worship to hear God's Word, pray, interact, receive the sacraments, confess, and receive forgiveness. Attending worship is going to a place where a number of conduits of grace converge.

Another gathering where conduits converge is a small group where God's people gather around his Word, prayer, service, and caring fellowship. Still another powerful gathering that God uses is a mentoring, discipling, or spiritual direction relationship between two Christians.

9. Christian Arts

Writers who explain the truths of Scripture and the wonder of God's work in the world open a conduit through which God's grace flows. Christian musicians who sing about God's love communicate his grace not only through their words but also through the language of melody and harmony. Painters, sculptors, those who work in stained glass, and other Christian visual artists capture the truth of God's gracious love in their works of art. Genesis 2:7 portrays God's forming of Adam as the action of a potter. God is an artist who created all the beauty that surrounds us, and he uses the beauty of other artists' works to channel his gracious love to those who pay attention.

Which Conduits Are Open and Which Are Blocked?

God's grace flows into care receivers' lives in many ways. Some people are more open to certain conduits than to others. Stephen Ministers look for the conduits of grace that are especially open in their care receivers' lives and work with those.

Note that a Stephen Minister's job is not to be a spiritual plumber, searching out clogged conduits and reaming them out to restore a free flow. Instead, Stephen Ministers look for the free-flowing con-

---

8 Foster, *Celebration of Discipline*, p. 7.

duits and use them to communicate God's love to their care receivers.

How might Stephen Ministers use open conduits to communicate God's grace to a care receiver? One way is to discuss what God is doing through a conduit in which the care receiver is actively participating. For example, if the care receiver is in a small group, the Stephen Minister might regularly ask how God is using the group to help the care receiver grow spiritually. Another way a Stephen Minister can use an open conduit is to encourage a care receiver to participate in it more. For example, a care receiver might remember times when God seemed very close when he or she prayed, but now he or she rarely prays. The Stephen Minister could gently encourage his or her care receiver to resume a discipline of prayer, always remembering to remain process-oriented—remembering that God is responsible for the results.

One way to know which conduits are open for a care receiver is to notice which conduits he or she takes advantage of. Does the care receiver go to worship? Does he or she read or hear the Bible, pray, practice other spiritual disciplines, belong to a small group, or enjoy Christian art? Where the answer is yes, those are conduits to use in your caregiving. Where the answer is no, it will be more difficult for your care receiver to receive God's grace in those ways.

Another way to discover free-flowing conduits is to ask the care receiver questions such as those in Reference Box F.

REFERENCE BOX F

Questions to Discover Free-Flowing Conduits

Are there times when you know God loves you more than you do at other times?

Does God's love become more real when you are doing any particular activities?

Is it easier to trust God when you are with any particular people? When you are alone?

When does God seem most real to you?

What has helped you experience God's love and joy in the past?

Sometimes, however, the assessment is not that simple. There will be people who regularly attend worship or a small group, hear God's Word, and place themselves at the receiving end of other grace conduits, but still have a lot of trouble hearing and believing that God loves them. In such cases God's grace is probably being blocked.

What Can Block Hearing and Believing?

Circumstances can block people from hearing and believing that God loves them, as can choices that people make. Often the blockages come from a combination of circumstances and choices.

Circumstances

People can encounter circumstances that make it very difficult for them to hear and believe that God loves them.

Ignorance

Some people don't know that God loves them and that Jesus died for them. Even in countries where most people have heard of Jesus, many still don't know what Jesus has done for them and their need for him. Since they don't know about Jesus, they don't turn to him when they really need him. As Paul put it, "How, then, can they call on the one they have not believed in? And how can they believe in the one of whom they have not heard?" (Romans 10:14a).

Oppression

There are places where people are prevented from going to church or reading the Bible. They risk persecution and punishment if they do. In such circumstances, people may have more trouble hearing and believing that God loves them. It is also true that God sometimes works through the fires of oppression to temper faith and make it as strong as steel.

Suffering

Some people suffer terribly. They may have diseases or injuries that cause great physical pain. They may suffer tragedies that bring unbearable emotional pain, such as seeing their children die. Such suffering can cause people to ask how a loving God could allow such pain and can cause them to doubt that God loves them.

Shame

People may be in circumstances in which they are terribly ashamed. They may have physical deformities that make them ashamed of their appearance. The cause of their shame might be something dreadful that a loved one has done, such as a parent whose child committed a terrible crime and was imprisoned. They may also be ashamed of something they have done and be unable to forgive themselves.

People who suffer such shame certainly need to hear and believe that God loves them, but their damaged self-image may prevent them from believing that anyone—including God—could possibly love them.

Despair

Other people are trapped in hopeless circumstances and don't believe their painful life can ever change. Examples include people who suffer abject poverty and live in squalid, violent conditions; people trapped in abusive relationships; and people who have been badly injured or have a disease and have lost control over their bodies. Their relentless pain may keep them from believing that God, who is the only one who could save them, really cares. They come to think that their lives have no meaning, and they see no hope for change.

Evil

Some people experience the horror of evil: through torture perpetrated by a government, through the violence of a rapist or a murderer, or through the hateful touch of an abusive parent. Elie Wiesel said his faith in God died when he experienced the evil of Nazi concentration camps.[9] Some people are so scarred by evil that they find it difficult or impossible to believe in a loving God.

---

9 Elie Wiesel, *Night* (New York: Bantam, 1960), p.32.

Evil Perpetrated in Jesus' Name

The worst evil is that which people do in the name of God. It is not hard to see how someone whose family was killed and whose home was destroyed by so-called "Christians" in an ethnic war would refuse to believe that Christ is a God of love. Regrettably, evil continues to be perpetrated in God's name, and such circumstances make it difficult for people who hear about that evil to believe that the Christian God loves them.

Choices

In addition to circumstances that keep people from receiving God's love, people make choices that block the free flow of God's grace in their lives and prevent them from hearing and believing that God loves them.

Refusing to Believe

Some people know about Jesus, perhaps they were even raised in the church, but they refuse to believe that God loves them or that the good news about Jesus' death and resurrection has anything to do with them.

Anger with God

Sometimes people become so angry with God over some tragedy or disappointment that they refuse to believe that he loves them. They choose to cling to their anger instead of finally letting go of it.

Unwillingness to Forgive

When people are unwilling to forgive others, they set up a roadblock to God's grace. Jesus told a parable to illustrate this point in which a king forgave one of his servants a huge debt, but that servant turned around and had a fellow servant thrown in jail for not repaying a small debt. Reference Box G contains Jesus' conclusion to the parable.

REFERENCE BOX G

The Wicked Servant

"When the other servants saw what had happened, they were greatly distressed and went and told their master everything that had happened.

"Then the master called the servant in. 'You wicked servant,' he said, 'I canceled all that debt of yours because you begged me to. Shouldn't you have had mercy on your fellow servant just as I had on you?' In anger his master turned him over to the jailers to be tortured, until he should pay back all he owed.

"This is how my heavenly Father will treat each of you unless you forgive your brother from your heart."

Matthew 18:31–35

Idolatry

Idolatry means putting something or someone in God's place. Jesus said, "'It is written: "Worship the Lord your God and serve him only"'" (Luke 4:8). An idol is anyone or anything that people value more highly than God, trust more than God, or serve instead of God. For many people, the idol is the self; they put themselves above God. When people continually put themselves in God's place, they try to play the role only God can fill. They block God's grace and instead just recycle their own pride, guilt, despair, or selfishness. What they need is the fresh input of God's gracious love.

Too Busy for God

A contemporary form of idolatry is being too busy to pay attention to God. Many people's lives are so full of demands—work, family, community, and even church—that they neglect to spend time with God. As people become busier, God's grace has less and less opportunity to flow to them. Their lives become spiritually barren.

Pride

C. S. Lewis wrote insightfully about pride: what it is, and how it gets in the way of people's relationship with God. Selections from Lewis's chapter called "The Great Sin" in *Mere Christianity* appear in Reference Box H.

REFERENCE BOX H

C. S. Lewis on Pride

There is one vice of which no man in the world is free; which every one in the world loathes when he sees it in someone else; and of which hardly any people, except Christians, ever imagine that they are guilty. . . . There is no fault which makes a man more unpopular, and no fault which we are more unconscious of in ourselves. And the more we have it ourselves, the more we dislike it in others.

The vice I am talking of is Pride or Self-Conceit. . . .

Pride is *essentially* competitive—is competitive by its very nature. . . . Pride gets no pleasure out of having something, only out of having more of it than the next man. We say that people are proud of being rich, or clever, or good-looking, but they are not. They are proud of being richer, or cleverer, or better-looking than others. . . . It is the comparison that makes you proud: the pleasure of being above the rest . . . .

Pride always means enmity—it *is* enmity. And not only enmity between man and man, but enmity to God.

In God you come up against something which is in every respect immeasurably superior to yourself. Unless you know God as that—and, therefore, know yourself as nothing in comparison—you do not know God at all. As long as you are proud you cannot know God. A proud man is always looking down on things and people: and, of course, as long as you are looking down, you cannot see something that is above you.[10]

Choosing Not to Participate in Christian Community

There are many reasons why people who consider themselves Christians don't attend worship, participate in a Christian small group, or find some other way to participate in Christian community. For some it is a matter of priorities; they don't choose to spend time that way and there are too many other activities they would rather do. Some are bored by church and can't relate to the music, the communication, and the traditions. While other churches or expressions of Christian community could fit them better, they don't know about those other options, and they aren't motivated to search.

These are just a few of the reasons why people choose not to go to church. Kenneth Haugk identifies 33 causes of

---

10 C. S. Lewis, *Mere Christianity* (New York: Macmillan, 1943, 1945, 1952), pp. 108–111.

inactivity in his course, *Caring for Inactive Members.*[11]

Guilt

While it may seem strange to regard guilt as a choice, sometimes it is. Sometimes people choose to hold on to guilt rather than to accept forgiveness. When they refuse forgiveness, they block the free flow of God's grace in their lives.

Sin

Sin is the general name for anything that separates people from God, but sin can be quite particular as a choice. People may cut themselves off from God's grace by choosing to continue some particular sin—for example, an adulterous relationship, a taste for Internet pornography, or choosing to hang onto hate instead of letting go of it. People may find it impossible to hold onto their sin and still relate to God, so they choose not to let God in at all.

Circumstances and Choices Are Often Combined

You can often understand people's choices when you know the circumstances they have been in. For example, a person may choose to remain angry at God because of the evil that he or she has suffered, or a person with exaggerated pride may have suffered and overcome deep shame earlier in life and vowed never to endure it again. Realizing and remembering that people's circumstances affect their choices and admitting that "If I had been through similar circumstances I might have

made similar choices" can prevent caregivers from falling into their own pride and blocking God's grace to themselves.

The Holy Spirit Breaks through Barriers

Perhaps you recognized from personal experience some of the barriers listed above. Everyone puts up barriers to God's love. The good news is that God breaks through our barriers and gets his grace to us in spite of our weakness and selfishness. As Paul put it, "For while we were still weak, at the right time Christ died for the ungodly. Indeed, rarely will anyone die for a righteous person—though perhaps for a good person someone might actually dare to die. But God proves his love for us in that while we still were sinners Christ died for us" (Romans 5:6–8 NRSV).

Thank God that he doesn't let our barriers stop his love. One of the ways God gets through people's barriers is by using Stephen Ministers to provide spiritual care, to love people even when they are at their worst.

▶ Helping People Hear and Believe

The key question for spiritual caregivers is: How can I ally myself with God's work in this person's life? Only God can meet God-sized needs, but God wants to use Christians as conduits of his gracious love to others. How can Stephen Ministers allow God to use them as spiritual caregivers? The remainder of this Preclass Reading concerns itself with that question.

---

11 Kenneth C. Haugk, *Caring for Inactive Members: How to Make God's House a Home* (St. Louis: Tebunah Ministries, 1990).

Being Caregivers Who Hear and Believe

Spiritual care providers must be spiritual care receivers. In order to help convey God's grace to others, Stephen Ministers need to be Christians who hear and believe that God loves them.

Take Your Own Spiritual Temperature

The first way to use the ideas in this Preclass Reading is to apply them to yourself. When you consider the seven signs of God's grace, what evidence of them do you notice in your own life? How are you aware of God's presence in your life? How open are you to changing and growing? What thoughts or behaviors show your own need for repentance, and where do you rate on a humility scale?

These are hard questions until you remember where they point. Everyone who asks these questions will see ways in which he or she needs even more of God's grace. Everyone who then prays for God's grace will find that God gives his love freely, and he is eager to give more of himself to you.

Avail Yourself of Conduits of Grace

As you pay attention to your spiritual temperature, you'll see your need to receive a steady supply of God's grace. Perceiving your need will drive you to conduits of grace: those places and activities where God always dispenses his gracious love.

Watch for Spiritual Pride

Some who take their spiritual temperature and avail themselves of the conduits of grace may be tempted to take pride in their spiritual accomplishments. Keep in mind Paul's words in Reference Box I, written to the Corinthians when they were tempted by pride.

REFERENCE BOX I

Boast in the Lord

Consider your own call, brothers and sisters: not many of you were wise by human standards, not many were powerful, not many were of noble birth. But God chose what is foolish in the world to shame the wise; God chose what is weak in the world to shame the strong; God chose what is low and despised in the world, things that are not, to reduce to nothing things that are, so that no one might boast in the presence of God. He is the source of your life in Christ Jesus, who became for us wisdom from God, and righteousness and sanctification and redemption, in order that, as it is written, "Let the one who boasts, boast in the Lord."

1 Corinthians 1:26–31 NRSV

Relying on God

Another part of allying yourself with God and his work in the care receiver's life is to rely on God to bring about the results he wants. You have regularly encountered this important principle of process-oriented caregiving in your Stephen Minister training, and there is good reason for the repetition. God is the Curegiver and you are a caregiver. You focus on the process and leave the results to God. God is the only one who can give the care receiver the healing and wholeness he or she needs, and your job is to do what you can, do the best that you can, and leave the rest to God.

Gospel-Centered Caring

Gospel-centered caring is caregiving that is firmly based in God's grace and seeks to communicate God's grace to others. It offers caregivers a way to ally themselves with God in the caregiving process.

Principles of Gospel-Centered Caring

Reference Box J contains some key principles of gospel-centered caring.

REFERENCE BOX J

Key Principles of Gospel-Centered Caring

- What people need most is a loving, trusting relationship with God.
- God alone builds this relationship, usually working through the presence, prayers, witness, and care of Christian caregivers.
- Gospel-centered caring doesn't begin with what a person must do; it begins with what Jesus has done for the care receiver and what the Holy Spirit continues to do.
- Gospel-centered caregivers' care is based on their growing awareness of their own need for God and of God's love at work in them.
- Gospel-centered caregivers are motivated by a sense of gratitude, not by a sense of fearful obligation.
- Gospel-centered caregivers communicate God's grace as best they can and so invite others to experience God's incredible goodness in Jesus.
- Gospel-centered caregivers try to show how God's love gives strength, hope, and courage to people in whatever circumstances they face.
- Gospel-centered caregivers struggle with the effects of sin, suffering, and

---

death in their own lives. They let their care receivers know that they are fellow strugglers.

- Gospel-centered caregivers never outgrow their need for God's grace.

Expressing God's Grace

Gospel-centered caregivers do the activities listed in Reference Box K to express God's gracious love for their care receivers.

REFERENCE BOX K

Ways to Express God's Gracious Love

Here are some ways that you as a gospel-centered caregiver can communicate God's grace and help care receivers believe that God loves them.

1. Seize every opportunity to reveal God's grace, especially when care receivers are experiencing their old sinful nature apart from Christ (see Galatians 5:13–24).

2. Create a safe place where care receivers can face the badness in their lives without damage to their self-respect.

3. Expect and accept resistance and regression on the part of care receivers (not to mention on your own part).

4. See grace at work, even when care receivers most deserve God's judgment.

5. Trust that God's goodness will destroy sin and evil.

6. Bless and do not curse. Forgive and do not return evil for evil.

7. Be sensitive, involved, nonanxious, and nonmanipulative in care receivers' presence. People don't have to protect themselves from gospel-

---

centered caregivers; they can open up and see their caregiver as an ally and resource.

8. Listen intently to others in order to understand their feelings, needs, and especially how they understand and relate to God. With great respect for care receivers' individuality, integrity, and personal responsibility, ask how you may be of help.

9. Diligently search for the good God has put within care receivers. See your care receivers as people who:

   ▸ possess the very righteousness and beauty of Christ (Isaiah 61:3; Romans 1:17; 3:21–26); and

   ▸ are therefore beyond all condemnation, blame, and shame: There is before God "no condemnation for those who are in Christ Jesus" (Romans 8:1).

10. Remain calm when faced with care receivers' badness, doubt, or other effects of sin or suffering.

11. Remain confident of God's goodness and gracious work within your care receivers.

12. Identify and express the good of care receivers' new nature, even when they express their badness.

13. Affirm whatever evidence of God's Spirit and work you can find in the midst of the problem.

14. Bring up with care receivers the possibility of changing their behavior in response to God's grace, and give them reasons for changing.

15. Affirm how good God is to his people, especially at the moment of their badness.

16. Affirm what care receivers most deeply long for, the desires that flow out of their new spiritual nature in Jesus Christ.

▶ Spiritual Caregiving Activities

So what might a Stephen Minister do to provide spiritual care, and how might Stephen Ministers choose what spiritual care activities might be appropriate to do with their care receivers?

Ways to Provide Spiritual Care

Keeping in mind the principles, attitudes, and actions of a gospel-centered caregiver, you can do the activities listed in Reference Box L to help your care receiver connect with conduits of grace in order to hear and believe that God loves him or her.

REFERENCE BOX L

Ways to Provide Spiritual Care

1. Share Scripture.

2. Worship with the care receiver.

3. Pray.

4. Meet physical needs in Jesus' name.

5. Listen as people confess sins and assure them of God's forgiveness.

6. Put the care receiver in touch with the pastor to receive the sacraments of the church.

7. Help the care receiver find ways to serve others.

8. Practice a spiritual discipline together and discuss it.

9. Help the care receiver become more involved in Christian community.

10. Engage in spiritual discussions in which you listen for and reflect spiritual concerns and witness about your own experiences.

11. Share and discuss Christian art.

---

12. Witness about your own experiences of God's love.

13. Bestow blessings.

14. Sing or listen together to recordings of hymns and spiritual songs.

This list is not exhaustive. You can probably think of other activities you can do with or for your care receiver to help the person hear and know that God loves him or her. You will consider some of these activities in more depth in the In-Class Sessions.

Choosing Which Spiritual Care Activities You Will Do

You wouldn't want to do all these activities with your care receiver. They don't all fit him or her and they don't all fit you. There are factors to take into account as you decide which activities you will do.

The Care Receiver's Needs

When you read *Christian Caregiving—a Way of Life,* you learned about some of the spiritual care activities in Reference Box L. You learned that you only offer spiritual care resources in order to meet the care receiver's needs, not to somehow meet your own needs. That point was reinforced in module 5, "Process versus Results in Caregiving."

Not all Christians relate to God the same way. For example, some people are very outgoing and hear God best in a large group of people, while others are most likely to receive God's grace alone or with just one other person. Some care receivers benefit from very concrete communication, such as a picture, while others prefer more abstract ideas and hear God as they read. Do your best to understand how your care receiver hears God, and then do the activities that work for him or her. Don't assume that what works for you will work for your care receiver.

Your Gifts and Experience

Take into account your own gifts and experience. Some Stephen Ministers have studied the Bible for years and are able to share many passages and stories that will be meaningful to their care receivers. Other caregivers are gifted artists and can share their creations with their care receivers and even create works of art with their care receivers.

While you consider the care receiver's needs first, also choose how to care based on your own experiences, gifts, and interests—conduits of grace that are comfortable and natural for you. Also be aware that sometimes you will stretch yourself and learn new ways of expressing God's grace in order to meet your care receiver's needs.

What Is Possible?

Of course, you can only do what is possible. Some care receivers may not be able to leave the house, so the only way to provide Christian community is to bring it to them. If your care receiver has physical problems, you probably won't suggest the spiritual discipline of fasting. Your common sense will help you know what is possible and what is not.

Experiment

You may not be sure whether a particular activity will help your care receiver hear and believe that God loves him or her. Therefore experiment. Describe several spiritual disciplines and see which ones your care receiver responds to. For example, you and your care receiver may pray every day for a week and then at your next caring visit discuss how it went. Or you and your care receiver might read the same Bible passages every day and talk once a week about what God is telling you.

No experiment is a failure. God is eager to give his grace to your care receiver (and to you), and you will learn from each experiment how your care receiver and you can best receive God's gifts.

Two Pilgrims Seeking God Together

You are not the leader and your care receiver is not the follower in spiritual care. You are both followers who are in need of God's gracious love and who receive God's gifts through Jesus. Be willing to accept gratefully your care receiver's witness to Christ's love, which will strengthen your faith. Make sure your care receiver knows that you are just as much a pilgrim as he or she is, and then enjoy each other's company on the journey.

Trust God for Results

As always, trust God for results. Remember that you are the caregiver and God is the Curegiver. He wants your care receiver and you to hear and believe that he loves both of you, and he has proved that he will stop at nothing, even to the point of sacrificing his only Son.

▶ Getting Ready for the In-Class Sessions

In the three In-Class Sessions you will work on spiritual care skills. Prior to each session, review this Preclass Reading, especially the seven signs of God's grace, the conduits of grace, and the ways people can block God's grace. Before the second In-Class Session review the section on "Active Listening" in the Preclass Reading for "The Art of Listening" on pages 44–50. Focus especially on the section on "Reflect Spiritual Concerns" on pages 49–50.

Some classes will learn this module in one long class or on a retreat. If that is the case for your class, review the section from "The Art of Listening" before your class or retreat.

For Further Reading . . .

Me, an Evangelist? Every Christian's Guide to Caring Evangelism
by William J. McKay

The word *evangelism* causes anxiety and fear for many Christians: "How do I share my faith? How do I talk about Jesus without sounding preachy?" McKay weaves together Biblical insights, practical caring skills, and an engaging story to offer a process-oriented solution. The ideal book for "reluctant evangelists" everywhere, *Me, an Evangelist?* shows how to joyfully, comfortably, and naturally live and share the love of Jesus with others in ways they will welcome.

To learn more or to order a copy, log on to www.stephenministries.org or call Stephen Ministries at (314) 428-2600.

Providing Spiritual Care

Outline and Focus Notes

Therefore be as shrewd as snakes and as innocent as doves.

Matthew 10:16b

Have the practical good sense of a snake, and be undevious or innocent as doves.

Matthew 10:16b, Willard

I. Snakes and Doves

FOCUS NOTE 1

The Snake and the Dove

These homely images [of the snake and the dove] begin to open up the positive side of an association with others that will help them without condemning them or forcing upon them good things that they simply cannot benefit from.

What is the wisdom of the snake? It is to be watchful and observant until the time is right to act. It is timeliness. One rarely sees a snake chasing its prey or thrashing about in an effort to impress it. But when it acts, it acts quickly and decisively. And as for the dove, it does not contrive. It is incapable of intrigue. Guile is totally beyond it. There is nothing indirect about this gentle creature. It is in this sense "harmless." The importance scriptural teaching places on guilelessness is very great. One of the traits of the small child, greatest in the kingdom, is its inability to mislead. We are to be like that as adults.[1]

II. Taking Your Own Spiritual Temperature

A. Looking Inward

---

1 Dallas Willard, *The Divine Conspiracy: Rediscovering Our Hidden Life in God* (New York: HarperCollins, 1998), pp. 230–231.

Looking for the Seven Signs

These seven scales are for the seven signs of God's grace from your Pre-class Reading. Mark each scale to indicate how much of that sign you see in your life. The statements at the ends of the scales describe extremes. Most people are somewhere in between.

1. Awareness of God's Presence

"I am aware of God's presence all the time."   "I am never aware of God's presence."

5   4   3   2   1

2. Faith

"I never worry because I am always sure that God is caring for me."   "I'm always worried and I never take risks because I can't trust God or others."

5   4   3   2   1

3. Hope

"I'm sure the future will be positive because God is in charge."   "I fear the future and feel despair at my inability to control it."

5   4   3   2   1

4. Love

"I always put God first and care for those in need."   "I look out for myself and only care for others when it serves my purposes."

5   4   3   2   1

5. Gratitude and Openness to Grace

"I believe God loves me because of Jesus, and I am thankful."   "If I fail, God won't love me, but if I am a good person, he has to love me."

5   4   3   2   1

6. Repentance and Humility

"I freely admit my faults and turn away from my sins when I become aware of them."   "I resent corrections. I believe that no one has the right to tell me how to live my life, not even God."

5   4   3   2   1

7. Community

"I love and serve others, share what God has given me, and seek others' guidance."   "I keep to myself, hoard my resources, and rely on my own judgment."

5   4   3   2   1

Which Conduits Are Flowing for You?

This grid is a way to understand better how much you use and benefit from the conduits of grace. The conduits of grace are listed below the grid, and each one has a number. Write all nine numbers on the grid based on how much you do them and how much God uses them. The farther to the right, the more you do the activity; the farther to the left, the less. The higher in the grid, the more God uses the conduit in your life; the lower in the grid, the less.

For example, if a person read the Bible only once or twice a month—which he or she considered to be not very often—but God used that occasional Bible reading to build his or her faith a little, then he or she would write a *1*—for Read or hear the Bible—where the asterisk is on the grid below. Here's another example. If a person worshipped five times a week—that's close to all the time—and God used that conduit almost all the time to help him or her hear and believe, then he or she would write a *2*—for Worship—in the top right, where the shaded box is.

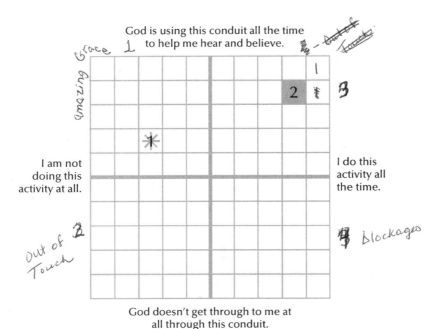

Conduits of Grace

1. Read or hear the Bible
2. Worship
3. Pray
4. Confess and receive forgiveness
5. Receive the sacraments
6. Meet Jesus in "the least of these"
7. Practice other spiritual disciplines
8. Get together with other Christians
9. Enjoy and discuss Christian arts

B. Conduits and Blockages

C. Your Own Blockages

Blockages

Preclass Reading pages 671–675

Circumstances

▶ Ignorance

▶ Oppression

●▶ Suffering

▶ Shame

▶ Despair

●▶ Evil

▶ Evil perpetrated in Jesus' name

Choices

▶ Refusing to believe

▶ Anger with God

▶ Unwillingness to forgive

▶ Idolatry

▶ Too busy for God

▶ Pride

●▶ Choosing not to participate in Christian community

●▶ Guilt

▶ Sin

Need to understand why?

Discussion Questions

Share as much or as little as you wish in response to some or all of the following questions:

1. What did you discover as you plotted your experience with the seven signs of God's grace on the scales in Focus Note 2?

2. What did you discover as you plotted your experience with the conduits on the grid in Focus Note 3?

3. What blockages in Focus Note 4 might be active in your life?

4. What might others do to provide effective spiritual care for you, to help you hear and believe that God loves you?

5. What seem to be some effective ways to help people hear and believe that God loves them?

D. Providing Spiritual Care

III. Looking Ahead

IV. Opening

V. Uncovering God-Sized Needs

A. Why Is It Hard to See Your God-Sized Needs?

FOCUS NOTE 6

Reasons It Is Hard to Recognize or Admit to God-Sized Needs

▸ Some people are embarrassed by their needs.

▸ There are those who are feeling so hurt and vulnerable that they can't risk more pain by recognizing or admitting to God-sized needs.

▸ Some are afraid that if they admit their true needs, they will feel overwhelmed.

▸ Some people deny their needs because they are secretly afraid that their needs cannot be met and if they acknowledge their needs they will be left in despair.

▸ There are those who disagree with God's assessment that they need a Savior and are therefore unwilling to admit that they have God-sized needs.

▸ Some believe that such information is private and inappropriate to share with anyone, so they keep their needs to themselves.

▸ There are those who refuse to recognize their needs because they believe they are self-sufficient, and admitting that they need a Savior doesn't fit their self-image.

B. Recognize, Reflect, Respond

1. Recognize

God-Sized Questions[2]

▶ **Identity**—Who am I? Who should I be?

▶ **Self-Esteem**—Am I lovable? Can I really like the person I am?

▶ **Meaning**—Why am I alive? Is there a reason for me to go on living?

▶ **Hope vs. Despair**—How can I face the future with hope and not dread?

▶ **Reason for Evil**—Why is there evil in the world? In my life?

▶ **Failure**—What if I fail? How could I live with myself?

▶ **Loneliness/Abandonment**—Am I really all alone in the world? What can I do about this aching loneliness I feel?

▶ **Addiction/Compulsions**—Is there any way to get out of this trap of addiction or compulsion I'm in? How can I stop doing things that are self-destructive?

▶ **Guilt**—How can I deal with the guilt I feel over what I've done?

▶ **Aging**—Why do I have to get old?

▶ **Purpose**—What am I going to do with my life?

▶ **Dissatisfaction**—Why doesn't my success bring me satisfaction?

▶ **Forgiveness**—How can I forgive people who have hurt me? How can I find forgiveness for the hurts I have caused?

▶ **Suffering**—Why do I, or people I love, have to suffer?

▶ **Broken Relationships**—Why do I fight with people I love?

▶ **Regrets**—Why do I do things I later regret?

▶ **Self-Doubt**—How can I handle the responsibilities I've been given?

▶ **Death**—Why do I, or people I love, have to die?

2. Reflect

---

2 William J. McKay, *Me, an Evangelist? Every Christian's Guide to Caring Evangelism* (St. Louis: Stephen Ministries, 1992), pp. 118–119.

Reflecting God-Sized Needs

Care receiver (CR): What am I going to do with the rest of my life? I was planning to spend it with Chris, but now *[he/she]* has left me and is going to spend the future with someone else.

Stephen Minister (SM): You're wondering what the future holds for you.

CR: That's right. I don't want to spend the rest of my life alone.

SM: The future can be frightening. Who knows what's going to happen?

CR: Yeah. It scares me. I could be miserable for the rest of my life and there's nothing I can do about it.

SM: Tell me more about how that makes you feel.

CR: It makes me feel pretty helpless.

SM: You feel frightened about the future and helpless to do anything about it.

CR: That pretty much sums it up.

Examples of Reflecting God-Sized Needs

Identity

"It sounds to me as if you have some questions about who you are and who God might want you to be."

Self-Esteem

"Am I right that you don't feel so great about yourself right now?"

Meaning

"It seems difficult for you to see what good can come from all this."

Hope and Despair

"Right now you're dreading what lies ahead of you, when you'd rather have hope that things will be okay."

Evil

"You're wondering why God allows so much evil in the world."

Guilt

"It seems that you're having trouble living with what's happened."

3. Respond

FOCUS NOTE 10

Do's and Don'ts for Responding to God-Sized Needs

Do

1. Be loving, gracious, and calm. Realize that needing God's love is the most normal condition in the world. Communicate to the care receiver that this is normal, that there is nothing to get upset about.

2. Pray for your care receiver.

3. Continue listening, reflecting, and exploring.

4. Witness to your care receiver, when appropriate, about how God has met your own or others' needs. You might also share a story from the Bible.

5. Assure your care receiver that God sees his or her needs and will graciously meet them.

6. Pray with your care receiver.

Don't

1. Don't panic. Don't become anxious or nervous. Remember that God is in charge. Don't let your feelings cause your care receiver to start feeling nervous or upset.

2. Don't become results-oriented. Continue your process-oriented caregiving and leave the results to God.

3. Don't try to persuade the care receiver to see the problem as you do. Rather, work with the care receiver to explore his or her needs.

4. Don't try to take control of the care receiver's spiritual life.

5. Don't pray with your care receiver in ways that really aren't prayer, where you pretend to be talking to God, but are really telling your care receiver what to do: " . . . and Lord, we know you want Fred to pray more, so please cause him to set aside a half hour every morning for nothing but prayer, and if he has any objections, please overcome them so he will follow through."

The Person of the Caregiver

This first module is called "The Person of the Caregiver" because it focuses on you, the person you are and the person you will become as God equips you to serve as a Stephen Minister. As important as all your skills will be when you enter into your caring relationships, the most important caring tool you will bring is yourself. Let me say that again. You—who you are, how you relate to others, how you care for and accept your care receiver, your trust in God—are the most important element you bring to the caring relationship. God will use you to bring Christ's healing to your care receivers.

VI. Skill Practice Exploring God-Sized Needs

Discussion Questions

1. How did it feel for *A* to explore this area of spiritual need?

2. How did it feel for *B* to facilitate that exploration?

3. What did *B* do that helped *A* better understand his or her need?

Discussion Questions

1. How did it feel for *B* to explore this area of spiritual need?

2. How did it feel for *A* to facilitate that exploration?

3. What did *A* do that helped *B* better understand his or her need?

VII. Looking Ahead

VIII. Opening

IX. How to Provide Spiritual Care

A. The Woman at the Well

Jesus Cares for the Woman at the Well

When a Samaritan woman came to draw water, Jesus said to her, "Will you give me a drink?" (His disciples had gone into the town to buy food.)

The Samaritan woman said to him, "You are a Jew and I am a Samaritan woman. How can you ask me for a drink?" (For Jews do not associate with Samaritans.)

Jesus answered her, "If you knew the gift of God and who it is that asks you for a drink, you would have asked him and he would have given you living water."

"Sir," the woman said, "you have nothing to draw with and the well is deep. Where can you get this living water? Are you greater than our father Jacob, who gave us the well and drank from it himself, as did also his sons and his flocks and herds?"

Jesus answered, "Everyone who drinks this water will be thirsty again, but whoever drinks the water I give him will never thirst. Indeed, the water I give him will become in him a spring of water welling up to eternal life."

The woman said to him, "Sir, give me this water so that I won't get thirsty and have to keep coming here to draw water."

He told her, "Go, call your husband and come back."

"I have no husband," she replied.

Jesus said to her, "You are right when you say you have no husband. The fact is, you have had five husbands, and the man you now have is not your husband. What you have just said is quite true."

"Sir," the woman said, "I can see that you are a prophet. . . . "

The woman said, "I know that Messiah" (called Christ) "is coming. When he comes, he will explain everything to us."

Then Jesus declared, "I who speak to you am he. . . . "

Then, leaving her water jar, the woman went back to the town and said to the people, "Come, see a man who told me everything I ever did.

Could this be the Christ?" They came out of the town and made their way toward him.

John 4:7–19, 25–26, 28–30

Providing Spiritual Care for the Woman at the Well

1. Which of the seven signs of God's grace are evident in the woman at the well? (See Preclass Reading, pages 662–664.)

> **The Seven Signs of God's Grace**
> 1. Awareness of God's presence
> 2. Faith
> 3. Hope
> 4. Love
> 5. Gratitude and openness to grace
> 6. Repentance and humility
> 7. Community

2. What might have blocked the woman at the well from hearing and believing that God loved her? (See Preclass Reading, pages 671–675.)

> **What Can Block Hearing and Believing?**
>
> | Circumstances | Choices |
> |---|---|
> | • Ignorance | Refusing to believe |
> | • Oppression | Anger with God |
> | Suffering | Unwillingness to forgive |
> | • Shame | • Idolatry |
> | Despair | Too busy for God |
> | Evil | Pride |
> | Evil perpetrated in Jesus' name | Choosing not to participate in Christian community |
> | | • Guilt |
> | | Sin |

3. How did Jesus provide spiritual care for the woman at the well?

4. Imagine a modern-day person like the woman. What might he or she be like?

5. How might you provide spiritual care to someone like the woman at the well?

6. Bonus question (if you have time): How would your care for such a person be different from the care that Jesus provided to the woman at the well, and why would it be different?

B. Skill Practice Providing Spiritual Care

X. Caregiver's Compass Review

XI. Looking Ahead

Prayer Partner Requests and Thanksgivings

My prayer partner is _____

Prayer requests and thanksgivings to share with my prayer partner

_____

_____

Prayer requests and thanksgivings shared by my prayer partner

_____

_____

STEPHEN
MINISTRIES®
SAINT LOUIS

2045 Innerbelt Business Center Drive
St. Louis, Missouri 63114-5765
Phone: (314) 428-2600
Fax: (314) 428-7888
www.stephenministries.org

Dear Stephen Minister,

Congratulations on completing your Stephen Ministry training.

Perhaps this training has illustrated for you that our growth as caregivers—and as disciples of Jesus—is a never-ending journey.

As you are commissioned and begin your caring ministry, your Stephen Leaders will meet with you for peer supervision and continuing education. These are vitally important times to strengthen and nourish you so that your caregiving continues to be compassionate, full of faith, skilled, trustworthy, and Christ-centered.

At Stephen Ministries St. Louis, we also provide other ways for Stephen Ministers to grow. Here are two of them:

The Rev. Kenneth C. Haugk, Ph.D.
Founder and Executive Director

The Rev. David A. Paap, Litt.D.
Program Director

Stephen B. Glynn
Director of Human Resources

The Rev. William J. McKay
Director of Project Development

Joel P. Bretscher
Director of Communications

Joel M. Keen, M.Div.
Pastoral Staff

The Rev. Kevin R. Scott, M.A.E.T.
Pastoral Staff

Joan M. Haugk, R.N., M.S.W.
Co-Founder
1947–2002

▶ **The *Stephen Minister Pages*.** Sign up at www.StephenMinister.org to receive *Care-Mail*, our monthly electronic newsletter. You'll find stories to encourage you, information to increase your knowledge, and practical tips and resources to help you improve your caregiving skills.

▶ **The Breakthrough Leadership Conference.** This in-depth, systematic training course is distinctly different from Stephen Ministry and is for leaders of all types—whether in businesses, congregations, or other organizations. Grounded in Christ-centered theology and sound psychology, it teaches the best leadership principles combined with practical skills to equip participants to break through to new levels of excellence.

If leadership is an important part of your career or your ministry at church, I encourage you to go on line (www.BreakthroughLeadership.org) or call us at (314) 428-2600 for details about this transformational conference. We'd be happy to send you a complete information packet and a DVD that features leaders—from both churches and businesses—who have attended the conference.

May God bless you as richly as you bless others in your caregiving journey.

Cordially in Christ,

David A. Paap

David A. Paap
Program Director